The Maleness of Jesus

Questions concerning the maleness of Jesus and the implications of this for women have been the subject of interesting theological conversation. Is Jesus' male personhood central to his meaning as the Christ or not? In this welcome volume Neil Williams provides a thorough discussion of this significant theological question and carefully draws out its implications for the church and the world demonstrating that the advent of Jesus is good news for all people.

> John R. Franke
> Clemens Professor of Missional Theology, Biblical Seminary, Hatfield, PA

This book is highly informative—but even more so—a mind opener. You will surely have to stretch your mind, whatever your present views are. Williams deals with the vast field of the problem in a very responsible and innovative way.

> Adrio König
> Head of Department of Systematic Theology and Theological Ethics (retired)
> University of South Africa

In this provocative and carefully nuanced book, Neil Williams tackles one of the most controversial issues among conservative Christians. His exploration of the theoretical and practical relevance of the maleness of Jesus balances serious theological analysis with a sensitivity to the pastoral challenges that surround this debate. Williams shows the similarities between the hermeneutical trajectory that characterizes arguments on this topic and other biblical themes, such as slavery and the Sabbath. Moreover, his attention to the larger matrix of theological issues—including the Incarnation and the Trinity—makes an important contribution that ought to be appreciated by all of those involved in this ongoing evangelical dialogue.

> F. LeRon Shults
> Professor of Theology and Philosophy, University of Agder, Norway

At first glance, it might seem that the question of the necessity of the maleness of Christ to the incarnation is an abstract theological issue. Williams shows just how important the issue is, not just for our understanding of redemption but also for our understanding of gender relationships. His book not only deftly addresses the question of Jesus' gender, but is a model for how to think through important theological and ethical issues with intelligence and civility.

> Tremper Longman III
> Robert H. Gundry Professor of Biblical Studies, Westmont College

This is a breathtaking book. Williams offers not only an invaluable excursus on the Sonship of Jesus and its implications for gender, role differentiation, marriage, and patriarchy, but it also offers a way of doing theology that invites many disparate voices and theological debates to the table. And rather than increasing cacophony, Williams judiciously draws out the competing views of each voice/view to a stunning symphonic shalom. For some, this work will be spurned as an accommodation to culture's shifting sands—but if so, Williams counters with a steady and gracious critique of all positions, including his own. There is no one path that is problem free. The way forward in this conversation on gender is with the kind of scholarship, wisdom, and grace offered by this courageous labor.

Dan B. Allender, Ph.D.
Professor of Counseling Psychology and Founding President, Mars Hill Graduate School
Author, *Sabbath* and *The Wounded Heart*

Williams combines uncommon common-sense and interdisciplinary synthesis to address a perennial challenge for some quarters of Evangelicalism: how male-centered modes of expression that characterize both Scripture and much of the history of the church must be in conversation with the social and scientific paradigms that have demonstrated clear explanatory power in recent generations. Williams is both courageous and careful in outlining his argument, steering clear of the anxious belligerence that often characterizes discussions on this topic. There is no other book I know of that combines such clear respect for Scripture, a participant's understanding of Evangelical concerns, and a dialogical temperament with important contemporary paradigms of thought. Williams truly raises the bar on the discussion of the "women's issue" and sets a new agenda for Evangelical treatments.

Peter Enns
Senior Fellow, BioLogos
Author, *Inspiration and Incarnation*

The Maleness of Jesus:
Is It Good News for Women?

Neil H. Williams

CASCADE Books • Eugene, Oregon

THE MALENESS OF JESUS
Is It Good News for Women?

Copyright © 2011 Neil H. Williams. All rights reserved. Except for brief quotations in critical publications or reviews, no part of this book may be reproduced in any manner without prior written permission from the publisher. Write: Permissions, Wipf and Stock Publishers, 199 W. 8th Ave., Suite 3, Eugene, OR 97401.

Cascade Books
An Imprint of Wipf and Stock Publishers
199 W. 8th Ave., Suite 3
Eugene, OR 97401

www.wipfandstock.com

ISBN 13: 978-1-60899-893-7

Unless otherwise indicated Scripture quotations are taken from the New Revised Standard Version Bible, copyright 1989, Division of Christian Education of the National Council of the Churches of Christ in the United States of America. Used by permission. All rights reserved.

Scripture quotations marked NIV are taken from the HOLY BIBLE, NEW INTERNATIONAL VERSION® NIV®. Copyright © 1973, 1978, 1984 by Biblica, Inc.™. Used by permission of Zondervan. All rights reserved worldwide.

Cataloging-in-Publication data:

Williams, Neil H. (Neil Harvey).

    The maleness of Jesus : is it good news for women? / Neil H. Williams.

    ISBN 13: 978-1-60899-893-7

    xiv + 290 p. ; 23 cm. Includes bibliographical references.

    1. Jesus Christ—Person and offices. 2. Patriarchy—Religious aspects—Christianity. 3. Women in Christianity. 4. Sex role—Religious aspects—Christianity.

BT708 W56 2011

Manufactured in the U.S.A.

For Lori

CONTENTS

Introduction	xi
CHAPTER 1: Summary of Various Views	**1**
Complementarian Position	2
Biblical Egalitarian Position	10
Christian Feminist Position	18
Post-Christian Feminist Position	28
Where Do We Go from Here?	36
CHAPTER 2: The Slavery Debate—Implications for Our Topic	**39**
Parallels Between Proslavery and Complementarian Arguments	41
Relevance of the Slavery Debate	59
CHAPTER 3: The Sabbath Debate—Further Implications for Our Topic	**77**
Summary of Different Views	78
Relevance of the Sabbath Debate	86
The Sabbath: A Changeable Institution	89
CHAPTER 4: Origins, Sex, and Evolution	**97**
Why Accept Evolution?	98
The Origins of Humankind and Sex	115
Hierarchies and Reproductive Strategies	119
Strength, Leadership, and a One-ton Gorilla	122
A Tale of Two Stories: The Gospel and Evolution	125
CHAPTER 5: Jesus' Maleness and Creation	**141**
Different Perspectives, Approaches, Emphases, Strengths, and Weaknesses	143
CHAPTER 6: Jesus' Maleness and His Sonship	**173**
The Sonship of Jesus	174
The Eternal Son	184

CHAPTER 7: What Have We Done with the Eternal Son? — 189

Is the Son Eternally Generated? — 189
Is the Son Eternally Subordinate? — 198
Is the Son Eternally Obedient? — 203
Is the Son from Above or from Below? — 205
Does *Son* Have Sexual Connotations? — 208

CHAPTER 8: The Eternal Son as God, and Jesus as God Embodied — 215

The Eternal Son as God — 215
Jesus as God Embodied — 217

CHAPTER 9: Jesus, Wisdom, and an "Eternal Daughter"? — 225

Wisdom in Proverbs — 225
John's Prologue — 231
An "Eternal Daughter"? — 234

Epilogue — 239

Bibliography — 241

Endnotes — 255

Introduction

At the center of Christianity is Jesus of Nazareth—whose maleness is used by many to justify male rule, to exclude women from leadership, and to tell us about the character of God. The maleness of Jesus is used to define God, deny women ordination, and support a so-called created order of male headship. Some of the largest denominations in Christianity use Jesus' maleness to secure the subordination of women and to emphasize that men represent Jesus better than women do.

This raises a number of questions that are the subject of this book. What is the meaning or significance of Jesus' maleness? Is it revelational of the character of God? Is it foundational for the gospel? Is Jesus' maleness associated with an ongoing created order of male priority? Or to ask these questions in another way, What would happen to our understanding of God, the gospel, or the created order if God were embodied female? What would change, and would it be for the better? Is revelation and salvation possible apart from a *male* redeemer? In a different time and culture, could there be a female incarnation?

These questions are essential for many, and for some the fundamental division is not "between those who are Christian and those who are not, but between those who believe that Jesus' male personhood is of the essence of his meaning as the Christ and those who do not."[1]

Although a contemporary theological debate, the question of whether Jesus could have been born a woman is not entirely new. For example, it was raised in the twelfth century by Peter Lombard and later by numerous commentaries on Lombard's work.[2] According to Lombard, Christ could have been a woman, but he took on the male sex because it is more honorable.[3] Later, Thomas Aquinas made the more radical claim—based on Aristotelian biology—that Jesus' maleness was a necessity because women are misbegotten males.[4] Today, none would claim that women are inferior in their being or nature. Nevertheless, in the church there are significant divisions over the meaning of Jesus' maleness, and many derive a variety of theological conclusions from his maleness, which makes it an important topic for contemporary theology.

There are other important reasons to consider this topic. The views that Christians have on the significance of Jesus' maleness are closely related to their overall views of women. And these views affect Christianity's task of love, justice, and reconciliation in a world that is characterized by the global marginalization, oppression, and abuse of women. This is surely one of the worst, if not *the* worst, social evils of our time, found in various forms—sex trafficking and slavery, genital mutilation, bride burning and honor killings, domestic violence by an intimate partner, female infanticide, sexual violence during armed conflict, and the servant status of many women. Even in cases where women may have escaped violence, they still suffer from economic and job inequities and sexual harassment. By any account, the abuse and marginalization of women is extreme and extensive. Women worldwide suffer psychological, physical, and sexual violence, most of it perpetrated by men. So no matter where theology is done or what context it addresses, the marginalization or abuse of women is found. Given this situation, is the *male* Jesus good news for women?

My general approach acknowledges that there is a place for both academic and practical books, but there is also a place for those that intentionally connect the two together. Michael Shermer, in his column in *Scientific American*, lamented the sharp divide in scientific literature between scholarly and popular books and called for more integrative scientific writing that "integrates data, theory and narrative into a useful and compelling work."[5] We may say the same regarding our theological literature: we need more integrative works. By integrative theology, I mean more than having a dialogue with other academic fields, such as the natural sciences; I mean being "useful and compelling"—that is, presenting material that is transformative and directly applicable for the church. Too often theology is done in the high-mountain altitudes where most cannot function or even breathe. Although there is much to admire about mountain climbers, life is lived in the valley. As for this life in the valley, it is hard for theology to serve the mission of the church if few can understand what is said or when many steps are needed to make concrete applications.

Here are a few further points on theology that influence my approach:

- Theology should be ecumenical. No one theology or theological system has the "whole truth and nothing but the truth." An ecumenical approach brings much-needed balance, humility, and an appreciation of diversity.
- Theology should be relational and serve the church; therefore it needs to be understandable and directly applicable. Theology can easily sacrifice much on the altar of irrelevance.
- Theology should seek to be compelling and transformative. This cannot be done by adopting a polemical approach, which is nothing more than a simplistic angry attack; nor can it be done by a "let's all just get along" or "ignore opposing viewpoints" approach, which doesn't promote the interests of justice or love.
- Theology should be interdisciplinary, drawing on areas within Christianity, such as biblical studies and practical theology, as well as disciplines outside, such as the natural sciences. An interdisciplinary approach provides further insight and keeps us

from a blinkered approach that limits our vision and hinders our engagement with the wider contemporary world.
- Theology should contain a strong narrative component—one that helps to join and integrate the material into a story worth telling.
- Theology should speak to the twenty-first century context, not to the seventeenth century or to the fourth century.

I write from an evangelical and Reformed position and trajectory, although I am sometimes critical of this tradition. This material is based on my doctoral dissertation in systematic theology completed in 1999 at the University of South Africa.[6] I am indebted to Adrio König, who supervised the original dissertation, for his stimulating interaction and kind friendship.

Thanks to Jeremy Phillips and Steve Taylor for their careful reading of this book and invaluable advice, and to Tremper Longman and LeRon Shults for their encouragement during various stages of writing.

Finally, many thanks to my children Matthew and Nathan and my wife Lori—who all make life worth living. This book is dedicated to Lori, who in her love for others reveals Jesus more than I do, in thankfulness for her life and cheerful spirit.

CHAPTER 1

Summary of Various Views

To provide a context for our topic, we will first outline four positions on the maleness of Jesus. This is not an extensive description of each position but a summary of the different ways people view the meaning and implications of Jesus' maleness. This outline will provide us with a basis for our discussion through the rest of the book.

But is it wise to divide people into different positions? It is notoriously difficult, and sometimes unwise, to categorize people. People are wonderfully diverse, and even within a so-called position there is variety; and no one person speaks for an entire group. There is always the risk of conflating an individual's view into one category or the danger of choosing the wrong name for a group—such as labeling people "traditionalist," when the church has had such a checkered history regarding women, and no one wants to identify with this history completely. Nevertheless, it is helpful to have some delineation between different views, and outlining various positions provides a good framework for understanding the conflict over Jesus' maleness.

I have divided the various positions and arguments into the categories of complementarian, biblical egalitarian, Christian feminist, and post-Christian feminist, though each position lacks homogeneity. I have also expanded the common meaning of *complementarian* to include views that stress that men represent Jesus better—particularly as priests or pastors. Furthermore, the categories are fluid, as some scholars are technically found in between categories and a number of people have substantially moved positions. There is even debate over whether some scholars are in the area they claim to be.[1]

So here are four views on Jesus' maleness with the recognition that I have trimmed here and clipped there and sometimes nudged or squeezed a person into a particular category. In such a controversial topic, it is easy to minimize or ignore the arguments of others, miss various qualifications, and generally fail to listen and understand. So effort is made to describe the positions in a manner acceptable to the representative people and to emphasize the strengths of each position.

COMPLEMENTARIAN POSITION

For complementarians the maleness of Jesus has theological significance and reveals God. In arguing against the ordination of women, J. I. Packer summarizes much of this position:

> Since the Son of God was incarnated as a male, it will always be easier, other things being equal, to realize and remember that Christ is ministering in person if his human agent and representative is also male.
>
> . . . That one male is best represented by another male is a matter of common sense; that Jesus' maleness is basic to his role as our incarnate Savior is a matter of biblical revelation. . . . The New Testament presents him as the second man, the last Adam, our prophet, priest, and king (not prophetess, priestess, and queen), and he is all this precisely in his maleness. To minimize the maleness shows a degree of failure to grasp the space-time reality and redemptive significance of the Incarnation; to argue that gender is irrelevant to

ministry shows that one is forgetting the representative role of presbyteral leadership.[2]

The Roman Catholic position on male priesthood and its representation of Christ, which is well known and documented, runs along similar lines.[3] Because Jesus was male, so a priest can only be male. To change to women priests would undermine and destroy this representational priesthood.

Complementarians have usually focused on the roles of men and women in church and family, where male and female relate in a complementary way, where the man is leader and the woman submits. It is more often assumed rather than argued that the maleness of Jesus is revelational of God.[4] Some complementarians, however, have specifically addressed the significance of Jesus' maleness and given reasons why Jesus had to be male.[5] We may summarize these reasons and other complementarian arguments below.

A Revelation Beyond Culture

Complementarians argue Jesus became male not only because of the patriarchal society but because his maleness was integrally related to God's revelational purpose. The maleness of Jesus is connected to "profound religious truths,"[6] and "God had a theological reason for sending Christ as a man."[7] They argue that there is revelational significance to Jesus coming as male, and the culture of that time, though relevant, does not ultimately determine this mode of revelation. Culture is thus viewed as secondary to revelation, in the sense that in the beginning God established a created order of Adam first and Eve second. At creation God determined certain features of this culture.

Jesus' maleness is not an accommodation to patriarchal culture but a reflection of God's character.[8] The maleness of God that we find in the Scriptures is "a revelation of the way things are."[9] Thus, any claim that Jesus' maleness was only cultural accommodation is to denigrate God's revelation.[10] This does not mean that the complementarian position ignores culture or is an ahistorical approach. Complementarians use the ancient Near East and Greco-Roman culture to demonstrate that precisely *because* of the culture of the day the maleness of Jesus and male portrayal of God *is* revelational. They observe that in Israel's world there were a multitude of other religions—Sumerian, Egyptian, Canaanite, Assyrian, Babylonian—and *all* had male and female deities.[11] Yet, Israel was different.

The male imagery in Scripture, although given in a patriarchal culture, is not only cultural, for it is given in an environment that accepted both male and female deities. In a similar manner, the Old Testament, unlike neighboring religions, did not allow women to become priests.[12] While acknowledging that God cannot be reduced to sexual differentiation, the position holds that God still *revealed* himself in this way.[13] So in logical progression, complementarians argue that to deny this revelational character of maleness is to deny the authority of Scripture.[14] Many complementarians say that any form of feminist theology has departed in some way from the truth of Scripture by adopting "not simply the secular movement's rhetoric and proposals, but some aspects of its basically nonbiblical world view as well."[15] Jesus' maleness is part of this revelation. Essentially, the male imagery is beyond culture.

The Permanence of the Language of Canaan

The second argument relates to the first and in particular to patriarchal language and discussions over analogy, metaphor, and simile. Complementarians argue that the scriptural language is permanent; so for Christianity to remain Christianity it must continue to use "the language of Canaan,"[16] which includes *Father* and *Son*. Complementarians insist that we cannot modify this language without fundamentally altering Christianity,[17] for God has chosen to reveal himself in this manner.[18] So to postulate a female incarnation or call the second person of the Trinity a Daughter would, in essence, be establishing another religion.[19]

The names *Father* and *Son* have abiding validity. They are names "from above" and not from culture. These names are the "opposite of a Feuerbachian projection."[20] "The Trinitarian names are ontological symbols based on divine revelation rather than personal metaphors having their origin in cultural experience."[21] This being the case, it is argued that the Son could only become incarnate as a male. A male incarnation is a necessity, and changing Son to Daughter would undermine the person of Jesus.[22]

Complementarians differ on how to argue for the permanence of the divine names. For some the debate rests on a distinction between metaphor and simile, where, for example, *Mother* is a simile but *Father* is a metaphor.[23] Therefore, God is *like* a mother but he *is* the Father. Others, however, go further to say that the names *Father* and *Son* are not metaphors, and not even analogies in a strict sense, but rather "catalogies." A distinction is made, at least by Donald Bloesch and Mary Kassian, between analogy and catalogy. Bloesch argues that names like *Father* and *Son* are more accurately described as catalogies—names not derived from our world but come from above.[24] There are particular metaphors or analogies taken from culture (from below), and then there are catalogies (from above) that describe who God *is*. These names are to be taken seriously and cannot be changed without recreating God.[25]

Apart from these differences, there is agreement that the words *Father* and *Son* are not cultural nametags, but a true expression of God's character. To alter these analogies would remove certain univocal (essential) elements of Father and Son, elements that cannot be changed without destroying what is essential to the analogy.[26]

Do these revealed divine names degrade and exclude women, or masculinize God? Complementarians argue that their position does not sexualize God. They repeatedly stress that "the biblical witness is clear that the living God transcends sexuality"[27] and that "this 'masculine' image of God does not have to be thrown out in order for Christianity to exist, for Christians to be truly emancipated."[28] They argue that their views do not make God male or encourage male superiority and that the use of male imagery is not anti-women.

Biblical Passages

The cornerstone of complementarianism is the creation account in Genesis 1–2. The creation narrative is used to establish a particular theological significance to the two sexes and to undergird the necessity of Jesus' maleness. Complementarian thinking invariably leads back to a "creation ordinance," which includes at least the following four elements:

1. In Genesis 1:27–28, Adam and Eve are created ontologically equal. There is sexual differentiation, but equality of being.
2. In Genesis 2:7, 18–22, Adam is created first and subsequently Eve. Eve, as a helper for Adam, is functionally subordinate.
3. In Genesis 2:23 and 3:20, Adam twice names Eve, indicating his authority over her.
4. Adam, as man, represents the entire human race.

It is argued that points 2 and 4 are specifically addressed and taught by Paul in 1 Timothy 2:11–15 and Romans 5:12–21 respectively. This creation ordinance, frequently referred to by complementarians,[29] establishes irreversible roles between male and female before the fall and establishes male rule. This divinely established order means that any matriarchal society is contrary to the creation structure, and any tampering with this order has serious consequences, including opening the door to homosexuality.[30] These unchangeable roles, which remain in effect today, have a direct bearing on the maleness of Jesus because of the theological significance given to the sexes at creation—a structure that has biological as well as theological differences.[31] A female incarnation would subvert this significance given to the sexes and undermine the divinely created order.[32]

After posing the question, "Must Christians apologize for the maleness of Jesus Christ?"[33] Susan Foh gives three reasons why Jesus had to be male: (1) 1 Timothy 2:12–14, (2) Romans 5:12–21, and (3) the Old Testament types.[34] These Old Testament types include men such as Adam, Abraham, Moses, and David who prefigure Jesus. The types also include the sacrificial system that required the sacrifice of male animals.[35] Romans 5:12–21 picks up one of these types and teaches that Jesus follows the pattern or type of Adam as the second representative of humanity. Adam was created first and is the head and foundation of the human race. Everyone is derived from him. Therefore, Adam, being male, necessitates the maleness of Jesus since Jesus follows the pattern of Adam as head and founder of a new humanity. But does this necessity of Jesus' maleness impinge on his ability to represent females? "No," reply complementarians, "representation and substitution need not imply identification."[36] As Adam represented all of humanity, so too can Jesus.

Complementarians use other passages, such as 1 Corinthians 11:3–16, Ephesians 5:21–33, Colossians 3:18–19, and 1 Peter 3:1–7, to teach irreversible complementary roles in which the husband is called to lead and the wife submit.[37] These passages all form part of the background to their view on Jesus' maleness.

A passage that is central to their position is 1 Timothy 2:11–15, where they argue that Paul prohibits women from eldership and having authority over men. This passage, unlike passages regarding slavery, is grounded in creation and has relevance for the maleness of Jesus. Jesus had to be male since women are prohibited, by virtue of creation, from the type of ministry in which Jesus engaged. Complementarians are unified in agreeing that the command in 1 Timothy 2:11–15 is permanent, since it is grounded in creation and the activity that is prohibited (women teaching and having authority) is transcultural.[38] Contrary to some feminists who argue that Paul appeals to creation to illustrate deception, complementarians note that Paul also refers to the situation *pre-fall*, where Adam was created first.[39] Similar to 1 Corinthians 11:3–10, Paul reasons in 1 Timothy 2:11–15 that priority in creation implies headship. There is also a correspondence with 1 Corinthians 14:33–36. Here it is argued that the injunction that women keep silent applies to the weighing of prophecies. The reason why women are not allowed to weigh such prophecies is because they are not to have authority over men.[40]

Trinitarian Theology

The complementarian argument is based on the creation ordinance, which in turn is grounded in the doctrine of the Trinity. As the biblical material directs complementarians to the creation account, the creation account takes them back to the character of God; so that the headship of Adam is not just a divine preference but is rooted in the nature of God. Robert Letham writes, "The priority and headship of the man over the woman rests not only on the doctrine of creation but also on the nature of the God whom man is to image. It is grounded ontologically in the being of God."[41]

Ultimately, the creation structure is grounded in the character of God and Trinitarian hierarchy where there is equality of being (ontological equality) but economic subordination (subordination in function or role). So the creation structure is established in the divine nature, a nature where the Father is head and the Son is subordinate to the Father. So in imaging God, Adam and Eve were equal in being and status, but in terms of roles (in church and family) Adam was head.[42]

Using classic theology, some complementarians say that the divine nature is such that the Father and Son have a relationship between them expressed in terms of *eternal generation*. From eternity there has been a generation of the Son by the Father, a generation that is part of the Trinity. Jesus' relationship with the Father on earth reflects this eternal generation of the Son by the Father. Therefore, Jesus coming as male traces its origin to the creation structure that in turn finds its origin in the Trinity. So the Trinitarian nature of God finds expression in the pre-fall creation structure and the male incarnation. Creation and incarnation could not be otherwise.

Authority

The complementarian position closely ties maleness with authority. John Frame provides a reason why God is referred to in primarily male terms: "Scripture describes God both in male and female terms, though the overwhelming preponderance of imagery is male. The reason, I think, is basically that Scripture wants us to think of God as *Lord* (Exodus 3:14; 6:3, 7; 33:19; 34:5ff; Deuteronomy 6:4ff; cf. Romans 10:9ff; 1 Corinthians 12:3; Philippians 2:11), and lordship, in Scripture, always connotes authority. Since in the Biblical view women are subject to male authority in the home and the church, there is some awkwardness in speaking of God in female terms."[43]

What is the origin of this link between maleness and authority? As with much of their argument, complementarians say that male authority is established in the created order where Adam is given authority over his wife, exemplified in his naming of her. They carry the connection between maleness and authority from creation, through the New Testament church, to us today. This tie between maleness and authority is not abolished by the gospel, and even a passage such as Galatians 3:28 does not eliminate all gender-based roles, including male authority.[44] Thus, they conclude that any attempt to subvert patriarchy expresses a desire to move away from authority.[45]

Part of the complementarian argument is based on permanent authority structures. Even though there is an ontological equality in the Trinity, there is also a functional hierarchy. This hierarchy is reflected in the male-female relationship as they image God, where man is given authority over woman.[46] Therefore, one reason for the male incarnation was to reveal authority. The maleness of Jesus reveals this authority, while incarnating as a woman would negate this authority. For complementarians, because the idea of authority and leadership is closely tied to maleness, it follows that Jesus had to be male to reflect this authority and the lordship of God. The argument is such: God gave man and not woman authority at creation, thus God reveals himself in male terms and a male incarnation because he desires to reveal himself as Lord.

Conclusion

The common ground in the complementarian position lies in the revelational character and necessity of a male incarnation. The basis for the complementarian argument is that God has revealed himself in Scripture as Father and Son, and the Eternal Son comes as a man. In doing so, he fulfills the Old Testament types and patterns. Other things being equal, men today still represent Jesus better than women. The revealed biblical language is patriarchal and this reflects an ontological reality. To move beyond Jesus being the Son to Jesus being the Daughter is to move beyond what is revealed. Furthermore, because men and not women are given leadership and authority—a role established in the created order—so Jesus had to be male. To say that the Son could incarnate as female undermines the revelation of God as Trinity, the created order of role differentiation, and many biblical types or patterns, including the analogy between Christ and his church.

BIBLICAL EGALITARIAN POSITION

Biblical egalitarians place themselves within the bounds of Scripture, biblical authority, and orthodoxy. Their views on Scripture and fundamental doctrines are close to complementarians.[47] They disagree with complementarians, however, and argue that the maleness of Jesus is only culturally and historically relevant. They also differ with feminists who depart from Christianity because of the perceived unchangeable maleness of God and patriarchal character of Scripture. Egalitarians believe that these feminists have adopted a position similar to complementarianism in that both view the Scriptures as unalterably patriarchal.

Cultural Reasons

Egalitarians argue that Jesus' maleness is culturally determined. Jesus became male in order to fulfill his mission in a patriarchal world.[48] Paul K. Jewett summarizes the egalitarian position: "There is nothing either in the concept of God, or in the concept of Incarnation, that leads by logical entailment to masculinity. Given the patriarchal society of Israel, the revelation of God naturally takes a patriarchal form. . . . It is not surprising, then, that God reveals himself to Israel as the 'Father' of 'his' people.

Being disclosed as the Father of Israel, it is likewise natural that God should send one called a 'son,' who naturally assumes male humanity."[49]

Jesus' maleness is because of the ancient patriarchal culture, so there is no theological necessity for Jesus coming as male. The reasons are historical and cultural.[50] A woman would have been ignored,[51] she could not have taught in the synagogue,[52] her testimony would not be believed, and she would have been ceremonially unclean on a monthly basis.[53] Furthermore, as male, Jesus could show a new way of relating—one that included respect and service. From a woman these characteristics were expected,[54] so only as a man could Jesus critique power structures and hierarchical systems.[55]

Regarding Jesus' maleness, most biblical egalitarians place maleness on a level similar to Jewishness. Speaking of Jesus' maleness, Ruth Tucker writes, "It was his *gender* identity, just as being a Jew was his *cultural* identity, and being a carpenter's son from Nazareth was part of his *social* identity."[56] Egalitarians stress the importance of taking serious consideration of the culture of the ancient world. In doing so, they argue that this culture gives sufficient reasons for Jesus' maleness. Given the patriarchal society, Jesus could not have carried out his ministry as a woman. In addition, they find no New Testament passage or teaching that draws theological implications from Jesus' sex.[57] Jesus' maleness is based on culture and not a necessity rooted in God.

Biblical Passages

When examining the creation narratives, egalitarians find an absence of any command from God or any other indication of male authority.[58] They argue that nowhere in the creation account is there an injunction concerning the rule of man over woman.[59] Instead, they underscore that the creation account teaches a mutual equality of being, with both male and female created in the image of God.[60] Eve as "helper" is not subordinate but one who comes alongside Adam as an equal partner.[61] Even Adam naming his wife "Woman" does not imply his authority and rule, but rather is a recognition of Eve's identity and equality.[62] In contrast to complementarians, egalitarians say that subordination came about because of the fall, not creation.[63] The fall is the beginning of male rule, not a change in the type or manner of rule.[64] Biblical egalitarians conclude that the creation account teaches an equality of being and function and gives no warrant for male leadership and authority. Thus, they find no established order in creation that necessitated Jesus being male.

There are differences among biblical egalitarians regarding the New Testament teaching on gender roles. Some deny that the New Testament requires a hierarchical or traditional model. Some believe that the New Testament in some places teaches a traditional model; nevertheless, this model was only applicable to the first-century church living in a patriarchal society. A few argue that there is a contradiction within Paul's teaching. All agree, however, that the modern church should teach and practice egalitarianism. The egalitarian view that Jesus' maleness is theologically indifferent is integrally related to their view that there is no theological difference between male and female—that the New Testament does not teach male rule as normative.

Some other passages they focus on include Acts 2:15–21, where the Spirit is given to all—male and female. They conclude that the "sex difference is irrelevant in the church."[65] Egalitarians appeal to 1 Corinthians 7:4, where Paul states that a wife has authority over her husband's body,[66] and therefore the only time Scripture uses the word *authority* in the marriage relationship is in the context of a mutual relationship.[67] Thus, it is argued that God gave both husband and wife authority in their relationship.[68] And in Ephesians 5:21–33 egalitarians argue that headship is a role where the husband, like Christ, is to give up his life, that is, to submit himself.[69] They find a similar concept in 1 Corinthians 11:2–16, where they argue that *head* serves as a metaphor for "source" or "origin" rather than "authority."[70] Here again, Paul is describing a mutual relationship, because he argues in 1 Corinthians 11:12 that every man has come from a woman.[71] For egalitarians, the biblical picture of marriage is one of equality through mutual submission.

Galatians 3:28 is the foundational verse for the egalitarian position.[72] Jewett refers to this verse as the "Magna Carta of Humanity."[73] Similarly, Grenz writes, "Egalitarians, in contrast [to complementarians], see Galatians 3:28 as the foundation for a new social order in the church. In their view this verse looms as the clearest statement of the apostle's own understanding of the role of women."[74] Galatians 3:28 must receive hermeneutical priority because of its overarching nature and its position within the Pauline corpus.[75] Egalitarians argue that this verse establishes the basis for the theological indifference of the sexes, as it lists male-female relationships in conjunction with slave-free and Jew-Gentile relationships. Here Paul teaches that racial, social, or sexual distinctions are immaterial in the new covenant,[76] although they stress that their position does not eliminate every distinction between the sexes.[77]

Trinitarian Theology

Egalitarians make a distinction between subordination because of nature and a temporary or voluntary subordination. As they oppose any rule-submission ordinance in the creation narratives, they deny that the persons of the Trinity relate to each other based on rule and submission. They agree that in the incarnation Jesus submitted himself to the Father, yet stress that his submission was voluntary. Egalitarians hold that the complementarian comparison between the Son submitting himself to the Father and the so-called wife's submission is invalid, since the Son voluntary submitted himself and the wife's submission is required.[78]

Egalitarians also oppose any relation between maleness and God's being. Jewett says that "an affinity between maleness and divineness remains the basic assumption behind every argument from the nature of God for the exclusion of women from the office of the ministry."[79] Egalitarians argue that complementarians have created an insurmountable problem by holding to the Trinitarian God who is beyond sexuality and yet maintaining a necessary male incarnation.[80] They believe that to argue for the theological significance of Jesus' maleness necessarily brings maleness into God's being and denigrates women. It also creates christological problems, for Jesus alone is the true image of God, yet he is male. Thus, they see only two options: either male reveals God more than female, or maleness is theologically insignificant.[81] Once again, when they look at the Trinity they conclude that Jesus' maleness does not reveal God's being; rather it is culturally defined.[82]

Jewett provides another argument by using the classic formulation of the Trinity. To support the view that the male incarnation is not a theological necessity, Jewett argues for the legitimacy of speaking of a Daughter instead of a Son. As classic theology spoke of the Father generating the Son, so we may speak of a Mother generating a Daughter.[83] He states that the only univocal element in the Trinitarian name—Father, Son, and Spirit—is that the second and third persons originate, as persons, from the Father. Therefore, it is legitimate to substitute a Mother-Daughter analogy, for it retains the univocal element of the original analogy, namely causation. Thus, for Jewett, we have left our conception of God unaltered since we have not changed what is true of the metaphor. For Jewett, this is legitimate because there are no sexual distinctions in the Trinity, only personal distinctions.[84]

Analogy and Metaphor

In her book *The Divine Feminine*, Mollenkott argues that the Scriptures do bring the "feminine principle into the Godhead."[85] Her work provides numerous different female pictures of God, such as a woman giving birth, nursing mother, midwife, mother bear, mother eagle, mother hen, and Woman Wisdom.[86] She also mentions that Jesus compared God with a female in Luke 15:8–10[87] and referred to himself in female terms as he wept over Jerusalem.[88] These female metaphors are important because they teach that God is not male. Jewett also argues that the female metaphors for God in the Bible are relevant. He notes that God has revealed himself as Mother as well as Father,[89] and when using female and male imagery for God the Scriptures (in both cases) are speaking analogically.[90] He argues that in the Scripture "to speak grammatically, 'he' is used of God as a *personal* pronoun, not a *masculine* personal pronoun."[91] Hence, in the created order male does not image God more than female.

Not all egalitarians agree with Mollenkott and Jewett regarding their search for female metaphors for God. Rebecca Groothuis believes this solves nothing, falls into the same difficulty as the complementarian position in that it sexualizes God, and in the end there are far more male references in Scripture.[92]

How do egalitarians address the imbalance between male and female metaphors for God in Scripture? Mollenkott observes that "it is perfectly natural for the Bible to contain a vast predominance of masculine God-language, springing as it does out of a deeply patriarchal culture."[93] Stanley Grenz says, however, that mere culture is not a sufficient answer for the male imagery in Scripture.[94] He suggests an answer: "The widespread use of male images indicates that God relates to the world primarily in a manner analogous to the human male. God is ultimately transcendent, creating the world as a reality outside of himself."[95]

Grenz is not expressing the general consensus. Most egalitarians argue that the reason why Scripture refers to God as Father is because a father in that culture had, among other things, power and authority. God as Father also presented a sharp contrast with other ancient religions. Egalitarians use this preponderance of male imagery to their advantage. They claim that given the patriarchal society, it is surprising that there are any female references to God. This leads us to an argument from exceptions.

Exceptions

Considering the patriarchal society in which the Bible was written, and the preponderance of male images, it is significant that there are exceptions. Given the patriarchal society where male was ideal, it is significant that we find female imagery for God.[96] Apart from female imagery for

God, egalitarians also find exceptions to male hierarchy. From the Old Testament, for example, they refer to the leadership of Miriam, Deborah, Huldah, and the Song of Songs. They find in the Song of Songs, a book written in a patriarchal society, a portrayal of a mutual marriage relationship with no male dominance or female subordination.[97]

Egalitarians also note a number of exceptions in the New Testament. Jesus had remarkable relationships with women,[98] and had women disciples,[99] and rather than assume the traditional male role, Jesus' life, as male, was one of submission and service.[100] Women were the first witnesses to the resurrection, and women shared in the outpouring of the Spirit on Pentecost (Acts 2:17). The daughters of Philip were prophets (Acts 21:9), and other women prophesied in the churches (1 Corinthians 11:5)—combining this with Paul's statement that the church is built on the foundation of the apostles and prophets (Ephesians 2:20). Women also labored together with Paul (Philippians 4:3), and some were his fellow workers (Romans 16:3). Other women were deacons (Romans 16:1), and many egalitarians read in Romans 16:7 the female form "Junia," not the male "Junias"—that is, a woman apostle, a woman with authority in the church.[101] Passages already noted, such as Galatians 3:28 and 1 Corinthians 7:1–6, are also regarded as exceptional to the patriarchal milieu. These exceptions demonstrate to egalitarians that the seeds of transformation are already present in the Scriptures. Since we find these exceptions in a patriarchal society, *how much more* should these exceptions now become the norm?

Authority

Biblical egalitarians affirm that people may have different roles, and they uphold the importance and relevance of authority structures.[102] They are convinced, however, that the church may not exclude women from positions of authority solely because they are women. For them there is nothing intrinsic to maleness that makes men better equipped to have authority. To support this claim, egalitarians refer to instances in Scripture where women have had authority. As noted above, they find women participating in all leadership positions. In the Old Testament mention is made of Miriam, Deborah, Huldah, Abigail, the wife of Proverbs 31, and the Song of Songs. In the New Testament they find the daughters of Philip, Priscilla, Junia, and Phoebe in positions of authority.[103]

Bilezikian notes that in the New Testament there were women converts, women apostles, women prophets, women teachers, women helpers, and women administrators.[104] Egalitarians claim that these women were clearly in positions of authority, which needs to influence our interpretation of 1 Timothy 2:11–15 and 1 Corinthians 14:33–36. Furthermore, Grenz writes, "Women did engage in prophecy. . . . In enumerating the gifts and offices in the church Paul lists prophecy ahead of teaching (1 Corinthians 12:28; Ephesians 4:11). From considerations such as these, egalitarians conclude that the prophetic office encompasses authoritative teaching and that it may even surpass the teaching office, at least within the early church. If this is so, they wonder, how is it that women can serve as prophets but not as teachers?"[105]

Egalitarians believe that complementarians find themselves in practical difficulty over this question of authority. Mary Stewart Van Leeuwen argues that complementarians, because of their unbiblical views on authority, get into the dilemma of "where to draw the line" regarding what is permissible for women to do in church. She observes that they do not allow women to teach adult men but permit them to teach children. Complementarians allow women to teach certain subjects at a seminary but not others. They prohibit women from preaching but let them go on the foreign mission field.[106]

Conclusion

Common to the biblical egalitarian position is that Jesus' maleness is only culturally and historically relevant. Jesus is the expressed image of God, and this cannot include his maleness, for it would imply that women are not in God's image. Men and women, however, equally reveal God, are equal in being, and are equally capable. Egalitarians do not minimize the differences between men and women, but state that there are no *established* leadership or headship roles based on gender. So there is no creation ordinance of male authority that is reflected in Jesus' maleness. They argue that to extrapolate Jesus' maleness beyond cultural relevancy to a theological necessity is to apply maleness to God's being.

Furthermore, they believe that passages that are exceptional to the normal patriarchal model demonstrate that Scripture contains the seeds of transformation. This is similar to the New Testament's handling of slavery, a topic we will discuss in the next chapter. Instead of explicit commands to abolish slavery, Paul mandated the submission of slaves to preserve the peace. Exceptions like the letter to Philemon and Galatians 3:28, however, persuaded the church to view slavery as contrary to God's purposes. Similarly, there are no commands to abolish headship-submission relationships, but the Bible includes sufficient exceptions to demonstrate that these gender-based roles are cultural. This being the case, we cannot derive any theological implications from a male incarnation.

CHRISTIAN FEMINIST POSITION

Christian feminists work for liberation within a Christian context, and they do not renounce Christianity as irredeemably patriarchal. Their starting point is the negative experiences of women—discrimination, oppression, abuse, marginalization, and invisibility. Christian feminism "begins from experiences and not from the revelation event."[107] And they reject "any Christology that smirks of sexism, or that functions to entrench lopsided gender relations."[108]

Contrary to post-Christian feminism, they do not view the maleness of Jesus as an insuperable problem. For most Christian feminists, the male incarnation, correctly interpreted, reflects their concerns. They depart from biblical egalitarianism in that they hold that in many places the New Testament does in fact teach and *require* patriarchy. They also disagree with complementarians, whom they believe teach the subordination of women, minimize the significance of experience and culture, and do not take seriously enough the human authorship of Scripture.[109]

Christian feminism observes how the church has changed its argumentation as Aristotelian biology was proven false—a biology that was used to hold that man is normative and woman inferior. They note that the church now generally affirms that women equally image God, yet it still maintains hierarchy. In making this observation, Christian feminists argue that the church cannot hold to the principle of mutual equality while, at the same time, enforcing particular inequalities where "one partner is always inferior to, dependent upon, [and] instrumental to the role of the other."[110]

Christian feminism denies that male is normative or is generic humanity.[111] They see no revelational significance to Jesus' maleness. Patricia Wilson-Kastner writes, "The maleness of Jesus is quite accidental to his meaning as Christ."[112] She continues, "No one can deny that Jesus the Christ was a male person, but the significance of the incarnation has to do with his humanity, not his maleness."[113] Other Christian feminists, such as Marjorie Suchocki, agree that to elevate Jesus' maleness to the revelation of God distorts the gospel.[114] Yet it is precisely this elevation of maleness that Christian feminism sees in the church at large. Jacquelyn Grant writes, "Women have been denied humanity, personhood, leadership, and equality in the church and in society because of the church's history of negative Christology. This negative Christology has resulted primarily from an over-emphasis on the maleness of Jesus. The maleness, in actuality, has become idolatrous. In fact, the maleness of Jesus has been so central to our understanding of Jesus Christ that even the personality of Jesus and interpretations of Christ have been consistently distorted. In effect, Jesus has been imprisoned by patriarchy's obsession with the supremacy of maleness."[115]

Christian feminists insist that to claim that Jesus' maleness is revelational diminishes the humanity of women and places the salvation of women into question. Rosemary Radford Ruether states a basic concern: "The critical principle of feminist theology is the promotion of the full humanity of women. Whatever denies, diminishes, or distorts the full humanity of women is, therefore, appraised as not redemptive."[116] In keeping with this principle, Christian feminists advance a number of arguments for maintaining the maleness of Jesus as only cultural, a particularity of the incarnation that has no ultimate revelational significance.

Kenosis of Patriarchy

Christian feminists, in contrast to complementarians and post-Christian feminists, do not believe that patriarchy is an essential part of Christianity.[117] They see in Jesus a person who repudiates patriarchy,[118] one who "rejects kingly and chauvinist understandings of the Messiah,"[119] one in whom we see the kenosis (emptying) of patriarchy. Christian feminism does not reject the male Jesus, for the Jesus in the Gospels is a "figure remarkably compatible with feminism."[120]

So although Jesus' maleness has been used to oppress women, Christian feminism emphasizes that in Jesus *as male* we see the destruction of this oppression. Ruether writes, "Theologically speaking, then, we might say that the maleness of Jesus has no ultimate significance. It has social symbolic significance in the framework of societies of patriarchal privilege. In this sense Jesus as the Christ, the representative of liberated humanity and the liberating Word of God, manifests the *kenosis of patriarchy*, the announcement of the new humanity through a lifestyle that discards hierarchical caste privilege and speaks on behalf of the lowly."[121]

Ruether expresses the view of many Christian feminists that, rather than identifying with the male religious hierarchy, Jesus was found identifying with women who were among the despised groups of society. Jesus did not assume the place of the male in that society. His relationships were not patriarchal, and his "self-identification and self-expression are in no way grounded in assumptions of male priority."[122]

Commenting on Ruether's "kenois of patriarchy," Rowan Williams writes, "If this is a viable theological idea, its force is that Jesus' maleness is important because, as a *crucified* or *marginal* or *powerless* maleness, it represents as dramatically as possible the 'otherness' and the judgement of God's Word upon the world's patterns of dominance. It does not manifest but subverts the 'maleness' of God. Its symbolic importance is not in being a timeless image but in its pertinence to specific social forms."[123]

Some Christian feminists, however, have criticized Ruether's kenosis of patriarchy. Elisabeth Schüssler Fiorenza makes the point that "Radford Ruether's argument reveals that she still codes Jesus' humanness in culturally masculine terms when she claims that his lifestyle discards hierarchical caste privilege. One can discard only what one has!"[124] Schüssler Fiorenza believes that such feminist discourse may "perpetuate kyriarchal mind-sets."[125]

Most Christian feminists, however, see Jesus as one who challenges society's view of established gender categories[126] and who proclaims a reversal of status systems.[127] "The Jesus confessed by the Christian creed is no chauvinistic champion of male supremacy. He is meek, humble of heart, an iconoclast bent on shattering all the idols that keep people from realizing their truest fulfillment."[128]

Finding these qualities in Jesus is essential for Christian feminists. They seek to find in Jesus "values and ideals which also are sought for and valued by feminists."[129] Finding such qualities unexpectedly leads some to argue that it is more significant that Jesus came as male. If Jesus was a woman, these qualities would not have been noticed. Instead, as a man, Jesus challenged the structures of power and authority[130] by refusing to adopt the typical male roles.[131] "He refused to lord himself over others, particularly over women."[132] Thus, Christian feminism does not abandon the male incarnation, for it reflects many of their concerns.

Christian feminists point to another feature of Jesus' life that undermines patriarchy: his use of *Abba* to address God.[133] They argue that Jesus confronted the culture's patriarchy and hierarchical structures by disparaging the titles *Rabbi* and *father* and by reinforcing the unique authority of God in heaven. Instead of further establishing patriarchy, Jesus' use of *Abba* undermined the patriarchal system by transferring authority away from the established patriarchal system, thus releasing people from domination. Moreover, Jesus' use of the term *Abba* is informal, stressing a loving relationship—a term that cannot be used to justify forms of domination.

Assumption and Redemption

In arguing against a necessary male incarnation, Christian feminism draws on the patristic dictum, "What is not assumed is not redeemed." Yes, Jesus was male, but his maleness was not an ultimate necessity. Christian feminists argue that Jesus' masculinity is to be viewed like other particulars of the incarnation, such as skin color, social class, or birthplace. What is revelational is Jesus' message, life, and humanity, not his maleness.[134] They emphasize that if the maleness of Jesus is necessary—because of God's nature or salvation—then women are excluded from this salvation.[135] If maleness is necessary, then femaleness is not "assumed," and thus women are not saved.[136]

Christian feminism stresses that Jesus' salvation redeems all humanity—male and female. Jesus' work of redemption is not restricted to certain groups: males, Jews, or the poor. It is universal in that it applies to all humanity and not to just one particular part of humanity.[137] A normative or necessary incarnation denies the universality of the incarnation and thus undermines the redemption and equality of women.[138] If women are to be included in salvation, we need two elements: (1) affirmation of the full humanity of Jesus[139] and (2) a denial of the *male* incarnation as an ontological necessity.[140]

For Christian feminists, a male incarnation does not grant special privilege to men whether in authority, holiness, or a closer identity with God. There is no ultimate reason why the incarnation could not be in female form. Thus, Christian feminists have few objections to the visible portrayal of a female Christ, even if it is only an attempt at consciousness raising.[141]

Trinitarian Theology

Christian feminists argue that the traditional metaphors may be changed. Without denying that Father and Son are relevant analogies, they argue for an inclusion of female metaphors such as Mother. Although we speak of God in images and metaphors, these images are all limited, and God is not identified by or restrained to any particular one. Furthermore, it is necessary to interchange these analogies because of the social effects of these predominant male metaphors that are used to entrench patriarchy, define reality, and oppress women.[142] The metaphor of God as Father is an example of a "good model gone astray,"[143] a metaphor made all-encompassing, and thus serves to institute patriarchy by going beyond the intention of the metaphor. Many argue that this metaphor was instituted by the dominant male culture that made God in its own image.[144]

For Christian feminists, the focus on male images for God is idolatrous,[145] for what is finite (maleness) is applied to the infinite.[146] If God is not male, feminists wonder why there is such opposition to using female images to speak of God.[147] God "transcends all images, words, and concepts";[148] and in transcending all images God is ultimately incomprehensible and mysterious—more unlike the image than like. So to insist on one particular image is to deny the incomprehensibility of God and the ultimate inadequacy of these images.[149]

They give other reasons for expanding our naming of God. Phyllis Trible notes the example of the postexilic change of YHWH to *Adonai*, providing warrant for a change.[150] Christian feminists also argue that the interchangeable use of Father and Mother is legitimate since the "image of God" includes both female and male.[151] God is not more male than female,[152] so "male has no special priority in imaging God."[153] They also regularly appeal to the medieval mysticism of Julian of Norwich, who argued for the metaphor of Jesus as our Mother.[154]

Christian feminists oppose a hierarchical Trinity—a hierarchy combined with the exclusive use of male images that establishes and reinforces male hierarchy and male as normative.[155] In addition, they note that the hierarchical view of the Trinity is often joined with the doctrine of immutability, further entrenching patriarchy. As such, some regard the doctrine of God's immutability as "anachronistic and dangerous."[156] In contrast, they stress relationship in the Trinity. They see no hierarchy in the Trinity, only a mutual, loving interrelationship of persons.[157] And like some biblical egalitarians, many Christian feminists argue that the traditional Trinitarian relationships, expressed in terms of a Father generating a Son, may be modified to Mother-Daughter without essentially changing our view of God.[158]

Two Opposing Biblical Traditions: Patriarchy and Liberation

Christian feminism divides the biblical material into two basic traditions: patriarchy and liberation. They argue for two traditions in Scripture: one is only cultural (patriarchal) and the other is essential. One part upholds and teaches patriarchy; the other speaks of liberation from oppression. Based on these opposing traditions, Schüssler Fiorenza writes, "At the same time the Bible has not served only to legitimate the oppression of white women, slaves, native Americans, Jews, and the poor. It has also provided authorization for women who rejected slavery, colonial exploitation, anti-Semitism, and misogyny as unbiblical and against God's will."[159]

On the one hand, the Bible is hierarchical, androcentric, and patriarchal; but, on the other hand, it contains a message of justice and liberation.[160] There are "texts of terror"[161] and texts of freedom. Of these two streams within Scripture, one is normative and the other is only cultural. Although they differ on precisely what constitutes the authoritative core (i.e., the texts of freedom), it is because of this twofold structure that Christian feminists believe they can work within a Christian framework.[1632]

Most Christian feminists argue that in particular places the New Testament does teach and require patriarchy. Passages such as 1

Corinthians 11:3–9, 1 Corinthians 14:34–35, Ephesians 5:22–24, and 1 Timothy 2:11–15 are patriarchal.¹⁶²³ Portions of the Pastoral Epistles and 1 Peter teach hierarchicalism.¹⁶⁴ There are many places in the New Testament that teach subordination,¹⁶⁵ and even Paul, who "affirms Christian equality and freedom," still "subordinates women's behavior in marriage and in the worship assembly."¹⁶⁶

There is, however, acknowledgement among Christian feminists that what is crucial is not these patriarchal texts but "the overall liberating perspective of our classic text."¹⁶⁷ Christian feminists find a significant antipatriarchal message in the Scriptures, a message that speaks of equality, liberation, and the full humanity of women. This liberation tradition is established in creation¹⁶⁸ and reiterated in the New Testament, particularly in Galatians 3:28 where Paul completely undermines sexual, class, and racial forms of domination.¹⁶⁹ This liberation tradition is as diverse as the female images for God, such as midwife and mother,¹⁷⁰ or the Song of Songs that affirms the equality and mutuality of the sexes with no hint of inferiority, subordination, or oppression.¹⁷¹

Sophia Christology

Christian feminists have proposed and argue for a *sophia* ("wisdom") Christology as an alternative metaphor.¹⁷² In so doing they seek to identify Jesus and Woman Wisdom.¹⁷³ Elizabeth Johnson has particularly developed this sophia Christology. She notes the relationship between *logos* ("word") and *sophia* not only in the Old Testament but also in intertestamental literature, such as the Book of Wisdom, Ben Sirach, and Baruch.¹⁷⁴

In intertestamental literature logos is identified with sophia, whereas in the Old Testament the two were seen as separate categories. It is argued that there was a development from the Old Testament, through Jewish wisdom literature, to Jesus. This development reaches its fulfillment in the New Testament description of Jesus, who is identified as the wisdom of God (1 Corinthians 1:30). In addition, in the New Testament Jesus equates himself with the female personification of wisdom (Matthew 11:19; Luke 7:35).

The identification of the figures of Logos and Sophia, however, is especially manifest in John's prologue, where Johnson argues that Logos and Sophia are interchangeable and that "the figure of divine Sophia shines through the Logos terminology."[175] Johnson, like many others, says that the closest parallels with the prologue are found in wisdom literature, and that the Logos in John's prologue is directly related to and based on the figure of Sophia.[176] It is argued that the New Testament portrays Jesus as the Logos of God who has the same function as Woman Wisdom in the Old Testament. Therefore, by including Sophia with Logos, this "opens up a possibility of a Christology which is not intrinsically androcentric."[177]

Johnson outlines the importance of the sophia Christology: "This foundational metaphor relieves the monopoly of the male metaphors of Logos and Son and destabilizes the patriarchal imagination. . . . Such a way of speaking breaks through the assumption that there is a 'necessary ontological connection' between the male human being Jesus and a male God, leading to the realization instead that even as a human man, Jesus can be thought to be revelatory of the graciousness of God imaged as female."[178]

Jesus as Sophia provides an alternate image of God. A sophia Christology thus has potential to break the hold of male metaphors for God and the insistence on the necessity for Jesus' maleness.[179]

Critique of Dualism

Part of the Christian feminist critique of a necessary and theological significant male incarnation is closely related to their general critique of dualistic thinking. Christian feminists are generally opposed to dualistic paradigms whether it is spirit-body, mind-matter, nature-culture, nature-grace, male-female, home-work, spirituality-carnality, or dominance-submission. They reject most dualistic forms, whether between superiority and inferiority,[180] or between the public and private sphere where men are in the public and women in private,[181] or where women are inferior and men superior,[182] or dualisms of spirit over flesh so as to downplay or ignore the body,[183] or even the dualism of the old and new Adam.[184] Their critique is that patriarchy is essentially dualistic,[185] with male presiding over mind, culture, and spirit, while women are assigned to body, nature, and submission. With such a dualism, men may therefore define culture and be considered to have superior reason. Mind and spirit are then considered far superior to body, so women then represent sexuality, carnality, and evil.[186]

Christian feminists believe that behind the insistence on Jesus' maleness is destructive dualistic thinking. This reasoning associates women with a subordinate, inferior body, thus making a male incarnation a necessity. According to this view, redemption can only be accomplished by a male savior. In contrast, Christian feminists argue that there was no such dualism in the original creation[187] or in the liberating message of the New Testament.[188]

Conclusion

Christian feminism argues that the male incarnation is historically contingent. There is little debate that Jesus was male, and Christian feminists use his maleness to their advantage. They note how Jesus redefined maleness and through his ministry radically opposed many patriarchal power structures. They insist that there is no essential connection between Jesus' maleness and the character of God. To make such a connection is to remove women from the plan of salvation and deny their full humanity. Such a connection also negates the significant liberation tradition in Scripture. Christian feminists believe that complementarians have based the necessity of Jesus' maleness on an inadequate use of analogy, a patriarchal mindset, and unbiblical dualistic tendencies.

Christian feminists view the Trinitarian relationships as nonhierarchical. The metaphors Father and Son do not necessitate Jesus coming as male since God is beyond masculinity. Therefore, God may equally be portrayed in female and male terms. Furthermore, changing metaphors to Mother and Daughter does not essentially change the generation formulation of classical theology.

Christian feminists also disagree with the post-Christian feminist position that Scripture is irredeemably patriarchal. While noting that there are numerous passages in the Scripture that support and teach patriarchy, Christian feminists argue that these have no normative value and allocate them to the realm of that particular ancient culture. What is normative is the great prophetic liberation tradition that speaks of the full equality and humanity of women as imagers of God.

POST-CHRISTIAN FEMINIST POSITION

Post-Christian feminists argue that Christianity and feminism are incompatible and irreconcilable—that one cannot be both Christian and feminist. Their critique challenges Christianity to its foundation. They abandon Christianity as a religion of the male, an irredeemable patriarchal religion where a great patriarch in heaven sends his son. They reject Jesus, the supreme male figure of this male religion. Post-Christian feminists argue that the maleness of Jesus is relevant in that it reinforces patriarchy and, as a symbol, powerfully influences its hearers. They argue that the "medium is the message"; thus Christianity cannot extract itself from this medium of its patriarchal past and continue to remain Christianity.

Post-Christian feminists strongly disagree with Christian feminists and biblical egalitarians, arguing that the biblical analogies and stories cannot be freed from patriarchy. The symbols at the heart of the religion—Father, Son, and a male savior—can never be changed. So Christian feminists are engaged in a futile endeavor, an attempt that either ends in syncretism or ignores significant parts of Scripture.[189] Post-Christian feminists agree with complementarians in arguing that Christianity is inherently patriarchal and that its symbols and metaphors are unchangeable. They believe, however, that complementarians are in an indefensible position, out of touch with the modern world, and have isolated their theology "in a cocoon separate from human knowledge, culture and society."[190] Complementarianism is inherently fallacious, oppressive, and sexist, "for that which 'complements' is always in some sense inferior to that which it complements."[191] In this "equal but different" scheme, it is always the female that complements the male and not vice versa.[192]

Post-Christian feminists reject Christianity's patriarchal past, its metaphors and stories, and its ultimate symbol in the person of Jesus. They believe that these have all contributed to and reinforced the notion that women are secondary and inferior—a fact born out through most of its history, where "Christian theology widely asserted that women were inferior, weak, depraved, and vicious."[193]

Christianity's Unbreakable Connection to a Patriarchal Past

According to post-Christian feminists, Christianity is patriarchal to its very core. Daphne Hampson writes:

> That Christianity is patriarchal is clearly the case. The long line of prophets, Jesus (who is central to the religion), the apostles and the leaders of the Church throughout history to the present have been men—almost without exception. Women are related to them as wives, mothers and companions. In the stories and parables of the New Testament men perform what were in that society men's roles and women women's roles. God is conceived in patriarchal terms: he is King, Lord, Judge and Father—all terms referring to male human beings in that society. Any exceptions to this overwhelmingly patriarchal nature of the religion are trivial.[194]

Furthermore, those passages and themes that are thought to support women's liberation are found, on closer inspection, to be quite patriarchal. They observe that the prophetic tradition, which is meant to strive for liberation, does not struggle against patriarchy. On the contrary, prophetic literature, for example Hosea, objectifies the female.[195] The prophets of the Old Testament who challenged many injustices never directed their criticism against patriarchy. Mary Daly writes, "Indeed, the imagery of Old Testament prophets was very sexist. There was a tiresome propensity for comparing Israel to a whore. . . . It did not occur to the prophets to decry Israel as a rapist—which would have been, behaviorally speaking, a more accurate description."[196]

Post-Christian feminists find other supposedly liberation texts to be very traditional. For instance, the story of Ruth does not portray female equality—Ruth still does what is expected of women in that culture,[197] and she still cannot be in a position of leadership at the gate of the city.[198] Similarly, the account of Mary and Martha would have significance only if a man was sitting at the feet of a woman.[199] And regarding Luke's account of the resurrection, Luke still confines women to a traditional role. The women who discover the empty tomb do not go and witness (contrary to Jewish law), but instead go and tell the male disciples.[200] Such examples of a closer examination of "liberation texts" confirm for post-Christian feminists the thoroughly patriarchal ethos of Scripture.

Post-Christian feminists also find this extensive patriarchy in the ministry of Jesus. They do not observe a "kenosis of patriarchy" in his life. They view Jesus as one who neither undermined patriarchy nor propounded feminist ideals.[201] So even though Jesus confronted Pharisees, he never challenged the inferior position of women. For instance, in analyzing Jesus' parables, post-Christian feminists note that women are marginalized. These women are in positions that patriarchal society assigned to them. Yes, Jesus helped women, but he also ministered to men. There was "nothing particularly exceptional about Jesus' behavior and attitudes towards women."[202] And even if they grant that Jesus countered patriarchal culture, this has little value because it is impossible to remove the overall oppressive patriarchal tradition of Christianity.[203]

Their argument is not only that the biblical text is patriarchal, but that this patriarchy is so interwoven into its entire message, including the core, that one cannot remove it. There is an unbreakable connection between Christianity and its patriarchal past. Christians have an anchor or a foot in history to which they always return. Since Christians hold that there is a revelation of God in past history—a special history culminating in Jesus Christ—to be Christian is to continually refer to that history, which is a patriarchal history. They claim that Christianity will always remain inextricably connected to patriarchy, and a person cannot discard this revelation while remaining Christian. Christianity, as a historical religion, cannot remove its concretion and forms[204]—it is simply impossible to remove the male imagery.[205] This is especially true regarding the metaphors for God, which are grounded in the normative and inspired texts of Christianity. Every time we read Scripture, we hear *Father* and *Son* being applied to God, we hear stories that enforce patriarchy, and we read of the savior Jesus—a male human being. One may find supplementary imagery, but the overwhelming imagery remains male.[206]

Post-Christian feminists argue that there is misogyny at the core and foundation of Christianity that cannot be removed. So they acutely disagree with Christian feminism, which "retranslates, skips over or reinterprets parts of the Bible that do not support human liberation."[207] Hampson illustrates the basic difference: "Christian feminists want to change the actors in the play, what I want is a different kind of play."[208]

Furthermore, they question whether Christian feminists are in fact remaining within Christianity. Hampson criticizes Ruether for never speaking of God but rather of "people's concept of God,"[209] and she writes that "one finds mention of Christ to be singularly absent from Schüssler Fiorenza's work."[210] Hampson also asks whether Sallie McFague's use of different metaphors such as the "world as God's body" is Christian.[211] Hampson believes it is not, and as such McFague "may construct whatever models for God she may wish."[212] For post-Christian feminists, this tellingly illustrates the incompatibility of feminism and Christianity and the futility of any attempt to reconcile the two. One cannot change the biblical symbols to their very foundation and remain in Christianity. Any attempt will result in failure, for Christianity always remains tied to the biblical texts.[213]

The Nature, Power, and Influence of Symbols

A fundamental reason why post-Christian feminists regard Jesus' maleness as significant and relevant is because of their view of the power and influence of symbols. Jesus' maleness continues to promulgate patriarchy, so they do not relegate Jesus' maleness to a category equivalent to race or class. Its significance is more profound. Christianity, being rooted in a patriarchal past, has male symbols for the divine.[214] It is a historical religion that is tied to that history with its symbols, metaphors, and stories. And these symbols are highly influential, inculcating and reinforcing certain beliefs so that today people view God "as an immaterial male spirit."[215]

These male symbols of Christianity continue to exert considerable influence over present culture and "are actively promoted by Western technocracy."[216] The pervasive influence of these symbols establishes and legitimates male authority and ensures that female power is squelched.[217] Therefore, a Goddess religion is appealing to some post-Christian feminists precisely because it "loosens the grip of masculine symbols upon the contemporary imagination."[218] Some find the symbol of Goddess necessary to counter patriarchy's destructive impact. As an alternative symbol, it affirms the legitimacy of female power, the female body, female initiative, and female relationships.[219]

God being symbolized by the male and Jesus being a male causes an insurmountable hurdle for post-Christian feminists. They don't believe that Christian feminists take seriously enough the central place of these images in Christianity. Feminists who work within Christian parameters have underestimated the impact, power, significance, and deep rootedness of these male images. To merely counter that God is beyond sex is inadequate, for these "symbols are effective at a subconscious and pre-rational level."[220] To illustrate their point, post-Christian feminists note that although complementarians affirm that God is beyond sexual differentiation they vigorously react to the suggestion of calling God "Mother." This response reveals that complementarians do hold that God is in some sense male.²²¹ Thus, Hampson concludes, "It is conservatives and feminist radicals who grasp the importance of symbolism. Both see that the fact that God, and Christ, have been seen as 'male' is crucial to the religion."²²²

Post-Christian feminists insist that the power and influence of these male images cannot be tempered or altered by an appeal to more female elements for God. This attempt by Christian feminists to find balancing female metaphors is counterproductive, for it merely serves to "enrich or enlarge our concept of the male."²²³ In other words, these female attributes are merely incorporated into the male God, without bringing any modification to his maleness. Instead, God's maleness becomes even more encompassing. Moreover, these attributes that God takes on are traditionally female roles, so this absorption "does nothing to change the conception of what are authentic roles for women."²²⁴

Hampson, for example, believes that Moltmann's appeal for a motherly Father is misguided and unhelpful—a position which merely incorporates female elements into the male.²²⁵ And any appeal to Mary or finding a female side of the Spirit is rejected, for these are also assumed under the male or into the male. The Father and Son outnumber the Spirit, and Mary's importance arises only out of her relation to Jesus.²²⁶ The Trinity allows no place for women, and so in Christianity "there is no symbolic place for articulate, self-actualizing woman, the equal of man."²²⁷

Beyond Christolatry

At the center of Christianity is the supreme symbol of a male Jesus, and this maleness cannot be evaded.²²⁸ In Christianity the Son becomes male, so it is clear that "salvation comes only through the male."²²⁹ Where biblical egalitarians and Christian feminists find liberation—for example in Galatians 3:28—Daly finds oppression, for both male and female are inextricably linked to being "in Christ," who is male.²³⁰ In addition, it is precisely this *male* savior who cannot save. Daly writes, "A patriarchal divinity or his son is exactly *not* in a position to save us from the horrors of a patriarchal world."[231] So she speaks of going "beyond Christolatry"[232]—that is, moving beyond deifying or glorifying Jesus' maleness, where this maleness is made essential for salvation and for our view of God. For Daly, a male savior cannot save women.[233]

Post-Christian feminists also observe that it is far easier to portray Jesus as a different race than sex.[234] The reason is that Jesus' maleness is regarded as more significant, for on this basis women are excluded from leadership, whereas those of a different race or class are not.[235] Because much of Christianity uses Jesus' maleness to exclude women demonstrates that God is viewed as male and could only incarnate in male form. Given this male incarnation, post-Christian feminists affirm that nothing can alleviate its patriarchal influence and significance.

Post-Christian feminists are thus critical of attempts to find female figures or motifs in order to have a more inclusive Christology.[236] They argue that these attempts will never achieve an equivalent place for women, for Jesus still remains male. Hampson notes that it is problematic for Christian feminists to look constantly at a male Jesus, thus their focus moves to women around Jesus.[237] Moreover, she claims that many Christian feminists do not have Christologies and questions whether it is possible for women to be content with a male savior.[238] This indicates to post-Christian feminists that those with feminist ideals will move beyond Jesus.

Women's Experience: A Rejection of Christianity's Truth and Moral Claims

The foundational starting point for post-Christian feminists is their experience[239] and a claim to autonomy. For them, thinking about God begins in experience,[240] and from this position of experience they reject Christianity's truth and moral claims. They argue that, starting from women's experience and autonomy, it is impossible to stay within Christianity. Because Christianity justifies patriarchy through male symbols and a male savior, it is neither true nor moral. Christianity is harmful, for it serves to "legitimize the inferior place of women in society."[241]

Christianity has propagated patriarchy, and post-Christian feminists note the evident immoral results of patriarchy, such as the history of male dominance characterized by an unholy trinity of rape, genocide, and war.[242] Post-Christian feminists conclude that Christianity is immoral because Christianity's conception of a male God and a male savior has led to violence and discrimination against women. Even if the situation is changed today, some wonder how God could have allowed only men in a previous age to have authority.[243]

Post-Christian feminist critique of Christian truth and morality extends into other areas. They find themselves in conflict with monotheism and covenant, both of which support hierarchical structures.[244] The idea of sacrifice is also abhorrent, and they observe that women "appear almost universally to dislike the theme of sacrifice."[245] Also, based on present experience, Hampson denies that the incarnation or resurrection is possible. Nothing can interrupt the causal nexus of history—the regularity of history and nature where one event follows the other.[246] So in formulating their position, priority is given to what women find valid in their "own experience without needing to look to the past for justification."[247] From this basis women can reclaim the right to name their reality—their self, world, and God.[248]

Conclusion

Post-Christian feminists regard Christianity as idolatrous: the symbols no longer make sense and describe reality, but instead support injustice and violence—and so have been revealed as idols. They conclude that Christianity is essentially a projection of the ideas and aspirations of men—the same religious system attacked by Feuerbach and Freud. Christianity, through its metaphors and symbols, teaches that God is in some sense male, and they cannot accept a religion whose logical implication is that male is God or that male is more godlike than female. Daly's well-known statement is applied in this context, "If God is male, then the male is God."[249]

Post-Christian feminists consider the maleness of Jesus to be relevant and an integral part of Christianity. Jesus' maleness is one of the unchangeable, central, powerful images of the religion. As a religious symbol, it is overtly and covertly influential, even to the subconscious level. As such, its power serves to legitimate patriarchy. In addition, Jesus' ministry does not curb this influence. Jesus, though benevolent to women, never confronted the oppressive patriarchy of his time. Thus, post-Christian feminists conclude that there is no Christology that is compatible with feminism.

WHERE DO WE GO FROM HERE?

At this point, it will be helpful to note some areas of agreement. Considering these different positions, there is consensus that Jesus was male—there is no debate on the historicity of Jesus' maleness. Related to this is an acceptance that the Bible refers to Jesus as the Son—although it is debated *why* he is called Son, what this means, and whether it is legitimate to speak of an Eternal Son. There is also agreement, at least in principle, that God is not male. Significantly, all positions affirm an ontological equality (equality of being) between female and male. Similar to the implications that God is not male, the implications of this equality are also disputed.

Across the spectrum of positions, there is also an agreement that some New Testament teaching, which was normative in the Greco-Roman culture, is no longer binding today.[250] Most agree, for example, that we should not require foot washing (John 13:14), greeting one another with a kiss (1 Corinthians 16:20), women to wear head coverings (1 Corinthians 11:3–16), a rigid application of Paul's instruction that women remain silent in the church (1 Corinthians 14:34–35), an abstaining from the meat of strangled animals and from blood (Acts 15:20, 29), prohibiting braided hair and gold jewelry (1 Timothy 2:9; 1 Peter 3:3), or taking wine for the stomach (1 Timothy 5:23).

The question of head coverings, for example, illustrates that these agreements are sometimes on a superficial level. Although most claim that women need not wear head coverings,[251] the reasons given are different. Complementarians view the command for head coverings to be a specific cultural application of the general principle of male headship that is established in creation.[252] Since head coverings were a particular symbol of women's submission in ancient culture, contrary to twenty-first-century culture, they can be abolished. The specific application is removed but the principle of male headship remains in place. Others argue, however, that the head covering command is given because of principles of love. It is a command to wear appropriate dress so as not to give undue offense.[253]

The reason why Paul refers to creation in 1 Corinthians 11:8–9 is also disputed. Complementarians argue that Paul is referring to the headship of Adam. Egalitarians argue that Paul is referring to Eve coming from Adam, that is, when Paul uses the word *head* in verse 3 he essentially means source. So it is disputed what principle is invoked from creation.

On a more fundamental level, the head covering debate illustrates two different approaches that may be summarized in this manner: (1) A principle established in creation is given a specific cultural command. (2) A specific cultural command is given a theological basis in creation. Although these may appear identical, the implications of the text are reversed. The first position argues that there is an unchanging principle of headship established in creation, which finds various cultural expressions. Since head coverings are only a cultural expression of female submission, and since head coverings no longer depict female submission in twenty-first-century culture, the specific law no longer applies. The principle of male headship remains, although with different cultural applications. The second position argues that because there is a change in application (head coverings no longer required), this demonstrates that particular commands can be given a theological basis. The passage illustrates that there are laws, though grounded theologically in creation, which are no longer normative.

Apart from these agreements—that God is not male, that male and female are equal in being, that Jesus was male and is called Son, and that there are some commands in the New Testament no longer applicable to us today—we have seen some remarkably different views on the meaning of Jesus' maleness. How can we go about answering some of the questions that we raised in the introduction? And how has the church in the past gone about solving similar difficulties and deciding what is just, good, and loving?

Theology has always had conversation partners. Here we need partners that will further our discussion and help us answer our questions. It is also helpful to have partners that illustrate how the church has wrestled with other issues and eventually decided on a particular outcome. In this first half of the book I have chosen three dialogue partners to direct, inform, and expand our discussion—helping us along as we seek to find some answers to our questions concerning the significance of Jesus' maleness. The first partner is the debate over slavery in the nineteenth century in North America. The topic of slavery regularly occurs in the gender debate, and there is considerable disagreement over the relevance of slavery. The second partner is the debate over the Sabbath. The Sabbath debate, though not usually referred to, is relevant because, like the gender debate, it also refers to creation. The third partner is an interdisciplinary conversation with science. Here we will expand our discussion beyond the theological discipline to incorporate ideas from other fields. All three partners will help carry our conversation a fair distance.

CHAPTER 2

The Slavery Debate—Implications for Our Topic

In the nineteenth century the church battled over the question of slavery. The conflict revolved around a central question: Is slavery a biblically approved and just institution (provided that slaves are well treated), or is slavery inherently un-Christian? The proslavery movement argued that the Bible supports the institution of slavery, while Christian abolitionists argued that enslaving people is contrary to the spirit of the gospel. The way people argued for either position provides a wealth of application and illustration.

The slavery debate leaves us with a historical example to consider, and living in the twenty-first century gives us the benefit of hindsight. The church worldwide rejects slavery and is concerned wherever people are enslaved. It considers enslaving a person to be antithetical to the good news of Jesus Christ. The church now condemns slavery, thus the general abolitionist hermeneutical approach, gospel understanding, and quest for justice has much to teach us.

Complementarians and post-Christian feminists argue that the slavery debate is different from our topic and mainly irrelevant. Complementarians consider slavery to be ultimately linked to culture and a fallen world, whereas they view male headship to be permanently established in creation. Therefore, complementarians view slavery as wrong, but they still argue for male headship. Since slavery is not grounded in creation, complementarians believe that it is largely irrelevant to the discussion. Likewise, post-Christian feminists find little relevance between the two debates. They view the eventual change of the church's view on slavery as more of a surface change, whereas they believe that their concerns relate to the core symbolism of the Christian faith.

In contrast, biblical egalitarians and Christian feminists argue that the slavery issue is similar to our topic and has significant implications. They find parallels between complementarian and proslavery argumentation;[1] and given these parallels, and the fact that the church now rejects slavery, they argue that the slavery question is relevant.

Let's now look at the slavery debate as it relates to our topic and, in particular, at the numerous parallels in argumentation between proslavery and complementarianism and between abolitionism and feminism. (Here I will use the term *feminism* or *feminist* to include biblical egalitarianism and Christian feminism when they would generally agree.) After outlining and interacting with some of these parallels, we will consider what areas are relevant or irrelevant for our topic. Regarding the overall slavery debate, for our purposes we are interested in similar argumentation and approaches and will only focus on the nineteenth-century debate in North America.

One caveat before we begin. Given the horrors of slavery, drawing any parallels with current positions is risky. One problem is guilt by association; implying that some people today are like nineteenth-century slaveholders creates the risk of alienating some people. There are remarkable similarities, however, between the slavery and gender debates, so we should not shy away from making associations and applications. The dangers should not make us withdraw from this discussion. And I want to emphasize that comparisons are made to illustrate similar *interpretive* methods and approaches in the debates. I intend no other comparison.

PARALLELS BETWEEN PROSLAVERY AND COMPLEMENTARIAN ARGUMENTS

The proslavery movement justified slavery from the universality of the institution. Viewing the swath of human history, they saw slavery existing in every age and concluded, in the words of Episcopal bishop John Hopkins (who was actually a Northerner), that slavery has "existed as an established institution in all the ages of our world, by the universal evidence of history."[2] The implication is that since slavery is universal it is part of the natural order of human existence and therefore must be legitimate. Similarly, complementarians appeal to the universality of patriarchy to defend male leadership. Based on Steven Goldberg's work *Why Men Rule*,[3] Bruce Waltke says that it is "a truism of anthropology . . . that male leadership is normative in every culture and that there is no evidence of matriarchy."[4] The suggestion is that there is something natural and proper about male leadership, since we find it across time and all cultures.

Universality, however, does not imply the goodness or inevitability of patriarchy—as Goldberg qualifies himself.[5] It also does not mean that men are better suited to leadership than women. On such a basis we could justify adultery from its universality, or we could conclude that since men are more likely to be involved in criminal behavior they are unsuited for leadership. In addition, egalitarians and Christian feminists hold that patriarchy came because of the fall—hence its universality. They argue, however, that the gospel should transform this worldwide patriarchy.

A related argument is from historical precedent. Proslavery advocates noted that the church had always given its consent to the lawfulness of slavery. Hopkins writes, "I *know* that the doctrine of that Church was clear and unanimous on the *lawfulness* of slavery for eighteen centuries."[6] Likewise, complementarians argue that the church has generally always held a complementarian view and that "until the twentieth century the Church universally understood Scriptures to teach male rulership in the Church."[7] Complementarians contend there must be good reasons for the church to hold this view for so long,[8] and "if Scripture does not mean what people have taken it to mean for centuries, then the Bible is obscure, and, due to its lack of clarity, it cannot possess the authority it once had."[9]

The argument from historical precedent—that is, "the church has always believed this"—carries significant weight. No one wants to overturn rashly what the church has understood and taught for most of its existence. Two things, however, need to be said at this point: (1) For most of its history the church has held that women are inferior by nature and therefore should not lead. This is not the complementarian position, which holds that women are equal in being. So complementarianism cannot be equated with the church's historical position. (2) In the case of slavery, it is now clear that some in the church were wrong in the past. So the argument from historical precedent is indecisive; and a cursory look at the church's history shows that it has been wrong on more than one occasion—for example, its anti-Semitism.

Unchangeable Character and Morality of the Institutions

As we saw in chapter one, complementarians appeal to creation to justify male headship. They regard male rule, at least in church and family, to have a permanent status because of its foundation in creation. Similarly, proslavery apologists believed that slavery was unchangeable, and they amassed considerable arguments by appealing to divine law, ordination, providence, prophecy, and indirectly, to creation. James Thornwell, for example, argued that in contrast to the "rights of man" approach, slavery was founded on divine law and providence.[10] This unchangeable law included the Decalogue and Paul's commands.

Slavery was also a condition founded in prophecy, such as the curse on Canaan in Genesis 9:25,[11] which demonstrated that God had ordained slaves to service.[12] Proslavery proponents considered slavery permanent, since divine order appointed people to different lots in life. They placed the institution of slavery on the same footing with relationships such as husband-wife, magistrate-citizen, and parent-child. Thus, "White Southerners tended to view most reform movements as heretical, because tampering with social relations that they believed had been ordained by God, such as slavery or the subordination of women to men, amounted to tampering with the will of God."[13]

Defenders of slavery also argued that slavery, by implication, was a condition inherent to creation, so that the slave was constitutionally suited to this position and made for service. In fact, an African was so well-suited for slavery that as a slave he was far happier, safer, and useful than in any other existence.[14] There was a common belief among slavery defenders that slaves were made for their position[15] and were not naturally fitted for the freedom that others enjoy.[16]

Related to this unchangeable character is the parallel claim of the morality of the institutions of patriarchy and slavery. Proslavery argued that because the Old and New Testaments never condemn slavery, any claim that slavery is evil is to assert that God approves of sinful behavior. To argue that the institution of slavery is immoral imputes evil to God.[17] Complementarians also note that the prophets never criticized patriarchy[18] and that no New Testament teaching condemns patriarchy.[19] Patriarchy is a moral institution, so a claim that it is evil implies that God approves of sinful behavior. Furthermore, it is argued that any claim that patriarchy is wrong is tantamount to claiming that revelation is distorted.[20]

Protection

In defending the institution of slavery, proslavery argued that the slave had to be protected, and the only way this could happen was by keeping him in servitude.[21] Hopkins elaborates, "In the view of the Southern slaveholders, therefore, the general emancipation of their negroes would not only be ruinous to the masters, but cruel, to the last degree, towards the slaves themselves; because it would thrust into the dangers and difficulties of freemen, millions of human beings who are entirely unfitted by nature for freedom, and who need the *protection* [italics mine] and government of their masters, even more than the masters need their labor."²²

Some complementarians have adopted similar argumentation. John Piper speaks of the need of men to protect women and this being a defining quality of maleness. In defining masculinity, he writes, "At the heart of mature masculinity is a sense of benevolent responsibility to lead, provide for and *protect* [italics mine] women in ways appropriate to a man's differing relationships."²³ It follows, therefore, that it is repugnant to many complementarians that women serve in combat. Tied into male identity is the view that men are to protect women.

In the case of slavery, the promise of protection and oppression went together. Often an oppressor provides fear and tyranny, and then promises protection. This promise of protection sounded loving, but it was foundational to a cruel system and based on racist views of Africans—that they were inferior in nature and ability. Slavery apologists failed to recognize that while claiming slaves needed protection, slaves essentially needed protection from their slave owners.

Likewise, why do women need protection, if it is not from evil men? In illustrating this need for male protection, Piper refers to a man protecting a woman who is being mugged by, presumably, a male assailant.²⁴ A characteristic of love is to protect the beloved, but why make this a uniquely male characteristic or calling? Surely, in each situation the person (female or male) should aid according to ability, with differing situations requiring diverse gifts of intelligence, strength, ingenuity, intuition, or verbal skills. Furthermore, if the focus is on men providing protection through their physical strength, all too often the only option considered is violence. Why not talk your way out of it? And in this case, perhaps a woman would do a better job of protecting everyone involved.

Equal but Subordinate

Proslavery advocates affirmed that slaves were equal but subordinate. Thornwell asks, "But where do the Scriptures teach that an essential equality as men implies a corresponding equality of state?"[25] While in principle holding that all people were in the image of God, proslavery held that slaves were in some way inferior. There was the belief that slaves were equal in being but were given different roles. So Robert Dabney held that the slave was in the image of God but did not have ecclesiastical equality.[26] Tellingly, H. S. Smith titled his work on racism in the southern United States (written in 1972) *In His Image, but . . . : Racism in Southern Religion*. He writes, "Religious leaders of the white South have always theoretically subscribed to the doctrine of the *imago Dei*, yet until at least well into the present century they, with rare exceptions, affirmed the inferiority of the Negro race and defended the traditional regional pattern of white supremacy."[27]

A similar transformation has occurred in the church. We know that through much of the church's history many viewed women as inferior in being. Today complementarians, while insisting that women are in no way inferior, still hold that women are "in his image, but . . ." They claim the full ontological equality of men and women but deny women leadership, at least in the home and church. Similar to proslavery advocates, complementarians argue that this equality of being is compatible with different roles or subordination. Men image God by having authority and women image God in their submission.[28] So both men and women resemble or image God, but in different ways.

The church eventually rejected the proslavery scheme of "equal but subordinate." Later we will return to whether it is in keeping with the gospel for complementarians to apply this "equal but subordinate" construction to women.

Emphasis on Specific Texts, Particularly Pauline

Defenders of slavery referred far more to Paul than to Jesus.[29] The texts they appealed to were mainly 1 Corinthians 7:20–24, Ephesians 6:5–9, Colossians 3:22—4:1, 1 Timothy 6:1–8, Titus 2:9–10, and Paul's letter to Philemon.[30] (A main non-Pauline text was 1 Peter 2:18–23.)

Proslavery arguments appealed to specific texts rather than to general principles of equality, love, and freedom. When challenged with a general principle of love like the Golden Rule, Thornwell responded, "The rule then simply requires, in the case of Slavery, that we should treat our slaves as we should feel that we had a right to be treated if we were slaves ourselves."[31] Proslavery incorporated principles of love into its system so that it even viewed the Golden Rule to support slavery.[32]

Complementarian argumentation also mainly appeals to Pauline literature, such as 1 Corinthians 11:2–16, 14:33–36, Ephesians 5:21–33, Colossians 3:18–19, 1 Timothy 2:11–15, and Titus 2:5. (Their main non-Pauline texts are Genesis 1–3 and 1 Peter 3:1–7.) Similarly, complementarians incorporate principles of love and equality into their system of thought. As we have noted, they view equality of being and subordination as compatible. Similarly, male headship is not conceived to be in conflict with love.[33] Overall, both positions claim that there are specific texts (particularly Pauline) that are not abrogated by an appeal to more general principles such as the Golden Rule.

Clear Meaning of the Text

The proslavery position held that these specific texts were clear and that there was no way around such plain meaning. Speaking of the abolitionists, Thornwell lamented, "While they admit that the letter of the Scriptures is distinctly and unambiguously in our favor, they maintain that their spirit is against us; and, that our Savior was content to leave the destruction of whatsoever was morally wrong in the social fabric to the slow progress of changes in individual opinions, wrought by the silent influence of religion, rather than endanger the stability of governments by sudden and disastrous revolutions."[34]

Similarly, complementarians ask the question, How would first-century Christians have interpreted passages that are at the forefront of the debate, such as Genesis 1–3 and 1 Timothy 2:8–15? Very similar to the way complementarians interpret them today.[35] Since these early

Christians would have some of the ancient patriarchal mindset, their interpretation would be along the same lines as complementarians.[36] The texts are clear today and they were clear to the earliest Christians; so feminist readings of these texts "cannot plausibly be sustained."[37]

Both proslavery and complementarianism argue that their positions are found in the clear or natural interpretation of the texts, the one that the church from the earliest of times accepted. They both note that opposing their positions is an argument from a "transformation principle," an argument that there are principles inherent to the gospel that over time transform these specific texts.

Negation of Clear Texts by General Principles

This builds on the previous point. There is a broad concern in proslavery and complementarian thought that an emphasis on general principles not only undermines these specific texts but also opens the floodgates of immorality. The fear is that if principles override the specifics everything becomes only cultural—all commands could be viewed as only cultural and anything may be permitted. Proslavery advocates were anxious that general principles would then be used to argue for any morality.[38] Similarly, complementarians are concerned that the emphasis on principles of equality and love, and using these principles to eliminate male headship, could justify homosexuality or at least leave no adequate defense against it. If these principles can negate the clear and specific commands for male headship, then people may use these principles to nullify any command.

Underlying the proslavery and complementarian concern of a drift into immorality is their establishment of the commands of submission in nature. Each position says that the commands for slave and woman submission (ethics) are founded in nature (ontology). It is therefore understandable that they resist a change of ethics. Proslavery resisted emancipation not only because of the clear texts but because they considered that the slave was suited by nature to his condition. Emancipation would then permit a slave to do something for which he is not suited by nature. Likewise, complementarians oppose egalitarianism not only because of clear biblical texts but because they believe these commands for headship and submission are based in creation. In other words, headship and submission define one of the created differences between the sexes and elucidate what is true by nature. Therefore, to negate headship is to minimize the differences between the sexes and thus open the door for homosexuality.

We will address the significant differences between the sexes later on. At this point we note that all positions agree that there are substantial differences between the sexes—including psychological, cultural, and physiological differences. The crucial question is this: Is male headship *one* of these *many* differences between the sexes? At least in the case of slavery, the proslavery slippery-slope argument was demonstrated to be wrong. The principles of equality, love, and freedom won the day without the church drifting into evil. In fact, if there was a slide, it was a slide into love, for it led to the abolition of an evil institution.

Countercultural Trend

Proslavery, like complementarianism, went against the prevailing trend in culture. Proslavery apologists readily acknowledged this. Hopkins recognized "how distasteful my sentiments must be, on this very serious question, to the great majority of my respected fellow-citizens."[39] Thornwell agreed and wrote, "Opposition to Slavery has never been the offspring of the Bible. It has sprung from visionary theories of human nature and society; it has sprung from the misguided reason of man."[40] Slavery defenders believed that arguments against slavery did not originate from Scripture but from the cultural context,[41] and they accepted that their position was contrary to that culture.

Given this position of proslavery, it is surprising that Piper and Grudem argue, "We must remember the real possibility that it is not we but evangelical feminists today who resemble nineteenth century defenders of slavery in the most significant way: using arguments from the Bible to justify conformity to some very strong pressures in contemporary society (in favor of slavery then, and feminism now)."[42] This is doubtful. Proslavery extensively claimed that the abolitionists were conforming to the culture and recognized that the cultural trend was contrary to slavery. Defenders of slavery supported the original status quo as complementarians do today. Piper and Grudem recognize that the present cultural influence is feminism, and since they oppose feminism their position is countercultural.

A further parallel is seen in that slavery defenders and complementarians have attempted to make their position more amenable to the culture. Smith notes that there was a development, especially by the time of the American Civil War, where proslavery apologists sought to develop a more humane slavery, correct abuses, and make it "less vulnerable to outside criticism."[43] Similarly, complementarians have dropped the term *hierarchy* and now use *complementarian*. Furthermore, many complementarians now hold that female submission is only required in church and family, and none would maintain that women are inferior in being, contrary to the church's historical position.

To imply that a position is wrong because it coincides with cultural developments is unpersuasive. Abolitionism is a case in point; the Copernican Revolution is another. Quite often, the cultural milieu shocks or catalyses some in the church to reexamine their interpretation and position.

Tendency to Ignore the Experience of Slaves and Women

There was a tendency in the proslavery movement to downplay the affliction of slaves. James McPherson notes that, in response to abolitionism, proslavery apologists emphasized that slavery had civilized Africans, given them security, been a blessing to them, and they were in fact "cheerful in their bondage."[44] (Some may remember similar arguments supporting apartheid in South Africa.)

In response to the question about the plight of slaves, Hopkins spends a chapter on the miserable condition of those living in England,[45] and he concludes that this "is a perfect demonstration that millions of people, descended from the superior races of mankind, are in a worse condition, by far, in free England, than the negro slaves of the South, in their social habits, in their sense of morality and religion, and in every other element of human comfort."[46] This is beside the point and diverts attention elsewhere. On another occasion Hopkins regards the question, "How would you like to be a slave?" as a "very puerile interrogatory."[47]

That complementarians undercut experience is shown in their general neglect of dealing with the persecution, abuse, or marginalization of women. For instance, there is no chapter in the main complementarian text, *Recovering Biblical Manhood and Womanhood*,[48] on spousal abuse, although the problem is found in the church and some men use biblical texts to justify their oppression—the same texts which the book uses to justify male headship. There is also no chapter examining and renouncing what the church has traditionally taught concerning the inferior status of women. Although it is easy to criticize what a book leaves out, given the importance that feminism places on the plight of women, it is an awkward silence that fails to address what is a foundational concern in feminist thinking.

As another example, Kassian, although sympathetic to the plight of women, regards the focus on bad experience as "consciousness raising"—a parallel to Mao Tse-Tung's approach to incite revolution.[49] Another way to view it would be to see raising awareness of injustice as an integral part of overturning evil, which Jesus did many times. Suffice to say that complementarians have not focused attention on the extensive persecution against women, such as the church's terrible history of demeaning women.

Opposing Argument Leading to an Abandoning of Christianity

Proslavery argued that the logical end of abolitionism would be a rejection of Christianity.[50] To support this claim they noted that there were ultra-abolitionists who rejected the Bible and who departed from Christianity,[51] and that such ultra-abolitionists had called for an antislavery Bible and an antislavery God.[52] Dabney refers to one person in particular who claimed that "his abolitionism is a prime moving cause with him to spurn Christianity."[53] Defenders of slavery viewed abolitionists as attacking the core of Christianity[54] and departing from the supremacy and authority of Scripture.[55] They believed that the logical end of this attack would be a departure from Christianity. Similarly, complementarians argue that feminists are on a path away from Scripture and Christianity.[56] To support this claim it is also noted that that there are post-Christian feminists who have departed from Christianity.[57]

Arising from the proslavery and complementarian belief in the clear meaning of certain texts, as well as their observation that the radical opposition has departed from Christianity, they classify the opposition as departing from Scripture and on a slippery slope to an outright abandonment of Christianity. The slavery debate, however, demonstrates that abandoning Christianity did not necessarily follow from an abolitionist position, since most Christians are now abolitionist, even though some in the past had claimed that their abolitionism led them to deny Christianity.

Denial of Ordination

In arguing against the public preaching of women, Dabney relates women and slavery. He writes, "So the canons of the early church forbade slaves to be ordained until they had legally procured emancipation; and doubtless they were right in this rule. But in Christ there is 'neither bond nor free.' If, then, the equality of these classes in Christ did not imply their fitness for public office in the church, neither does the equality of females with males in Christ imply it."[58] As proslavery advocates opposed the ordination of slaves,[59] so complementarians also deny women ordination, a position based on 1 Timothy 2:11–15.[60]

Current Situation Abolished in the End Times

Proslavery was not in favor of perpetual bondage and desired that the institution eventually be abolished.[61] Thornwell conceded, "That the design of Christianity is to secure the perfection of the race is obvious from all its arrangements; and that, when this end shall have been consummated, Slavery must cease to exist is equally clear. . . . In this sense Slavery is inconsistent with the spirit of the Gospel."[62] Defenders of slavery acknowledged that the consummation would abolish slavery. But this fact was insufficient to overturn the present social order. For proslavery advocates, the spirit of the gospel and the future world did not overturn the present established roles in a fallen world.

Most complementarians agree that the eschaton will abolish our present marriage and church structures. And as with proslavery, this fact does not overturn the present created distinctions of male headship and female submission. For complementarians, feminists are guilty of an over-realized eschatology—an attempt to remove created distinctions between the sexes that will only be removed at the end times.[63] So although male headship will be removed in the coming age, this does not mean that we should remove it today. Principles such as those found in Galatians 3:28, although true in the eschaton, do not overturn the present created distinctions.[64]

The power of this argument fades in light of theological developments that lay emphasis on the *primacy* and *efficacy* of the future. According to Anne Carr, God is not so much up *above* us, but up *ahead* of us.[65] Theologians call this by various names: ontological eschatology, futurity, the power or ontology of the future, or God as the Absolute Future. Contemporary theology has gone back to the future, with the emphasis not on the past, or even the present, but on the future that draws us, enlivens, gives hope, and provides vital ethical implications. With this perspective, the good news is the inbreaking of the future. The future of complementarianism is its abolishment, so why not work toward it now?

Numerous parallels exist between proslavery and complementarian argumentation, and their striking similarities indicate more than coincidence. Furthermore, we can see this connection where some complementarians continue the proslavery argument and maintain that slavery is not intrinsically evil. Foh asks, "If slavery is wrong, why didn't someone—Jesus or the apostles—say so? Instead of condemnation of slavery *per se*, in the New Testament we find the clear denunciation of the abuses resulting from and associated with slavery. A distinction should be made between the institution itself and the abuses associated with it; denunciation of the abuses related to slavery does not concern the legitimacy of slavery itself."[66] This does not mean that Foh and others support nineteenth-century forms of slavery. Our interest lies in the similar argumentation and hermeneutical approach. The number of parallels, the close similarity in argumentation, and the fact that some complementarians continue the proslavery argument demonstrate that the parallels between proslavery and complementarianism are related. The relevance of these parallels remains to be examined.

Parallels Between Abolitionist and Feminist Arguments

Why did Paul not confront slavery and expose it as evil? Albert Barnes gives the reason as expediency. Slavery and ancient culture were so entwined that to remove slavery would be disastrous. He argues that in a similar manner the New Testament does not confront the civil government that was also extremely wicked.[67] The argument from expediency is prevalent in biblical egalitarianism,[68] and we also find it in Christian feminism. It claims that Paul's commands for submission of slaves and women were to keep the peace and to help the oppressed live under harsh conditions.[69] There would have been significant social upheaval if Paul had openly undermined slavery and patriarchy—something akin to arguing for the abolishment of computers in our day. Instead, Paul commands slaves and women to submit, thus preventing a destructive conflict that would have arisen given the enmeshment of slavery and patriarchy in that culture.

The argument from expediency has a couple of weaknesses. First, it assumes that a person like Paul was an abolitionist but restrains himself—that Paul thought through the problem, realized that slavery was wrong, but decided not to address it because of the widespread social upheaval and conflict that would arise. But we know that Paul was unafraid to confront major issues. Paul, as a person of his time, was not a closet abolitionist. He did not consider abolishing slavery; however, when Paul applies the gospel to various situations he goes beyond his culture. Paul sees some problems with the treatment of slaves, so he urges slave owners to treat slaves with love (Ephesians 6:9; Colossians 4:1); and he asks Philemon to receive his runaway slave no longer as a slave but as a brother (Philemon 16). In doing so, Paul plants gospel seeds that in time came to fruition under the Spirit and helped to change the conscience of the church. In this sense, Paul faithfully served a gospel bigger than his own vision.

Second, the great social movements to abolish slavery and bring equal rights to women went against entrenched societal institutions and systemic evils. If Paul did not confront particular issues because of practical considerations such as causing social upheaval, why support, say, abolitionism? In other words, the argument for expediency raises the question whether we should ever fight against entrenched social evils, because in doing so we may cause considerable social unrest.

Applying Specific Texts

Abolitionists appealed to specific passages, which if put into practice would abolish slavery. One of the preferred texts concerned kidnapping. As early as 1700, in *The Selling of Joseph*—the first abolitionist tract to appear in the future United States—Samuel Sewell drew attention to

Exodus 21:16 and the capital offense of kidnapping.[70] This argument was taken up by people like Barnes, who attempted to demonstrate that the Mosaic law did not fundamentally approve of slavery, since it opposed kidnapping (Deuteronomy 24:7) and most slavery came through kidnapping.[71] He believed that a rigid application of this law would abolish slavery. For Barnes, the Mosaic law secured many rights for slaves and regulated slavery to make the institution more bearable.

Similarly, when discussing Ephesians 6:5–9 Barnes reasons that Paul expresses the relationship between master and slave in such a manner as to secure the abolition of slavery. Concerning Ephesians 6:9, he says, "He [Paul] taught them [masters] their duty towards those who were under them, and laid down principles which, if followed, would lead ultimately to universal freedom."[72] In expressing the relationship in this way, Paul transforms the relationship between slave and master—a transformation that would in turn lead to emancipation. Even though Paul did not directly confront slavery, he urged a way of relating that when put into practice would transform and eventually overturn slavery.

Feminists adopt a similar argument. They argue that passages such as Galatians 3:28 or Ephesians 5:21–33, if rigorously applied, would abolish patriarchy. A thorough application of Galatians 3:28 would lead to ecclesiastical equality, like what was achieved for Gentiles and slaves. Similarly, Ephesians 5:21–33 correctly applied would, in practice, work out as an egalitarian marriage. The husband giving up his life would effectively abolish complementarianism.

There is, however, an important difference between abolitionist and feminist arguments. Whereas abolitionists sought to remove the institution of slavery, feminists address the issue of submission within the institution of marriage. In other words, feminists want to preserve the institution of marriage but strive for a transformation of the structure within the institution. They desire the abolishment of the institution of patriarchy, which is different from the institution of marriage. Abolitionists, however, attacked the institution of slavery as well as the structures within it.

Appeal to a Historically Relevant Issue

As the gender debate refers to slavery, the slavery debate referred to polygamy. Abolitionists argued that the Bible allowed for polygamy, though the people of God came to view it as sinful—like the issue of slavery. They argued that in the same way polygamy was eventually declared to be sinful, though it was permitted and regulated, so should slavery be declared evil. Defenders of slavery denied this association, claiming that the Bible established slavery in prophecy and divine law[73] but that polygamy had no such sanction.[74]

In other words, proponents of slavery viewed the institution of slavery as permanent and polygamy as only cultural. Similarly, complementarians view the institution of male headship as normative and slavery as only cultural. As divine law, providence, and prophecy functioned to justify the morality of the institution of slavery, so the creation ordinance is used to justify male headship. Feminists appeal to what complementarians do not support, namely slavery, and argue that complementarians are inconsistent—that is, they should argue for slavery. Abolitionists appealed to what defenders of slavery did not approve, namely polygamy, and maintained that they were inconsistent—that is, they should tolerate polygamy.

In response to these associations, proslavery advocates and complementarians deny the correlation with polygamy and slavery respectively:

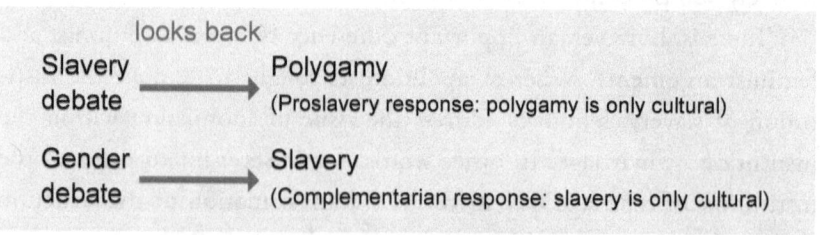

Both defenders of slavery and complementarians claim that the connections are irrelevant and that polygamy and slavery are different issues—their position being that one is permanently established and the other is only cultural. Furthermore, contrary to proslavery arguments that polygamy was only cultural, abolitionists found legislation governing polygamy in Exodus 21:7–10 and Deuteronomy 21:15–16 and 25:5–10.[75] Abolitionists argued that the Bible established polygamy in divine law and thus had a theological basis, like slavery. Similarly, feminists refer to texts, such as 1 Peter 2:18–21, which establishes slavery in the work of Christ,[76] and gives slavery theological underpinnings. Thus, feminists argue that those who justify male headship should also justify slavery.

Emphasis on Principles of Equality, Love, and Freedom

Abolitionists appealed to three main principles: equality, love, and freedom. They argued that these principles formed the foundation of a transformation dynamic that works itself out in the course of history. Abolitionists appealed to the principle of equality—that God made all people in God's image.[77] They argued that everyone is created equal[78] and has equal rights, such as the rights to property and marriage. All have a common nature (Acts 17:26), a nature that Jesus took on, so that no one is by nature inferior.[79] They also appealed to the principle of love and "readily acknowledged that Jesus did not condemn slavery in so many words, but always insisted that he laid down general principles that could not be reconciled with involuntary servitude. Above all else, they pointed to the law of love (Matthew 22:39) and the Golden Rule (Matthew 7:12) as subversive of the bondage system."[80] Finally, abolitionists appealed to the principle of freedom. In Scripture they found the principle of seven-year release, jubilee, freedom for the oppressed (Isaiah 58:6),[81] deliverance of the captives,[82] and Paul's message of freedom. Paramount was the deliverance from slavery in Egypt, which is a paradigm of what God does and how much God hates slavery.[83]

It is these three principles of equality, love, and freedom that form the basis of a transformation dynamic that brings changes through gradual development. Barnes writes, "It is in this way that God has in fact removed most of the evils of the world by a *gradual* development of principles which strike on great wrongs existing in society, thus preparing the world for the higher development of his will."[84] He continues, "There are certain things, in accordance with this view, which are evil and wrong, but which require patient *instruction* and much *discussion of principles* before the wrong will be perceived, and where, if denunciation be employed instead of argument, the whole object will be defeated."[85] Barnes concludes, "The principles laid down by the Saviour and his Apostles are such as are opposed to Slavery, and if carried out would secure its universal abolition."[86]

Looking back at the debate over slavery, feminists find a direct correlation between their concerns and abolitionist arguments.[87] For instance, Ruether sees her approach of emphasizing the liberating prophetic tradition as similar to abolitionist reasoning. She writes, "Christian churches in the 19th century pushed to the side texts that justified slavery. They brought to the center the texts that present redemption in the root meaning of liberation from slavery. They did this in order to reject the church's long historical tradition of justifying slavery as an institution and to champion the abolition of slavery, when it became evident to the 19th century conscience that this was the right thing to do. Today no Christian church would cite these texts justifying slavery as normative, though they remain in Scripture."[88]

Similar to abolitionists, feminists place primary importance on the principles of equality, love, and freedom. They argue that the spirit of the gospel and moral principles are opposed to the institution of patriarchy. It is only, however, in the course of history that the outworking of these principles finds expression. Feminists conclude that these principles must receive priority as we seek to understand and apply the gospel today.[89] Of course, there is no need to make a dichotomy between biblical principles and specific texts. The two are not opposed to one another, since moral principles influence our interpretation of specific texts and vice versa. And as we have seen, abolitionist arguments went beyond an appeal to principles, invoking many specific texts, such as the prohibition against kidnapping and oppressing people,⁹⁰ or the importance of paying people for their work. The point, however, is that proslavery and abolitionism *stressed* a particular approach. With a similar approach today, complementarians focus on specific texts while feminists focus on moral principles and their application.

Ultra-abolitionism and Post-Christian Feminism

One broader and important parallel deserves mention. In both the slavery and gender debate there was a radical group—ultra-abolitionist and post-Christian feminist respectively—that departed from Christianity. In each case the radical element agreed with their opposition—that the Bible supports the institution of slavery or patriarchy. Proslavery arguments led some to reject Christianity. In leaving Christianity a few agreed with slavery defenders that the Bible was proslavery. Similarly, post-Christian feminists agree with complementarians that the Bible teaches and legislates patriarchy, therefore they reject Christianity.

The parallels between abolitionist and feminist argumentation are clear. They were clear to women of the nineteenth century who saw the connection between the abolitionist position and their concerns.⁹¹ The parallels are clear to feminists today and they form part of their argument: (1) they are justifying an appeal to the priority of moral principles, and (2) they are following an approach that in the case of slavery proved to be correct.

RELEVANCE OF THE SLAVERY DEBATE

Complementarians say that the associations with slavery are irrelevant. Piper and Grudem write, "Therefore, while it is true that some slave owners in the nineteenth century argued in ways parallel with our defense of distinct roles in marriage, the parallel was superficial and misguided."⁹² Complementarians argue that these similarities may be interesting but are inconsequential, because slavery and male headship are two separate issues. Post-Christian feminists also agree that the analogy to slavery is irrelevant because patriarchy is far more embedded in Christianity, even to the extent of the divine names. The supreme images are patriarchal and not images expressed in terms of slavery.

Four main objections arise from complementarians when any comparison is made between them and defenders of slavery. They argue that their position cannot be compared with proslavery because of the following considerations.

1. Slavery and hierarchical marriage are not the same; they are quite different institutions.
2. Slavery in New Testament times was different from what we find in the nineteenth century. When the Bible addressed slavery, it was lenient because it addressed an institution that was unlike and far milder than slavery in the American South.[93] Thus, proslavery was wrong to use the Bible's tolerant view on ancient slavery to justify a harsh and cruel form of modern slavery.
3. The Bible only regulates the institution of slavery; it makes no comment about the institution as such. The Scriptures do not establish or approve of the institution of slavery (unlike hierarchical marriage).
4. Related to points one and three, hierarchical marriage is a permanent and good creation ordinance, whereas slavery is immoral, impermanent, and arose in a fallen world.

At this point we can answer objections one and two. The first objection that slavery and marriage are different is a given. Everyone agrees that marriage and slavery are different and not of the same order. And no one argues that we should abolish marriage, as we have done with slavery. On this, we all agree. Regarding slavery, abolitionists fought to abolish the entire institution. They viewed slavery as always a sin, even if masters treated their slaves well.[94] The institutions of slavery and marriage are different in that marriage continues as a good institution, whereas slavery arose from human sin.

Nevertheless, what remains are some remarkable similarities between proslavery and complementarian arguments and hermeneutical methods. To claim that these parallels are irrelevant, simply because the institutions are different, is special pleading. For instance, the debate is not over comparing slavery and marriage but comparing the same "equal but subordinate" schemes essential to both positions. These schemes require subordination because of being a slave or a woman. Furthermore, because everyone agrees that slavery and marriage are different, the debate is this: slavery is inherently subordinationist and hierarchical, but marriage may *not* be.

Regarding the second objection, we can say two things. First, even if slavery in New Testament times was unlike nineteenth-century slavery, we still have the parallel arguments and interpretive approaches of complementarians and proslavery advocates. Even if ancient slavery was quite different, proslavery theologians still interpreted the biblical text in a manner that has noteworthy parallels to complementarians today. It would still be a worthwhile exercise to compare the two.

Second, the objection of point two rests on whitewashing ancient slavery. Although there are exceptions, slavery in New Testament times was dehumanizing, violent, and terrifying. Yes, there were slaves in important positions, but "even the most privileged slave . . . could be quickly sold, or stripped and whipped, or raped, or sometimes killed at the whim of an owner."[95] Here are some features of slavery in New Testament times:

- Slaves were pieces of property. Roman law classified a slave as property.[96] The slave's body belonged to the slaveholder, so the slave could be abused at will or profited from by being forced into prostitution.[97] As a piece of property, most slaves had no honor and little self-identity—for example, a crime committed against a slave was seen as an assault not against the slave but against the slaveholder.
- Slaves endured sexual abuse. The sexual abuse of slaves was rampant.[98] Jennifer Glancy writes, "Sexual access to slave bodies was a pervasive dimension of ancient systems of slavery. Both female

and male slaves were available for their owners' pleasure."[99] And "since Roman society placed little value on men's sexual abstinence, young men often satisfied their sexual desires with household slaves or prostitutes (who were typically slaves)."[100] Slaves were to be sexually available, and the number of children born from such abuse points to its widespread and unrestrained occurrence.[101]

- Rome in its military conquests abducted multitudes of slaves from other nations. Julius Caesar helped himself to a million people from Gaul.[102] Captives from the spoils of war provided a steady influx of slaves that kept some slave markets operating at full capacity of some twenty thousand slaves a day.[103] Of course, those born to slaves became slaves themselves—further increasing or replacing the numbers.

- Slaves were legally tortured. Only slaves and noncitizens could be tortured.[104] And worse still, "Questioning slaves by the use of torture was both routine and required under the criminal law of Rome (and Athens)."[105] But why require the torture of slaves when questioning them? The reason is that slaves are by nature bad and deceitful.[106] So it was believed that the only way to get the truth from a slave was through torture. In addition, Roman law "provided that if a slave murdered his master, all the slaves in the household must be questioned under torture and then executed."[107] When a household slave killed a Roman prefect in AD 61, the authorities crucified all four hundred household slaves, including children.[108]

- Slaves endured horrific working conditions in the mines. Slaves did most of the mining throughout the empire, and Roman mines were notoriously inhumane.[109] Provided that Rome kept up a steady supply, slaves usually suffered under the cruelest conditions, working long hours in chains until death relieved them.[110]

- The majority of gladiators were slaves.[111] Their violent existence is exemplified by the events surrounding Spartacus, whose famous revolt was eventually crushed by the Romans, who promptly crucified about six thousand of these slaves along the Appian Way.

The Stoic writer Seneca (c. 4 BC–65 AD) describes typical Roman masters as "excessively haughty, cruel, and insulting,"[112] so a master has as many enemies as he has slaves. In addition, most slaves in the empire were never freed.[113] So it is unsurprising that J. A. Harrill concludes, "Despite claims by some NT scholars, ancient slavery was not more humane than modern slavery."[114] If we are looking for differences between ancient and nineteenth-century American slavery, we have to look no further than the color of our skin. The main difference was racism. And as for which system was worse, David Davis writes, "Even the harshest Southern lawmakers in the United States did not copy Roman laws allowing naked slaves to be put in an arena to fight hungry lions or ruling that if a slave raped a free virgin, molten lead was to be poured down his throat."[115]

What benefits do complementarians get by claiming that slavery in New Testament times was mild? (1) It allows them to distance themselves from the proslavery approach. If ancient slavery was mild, then proslavery made a huge interpretive mistake by likening ancient and modern forms. (2) It lessens the challenge that comes to their interpretive methods. If ancient slavery was brutal and the New Testament did not condemn the institution, can a complementarian hermeneutic demonstrate that slavery is immoral?

But as we have seen, slavery in New Testament times was cruel, which leads me to view these two supposed benefits as liabilities. First, proslavery used a particular method of interpretation to argue for the continuation of slavery, a method that has close parallels to complementarianism. Complementarian and proslavery approaches are close, but proslavery got it wrong. Second, since ancient slavery was cruel, complementarians have to adopt a different method of interpretation if they wish to argue against slavery. (We will look at some examples of this shortly.) This throws their overall interpretative method into question and uncertainty.

Since ancient slavery was cruel and since the Bible does not condemn slavery, what hermeneutic allows us today to condemn slavery? Certainly not the one adopted by slavery defenders, nor its parallel adopted by complementarians to argue for male headship.

Returning to the four objections complementarians have to comparisons of their position with the proslavery position, we have covered points one and two. We will cover point three shortly and address point four more fully in the following chapters. So what is the relevance of these parallels between complementarianism and proslavery?

Parallel Arguments Are a Warning

As we look at the slavery debate we have the benefit of hindsight. The whole church now sees slavery as morally incompatible with the gospel. Abolitionism won. But not long ago a significant section of the church amassed biblical arguments for slavery. Not only were they wrong, but they were wrong on the most important social issue of their day. This cautionary tale is relevant when we find ourselves today facing similar arguments and hermeneutical methods. Given the errors of the proslavery position, when we encounter arguments such as women need "protection" or women are "equal but subordinate," we should pause and not have an attack of historical amnesia.

The parallel arguments alert us to possible parallel mistakes. For instance, both complementarians and slavery defenders have arguments from historical precedent—that the church always supported their position. On closer examination, however, we find that this was not the case with slavery. Rodney Stark summarizes, "Although it has been fashionable to deny it, antislavery doctrines began to appear in Christian theology soon after the decline of Rome and were accompanied by the eventual disappearance of slavery in all but the fringes of Christian Europe. When Europeans subsequently instituted slavery in the New World, they did so over strenuous papal opposition, a fact that was conveniently 'lost' from history until recently."[116] This included opposition to slavery from

Dominican and Jesuit missionaries and the "condemnations of successive Popes, for example, Paul III in 1537, Pius V in 1567, and Urban VIII in 1639."[117] Many popes repeatedly issued papal bulls that condemned slavery under threat and pain of excommunication.[118]

For the proslavery argument from historical precedent to work, defenders had to throw a can of paint at a canvas that erased crucial parts of the picture. Similarly, complementarians claim to have historical precedent for their position. But their view is also different from what we find in the past. Many people in the past viewed women as inferior in being—an opinion no complementarian would hold today, and most complementarians apply their views *only* to church and family.

This caution extends beyond these parallel arguments to particular ways of viewing the world, God, and the Bible. The proslavery method of interpretation and understanding of the gospel and the continuing work of the Spirit preserved their hierarchical views, their personal identity, and their understanding of how Scripture is authoritative. These defenders of slavery minimized the significance and persuasive moral force of gospel principles—the image of God, love, freedom, and the impartiality of God. Their dualistic views of the gospel and humanity allowed for a split between personal and social change; so they allowed for the former but were comfortable with injustice.

The topic of slavery is relevant because it helps us establish the validity or importance of various arguments. In addition, it helps to disclose particular lines of reasoning, certain emphases and methods of interpretation, and different views about God, humanity, and the Bible.

Change of Hermeneutic

How do complementarians argue that the institution of slavery is immoral? Consider Piper and Grudem's reasoning:

> The preservation of marriage is not parallel with the preservation of slavery. The existence of slavery is not rooted in any creation ordinance, but the existence of marriage

is. Paul's regulations for how slaves and masters related to each other do not assume the goodness of the institution of slavery. Rather, seeds for slavery's dissolution were sown in Philemon 16 ('no longer as a slave, but better than a slave, as a dear brother'), Ephesians 6:9 ('Masters . . . do not threaten [your slaves]'), Colossians 4:1 ('Masters, provide your slaves what is right and fair'), and 1 Timothy 6:1–2 (masters are 'brothers'). Where these seeds of equality came to full flower, the very institution of slavery would no longer be slavery.[119]

We should remember that proslavery advocates used many of the passages mentioned above to justify the institution of slavery—that slavery was legitimate if masters treated slaves humanely. Piper and Grudem's argument against slavery, however, depends on the "seeds of equality," undoubtedly an abolitionist approach!

Rather than an isolated case, this is a staple argument of complementarians. When comparing slavery and marriage, Edmund Clowney writes, "Why, then, does not the loving submission of the wife and the sacrificial love of the husband subvert the structure of authority in the marriage relationship? Because slavery is an enforced relationship that is altered in its *essence* by mutual love, while marriage is itself a relationship of love ('one body'), a relationship brought by grace to fulfill God's design in the roles appointed by his creation."[120] So the principle of love transforms slavery to its core. And as one more example, Dorothy Patterson, speaking of "fundamental ethical principles," says, "These biblical principles, though not explicitly applied to slavery [in the Bible], if generally acknowledged and appropriated, must eventually lead to its abolition."[121]

The proslavery position viewed slavery as firmly established in divine providence, prophecy, order, and law and therefore not undermined by principles of love, equality, or freedom. Similarly, complementarians view male headship as firmly established in creation and not undermined by various principles. Nevertheless, in rejecting slavery Clowney uses abolitionist reasoning such as principles of equality and love to argue why slavery is wrong. While denying that the principle of love destroys male headship, he affirms that the principle does destroy slavery. For Patterson, there are foundational ethical principles that abolish slavery. For Piper and Grudem, it is the "seeds of equality." This leads to an intriguing point: we have seen numerous parallels in argumentation between proslavery and complementarianism, yet in rejecting slavery as a moral institution complementarians use *abolitionist* reasoning to explain why slavery should no longer continue.

Most complementarians reject slavery, but the hermeneutic used to repudiate slavery is along the lines of principles and not specific texts, which is opposite to their argument for male headship. It appears that they can only say that slavery is immoral by an appeal to general principles—an approach that would have been dismissed by proslavery apologists. Given the extensive parallels between proslavery and complementarianism, a more consistent approach would maintain that slavery, as an institution, is moral because of the Bible's specific commands and lack of denunciation. In other words, if complementarians applied similar methods of interpretation to slavery as they do to male headship, they would support the institution of slavery. Yet, their condemnation of slavery by an appeal to moral principles demonstrates their inconsistency in denouncing a feminist hermeneutical approach that focuses on principles.

The Theological Basis of Slavery

Proslavery advocates dismissed the polygamy analogy as irrelevant and argued that polygamy was only cultural and regulated by God. Likewise, complementarians treat the slavery analogy as irrelevant and argue that slavery was only cultural and regulated by God. In other words, according to complementarians the Bible does not support or establish the institution of slavery; it only gives commands to masters and slaves to make the institution more humane. Slavery is only cultural, because the New Testament only establishes slaves' submission, *not* the institution. Complementarians hold that slavery was not established in creation, and neither was there a "permanent moral command" associated with slavery.[122]

Proslavery apologists did not view slavery in this manner. As we have seen, defenders of slavery had amassed numerous biblical arguments for the establishment of slavery. So convinced, they argued that their opponents were departing from Scripture and giving into cultural pressure. Proponents of slavery even found support for their position in the first table of the Decalogue (Exodus 20:10, 17; Deuteronomy 5:14).[123]

Does the Bible establish the institution of slavery? Do the Scriptures give slavery a theological basis? In fairness to the proslavery position, the New Testament commanded slaves' submission and made no comment about the immorality of the institution. The Bible connected slavery with theological principles, such as the calling of God and work of Christ (1 Peter 2:18–21). In the great hymn of Philippians 2:5–11, Jesus, who was in the form of God, takes on the form of a slave (Philippians 2:7). Significantly, slavery is applied to the divine names (Colossians 4:1; Ephesians 6:9; 2 Timothy 2:21), where God is referred to as "Master." In addition, Christians are referred to as "slaves of righteousness" (Romans 6:18), "enslaved to God" (Romans 6:22), and "a slave of Christ" (1 Corinthians 7:22; cf. Colossians 4:12). Paul regularly referred to himself as a slave in this sense (e.g., Romans 1:1; Philippians. 1:1; Galatians 1:10). And following Paul's example, Christians are urged to become "slaves" to other people (1 Corinthians 9:19; 2 Corinthians 4:5; cf. 1 Corinthians 11:1). All of this provides a theological basis for the institution of slavery. It is special pleading to claim that this only applies to the regulation of slavery and not to the institution itself—a distinction the New Testament does not make.

Slavery is cultural and temporary, but the Bible gives it a theological basis while that cultural situation continues. This demonstrates that at least some issues, though only cultural, are firmly established theologically. As slavery continued, the theological basis appeared to some to legitimize and permanently establish the institution of slavery; yet principles of equality, love, and freedom eventually brought liberation.

Abolitionists demonstrated that slavery was only cultural by an appeal to principles, not by separating the institution and the structure within it. This explains why the debate between proslavery and abolitionism reached an impasse. Both positions had biblical arguments and strong theological positions—one appealing to the theological basis, and the other to general gospel principles. They reached no consensus, not only because of differing hermeneutical approaches but also because of underlying presuppositions such as the superiority of one race over another.

In fact, the outcome of slavery was decided not by theological debate but by civil war. As Mark Noll wryly observes, "It was left to those consummate theologians, the Reverend Doctors Ulysses S. Grant and William Tecumseh Sherman, to decide what in fact the Bible actually meant."[124] Both positions used the biblical material in a comprehensive and persuasive manner to support their position. McPherson writes, "By 1860, however, the Bible argument was pretty well played out. Thirty years of controversy had only shown that the Bible could be quoted effectively on both sides of the slavery issue."[125] The error of the proslavery position, however, was to use the theological basis to permanently establish the institution.

Gospel Application

Drawing on the slavery debate, we can make the following further applications:

1. The fact that a significant section of the church was wrong on slavery opens up the possibility that the church may be wrong in other areas. Given that conservative theology in America set forth the proslavery position with such moral certainty should alert us to the possibility of major errors in all theological systems, including our own.
2. Realizing and repenting of the evil of one injustice can open our eyes to other injustices and spur us to work for further transformation. A relevant example is found in the life of the Puritan Samuel Sewall (1652–1730), one of the judges who presided over the Salem witch trials.[126] After the trials

had come to an ignominious end and twenty people had been sent to their deaths, Sewall was cut to the heart and publicly repented for his role—the only judge to do so. He realized, however, that his repentance needed to be a process; and his subsequent life showed a remarkable transformation with his concern for slaves, Native Americans, and women. After his public apology in 1697 Sewall turned his attention to the plight of slaves. In 1700 he wrote and published *The Selling of Joseph*,[127] the first abolitionist tract printed in America. Sewell went on to champion the rights of Native Americans and women during a time when most considered them savages or inferior. His essay *Talitha Cumi*[128] argued that both women's and men's bodies will be raised in the resurrection, contrary to the widespread belief that everyone would be raised male and that heaven would be male. It is remarkable to read an article written by a man in 1724 that begins with Galatians 3:28—"there is no longer male and female; for all of you are one in Christ Jesus"—and ends by speaking of the rights of women. It is even more remarkable given Sewell's past.

3. Considering views on slavery, we see that change takes time. In 1995 the Southern Baptists, at their 150th convention, repudiated slavery and repented of their participation in it. They did so by appealing to equality and that all people are made in the image of God.[129] Likewise, in 2002 the Presbyterian Church in America (PCA), at their 30th general assembly, condemned chattel slavery and repented of their involvement. They also appealed to principles of love and freedom.[130] Ironically, at the same assembly this denomination registered their opposition to women in combat, stating that it is the biblical duty of men to protect women. Instead of directing their energy toward the evils of war, they emphasized their male identity as protectors of

women. And in 2006 the Church of England apologized for its role in the trans-Atlantic slave trade. One lesson from slavery is that it takes time for communities (ours included) to change their established or official views and to realize that some hallowed positions are contrary to the gospel and the Spirit of God.

4. As the Bible challenged the evil within slavery, the same challenge comes to patriarchy. Even though it was debated whether the institution of slavery was evil, the Bible clearly addressed sins that happened within slavery. Likewise, although it is debated whether patriarchy is evil, the Scriptures clearly denounce the sins that can occur within marriage or between the sexes—abuse, oppression, contempt, selfishness. The slavery debate is relevant in that, by association, it draws our attention to the sins that can occur within marriage or between the sexes and at least exposes those who use male headship to justify any of the above sins—a point with which all positions agree.

In addition to the evils found within slavery, the gospel also indicts the broader proslavery society of the American South. This provides lessons for us today, since this form of slavery, like apartheid in South Africa, was upheld by theological reasoning and was tied to male identity. And like apartheid, the defense of slavery is a sad story about the preservation of a brutal society.

What did slavery give to white men? Control, power, and authority over others. Privilege, liberty, and reputation. Access to wealth and property, with its attendant security.[131] These things defined white men, who sought to preserve this identity at all costs—even to the extent of waging war. Although it is sometimes popular to ignore or deny the fact, slavery was the principle cause of the American Civil War.[132] James McPherson devotes a full third of his book on the

Civil War, *Battle Cry of Freedom*, to the events leading up to the war. Most revolved around slavery—including the right to own slaves,[133] the fugitive slave law (requiring runaway slaves to be returned to their masters),[134] whether new states added to the Union should be slave or free,[135] the right to take personal property (i.e., slaves) to another state,[136] and the numerous compromises over slavery made by Congress to prevent secession or war.[137] The issue of slavery not only split denominations, such as the Baptist and Methodist,[138] it rent the country in two.

In addition, the common soldier in the Civil War viewed the reason for the war as slavery. In her book *What This Cruel War Was Over*, Chandra Manning has shown, by scouring soldiers' letters and diaries, regimental newspapers, and other material, that "no matter which side of the divide a Civil War soldier stood on, he knew that the heart of the threat, and the reason that the war came, was the other side's stance on slavery."[139] For Manning, the continued existence of slavery was essential to maintain Southern men's identity and social structures. They understood that abolitionism would destroy their sense of manhood and the fabric of their society.[140] So their survival depended on fighting this war, and it even motivated Southerners who were not slaveholders to continue fighting.[141] The result was that many men would fight to the death to preserve their identity.

5. The slavery debate reminds us that we all *eisegete* (read into the text) as well as exegete (read out of the text). Based on our goals, gospel understanding, openness to the Spirit's leading, culture and community, assumptions and interpretive methods, we are selective about what we see and emphasize. We reread texts, reinterpret, and shuffle things around. For good reasons, most abolitionists chose the Exodus theme, "I am the God who brought you up out of Egypt," as the

great example of how much God loves freedom. They did not choose, for example, the destruction of the Canaanites by Israel, as it found its freedom, as a basis for launching a holy war against slaveholders. Some abolitionists, however, did privilege other texts. The famous and violent abolitionist John Brown took a fancy to other passages.[142] He emphasized that God had drowned Pharaoh's army, and his favorite texts were an "eye for an eye" and "without the shedding of blood there is no remission of sin."[143] Today there is no "plain reading" (whatever that may mean) of the New Testament slavery texts. Under the continuing work of the Spirit and influenced by the gospel principles of love, freedom, equality, and justice, the church community has transposed the slavery texts. What was once so obvious and important to proslavery is now peripheral to the entire church community.

How may we summarize and illustrate this approach? How can we incorporate the emphasis on the gospel, the Spirit of God, the biblical text, and the church community? We can see from the abolitionist movement that the gospel story undergoes development. There is the recognition that the Holy Spirit is still leading the church into all truth, that Jesus had much to tell us but some things would have to wait for the unfolding drama of the gospel. So, learning from the abolitionist movement, we should make a distinction between the gospel story and the text of Scripture. We even find this distinction in the text itself—for example, in Ephesians 1:13, where Paul writes, "In him you also, when you had heard the word of truth, the gospel of your salvation, and had believed in him, were marked with the seal of the promised Holy Spirit." This "word of truth" is not referring to the Bible as we have it, for most of the New Testament wasn't written at this stage. This "word" is the gospel story (cf. 1 Peter 1:22–25) that Paul lives by and unpacks in his letter to include God's "armor" of faithfulness, righteousness, salvation, peace, and truth

(Ephesians 6:10–17). It is this gospel story, this "word"—the "sword of the Spirit" (Ephesians 6:17)—that we should take up and live by.

In the words of Richard Hays, "Gospel interprets Scripture; Scripture interprets gospel."[144] Our interpretation of the Bible is dynamic and involves many factors. After an extensive analysis of Paul's interpretation of the Old Testament, Hays writes, "True interpretation depends neither on historical inquiry nor on erudite literary analysis but on attentiveness to the promptings of the Spirit, who reveals the gospel through Scripture in surprising ways. In such interpretations, there is an element of playfulness, but the freedom of intertextual play is grounded in a secure sense of the continuity of God's grace: Paul trusts the same God who spoke through Moses to speak still in his own transformative reading."[145]

Hays' interpretive method resonates with the abolitionist reading of Scripture. Joining this with Robert Jenson's view that the church and gospel "mutually determine each other,"[146] we have a threefold dynamic relationship where, under the authority and in the presence of the Spirit, these three—the church community, Scripture, and gospel—interrelate and interpret each other.

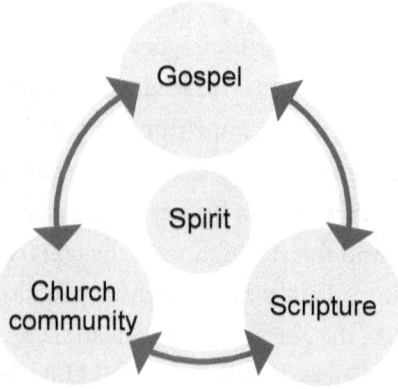

These distinctions between gospel, Scripture, and church community are not absolute or sharp, for they are all integrally connected. How does this relate to the slavery debate? The Bible didn't condemn the institution of slavery, but the gospel as understood by the church today does.

This happened in the presence and under the authority of God's Spirit. The proslavery position is one interpretation of Scripture. At one time it made sense to some people as a clear, simple, and reasonable reading of the Bible. But the abolitionist reading is the far better understanding and explanation of the gospel—something that the church community now affirms. As the church community lives the transforming life of love, freedom, and holding all people as imagers of God, it better interprets the text it is reading, it better understands the gospel, and it lives more in step with the Spirit.

CONCLUSION

We have seen the strengths of each position in regard to the slavery debate. The strength of proslavery was the grounding of slavery in divine law, ordination, prophecy, and providence. Likewise, the strength of the complementarian position is the grounding of male headship in creation. In contrast, the abolitionists' strength was their focus on the implications of the image of God, love, and freedom. Similarly, feminists' strongest arguments lie in the principles of equality, love, and freedom—principles that form the foundation of a transformation dynamic. The strength of the one is the weakness of the other. There are also differing emphases: while proslavery and complementarianism stressed particular texts, abolitionism and feminism placed additional value on culture and experience.

What about these differing approaches? Is one superior to the other? Abolitionist reasoning won the day—with argumentation that even complementarians use today. But the slavery and gender debates have their differences. The issue of slavery, though relevant in many ways, does not entirely solve our problem. Patriarchal metaphors are more deeply embedded into Christianity.[147] Jesus didn't own slaves, but he did have twelve male disciples. The Trinitarian name includes Father and Son. It is easier to argue against slavery than against patriarchy. In the creation narratives, we see that marriage (unlike slavery) is good. Is there a complementarian structure established in the creation narratives—and if so, may it be transformed? This leads us to a discussion concerning the Sabbath, which is considered by some as another creation structure or ordinance that remains in effect today.

CHAPTER 3

The Sabbath—
Further Implications for Our Topic

Sabbath-keeping is central to the Old Testament. We find it in the creation narratives when God rests on the seventh day. We find it as one of the Ten Commandments. And we find it in Isaiah's vision of the new heavens and the new earth (Isaiah 66:22–23). Sabbath-keeping was essential for a Jew's covenant obligation. But there is debate whether there is any place for the Sabbath in the Christian community. The debate over the Sabbath, like slavery, illustrates how the church has wrestled with deciding what is good, just, and true for today.

Does the Sabbath continue? What change, if any, has come to the Sabbath because of the new covenant? Is the Sabbath a creation ordinance—and if so, may it be transformed or abolished? Is there any relationship between the Sabbath and "the Lord's day"? There is by no means agreement on these questions. Such disagreements are understandable, since the Sabbath debate revolves around perennial theological discussions such as the relationship between the old and new covenants, the relationship between creation and redemption, and the role of the Mosaic law in the New Testament.

The topic is of interest to us because there are parallels between gender and Sabbath debates. The Sabbath and male-female distinctions are found together in Genesis 1–2. In addition, many complementarians view the Sabbath, like marriage and male headship, as a creation ordinance. Thus, similar to the gender debate, the Sabbath discussion ultimately traces back to creation and raises the question of whether there is a God-established permanent structure.

SUMMARY OF DIFFERENT VIEWS

Before weaving implications of the Sabbath discussion into our topic, it will be helpful to outline the different positions on the Sabbath. The views we will discuss are called Seventh Day, Sunday-Sabbath, Lord's Day, and No Day.[1]

Seventh Day

The seventh-day position argues for the permanence of the Sabbath based on creation, moral law, and the overarching covenant God has made with his people. First, those who hold this position argue that the creation account establishes a perpetual order to the Sabbath.[2] The Sabbath continues because it is tied to creation[3] and identified with the seventh day in Genesis.[4] It is this seventh day that was blessed and sanctified at creation.[5] Since the Sabbath is based in creation it is not limited to Israel or to a particular time. What was established at creation by God's example may not be modified, except by a clear command. Since there is no such command, the Sabbath must continue in this present age. In addition, the Sabbath awaits its consummation—"A sabbath rest still remains for the people of God" (Hebrews 4:9).[6]

Second, the Sabbath is permanently established in the Ten Commandments (Exodus 20:8–11). This moral law is a manifestation of the character of God, so it is abiding, holy, and spiritual. The command to observe the Sabbath, including the specific reference to the "seventh day," ultimately goes back to creation and to God's example of resting on the Sabbath.[7] When we come to the New Testament, we find that none of the Ten Commandments are abolished,[8] so to change from Sabbath to Sunday or to abolish the Sabbath is to modify one of God's permanent commands. Such an alteration warrants clear teaching, of which there is none in the New Testament. And even Jesus' attitude toward the Sabbath demonstrates that "the question was not, Should the Sabbath be kept? Rather, it was, How should the Sabbath be kept?"[9]

Therefore, seventh-day adherents criticize those who use the fourth commandment to justify Sunday observance. Samuele Bacchiocchi asks, "How can the fourth commandment . . . be legitimately applied to Sunday, when it is the seventh and not the first day that the commandment demands to keep holy?"[10] The position argues for a thorough application of the moral law, the law that was never revoked and that continues even beyond the ordinance of marriage to the new heavens and new earth (Isaiah 66:22–23).

Third, the Sabbath is based on covenant. It is, in fact, "a sign of an 'everlasting covenant' (Exodus 31:16) in which God bound Himself to His covenant people."[11] It is a "covenant sign through which God has pledged that the present proleptic experience of freedom, liberation, joy, and communion on the weekly Sabbath is but a foretaste of the ultimate reality in the glorious future."[12]

Given this foundation of the Sabbath in creation, moral law, and covenant, seventh-day advocates find fault with various Sunday positions, especially those that stress a creation ordinance and moral law. For example, Hans LaRondelle criticizes John Murray for holding to the Sabbath as a God-instituted creation ordinance and holding to the fourth commandment and yet claiming that there is a transfer from Sabbath to Lord's Day.[13] He believes that this position, like other Lord's Day theologies, ends with an "un-Biblical dichotomy between the work of the Creator and the work of the Redeemer, the Re-Creator."[14]

How does the seventh-day position respond to New Testament passages that apparently go against their position? Their interpretation can be illustrated with some examples. For instance, they argue that the gathering at Troas on the "first day of the week" (Acts 20:7) was at night and was a farewell gathering for Paul;[15] it was a special meeting.[16] Besides, Paul met many more times on the Sabbath.[17] Romans 14:5–6 is not referring to the Sabbath but to various ceremonial days, possibly fast days.[18] Paul, who upheld the moral law, would hardly be abrogating the fourth commandment. Likewise, in Colossians 2:16–17 Paul once again is referring to festival days and ceremonial Sabbaths.[19] In 1 Corinthians 16:1–2 Paul is not describing a church service,[20] and the believers were to *privately* put aside money.[21] Finally, to argue that John is referring to Sunday in Revelation 1:10 ("the Lord's day") is reading the patristic usage into the text.[22]

Seventh-day adherents find no New Testament passage abrogating the Sabbath. They also find it telling that the Sabbath is not mentioned as a controversy at the Jerusalem council recorded in Acts 15. Walter Specht writes, "It is significant that the matter of Sabbathkeeping is not mentioned as an issue at this conference. Had there been a movement on foot to do away with the Sabbath or to change the day of worship to Sunday, there would no doubt have been considerable debate and bitter contention on the part of the large number of Jewish Christians who were 'zealous for the law' (Acts 21:20)."[23]

If Paul repealed the Sabbath, it surely would have caused difficulties for many in the church. The absence of any mention of conflict over the Sabbath indicates that it continued to be observed. Bacchiocchi concludes: "The adoption of Sunday observance in place of the Sabbath occurred, not in the Jerusalem Church by apostolic authority to commemorate Christ's resurrection, but rather in the Church of Rome during the early part of the second century, solicited by external circumstances. . . . The difference then between the seventh-day Sabbath and Sunday is not merely one of names or numbers. It is rather a difference of authority, meaning, and experience. It is the difference between a *man-made holiday* and *God's established Holy Day*."[24]

Sunday-Sabbath

The Sunday-Sabbath position adopts similar argumentation as seventh-day. The difference occurs in the transfer from the seventh to the first day. In arguing for the observance of the Sabbath, John Murray says that the Sabbath is grounded in (1) the creation ordinance, (2) the divine example, (3) the Decalogue, and (4) the example of Christ, who did not abrogate the Sabbath and confirmed that the Sabbath was made for humanity.[25] For Murray, the creation ordinance and moral law are not obsolete.[26]

This position, however, disagrees with the seventh-day conclusion. Murray continues to argue for a Sunday observance based on the work of redemption accomplished in the resurrection.[27] He concludes, "Jesus rose from the dead on the first day of the week (cf. Matthew 28:1; Mark 16:2, 9; Luke 24:1; John 20:1). For our present interest the important feature of the New Testament witness is that the first day of the week continued to have *distinctive religious significance* (cf. Acts 20:7; 1 Corinthians 16:2). The only explanation of this fact is that the first day was the day of Jesus' resurrection and for that reason John calls it 'the Lord's day' (Revelation 1:10)."[28]

As another example, Greg Bahnsen, following Murray, affirms that the Sabbath is permanently established in a creation ordinance and the moral law.[29] In view of the Sabbath's continuing validity founded on creation and moral law, all people are required to observe it. In the new covenant, neither Jesus nor the New Testament writers overturned this institution. Jesus only removed the legalistic interpretations of the Sabbath. In answering why the Sabbath is changed to Sunday, Bahnsen writes that "the New Testament does distinguish the *first* day of the week from the other six (1 Corinthians 16:2; Acts 20:7) and denominates it 'the Lord's Day' (Revelation 1:10)."[30]

The Sunday-Sabbath position permanently establishes the Sabbath by virtue of creation and the moral law.[31] As such, the Sabbath continues in the present age and points toward a fulfillment in the eschaton—a Sabbath rest for the people of God (Hebrews 4:9–11). Since this rest is still a future reality, the sign remains.³² There is, however, a change of day recorded in the New Testament where Christians met on the first day of the week (Acts 20:7, 1 Corinthians 16:2). There is a transition from Sabbath to Lord's Day because of the resurrection. This change of day in the new covenant is essentially a ceremonial change.³³ The principle of the Sabbath found in creation and the moral law still remains. Although agreeing in much argumentation, the Sunday-Sabbath position criticizes seventh-day adherents for not taking sufficient account of the flow of redemptive history and the Spirit who leads into all truth.³⁴

Lord's Day

In considering the Lord's Day position, we will look at two differing approaches. One approach finds some continuity between the Sabbath of the old covenant and the Lord's Day of the new covenant; and the other approach finds no continuity, no transformation, of the Sabbath into the celebration of the Lord's Day.

Transformation of the Sabbath. The "transference of the Sabbath" approach attempts to find middle ground between the continuity and discontinuity of the old and new covenants.³⁵ Paul Jewett argues for this position and seeks to secure a midpoint between the rejection of the Sabbath by the Reformers and the acceptance of the Sabbath by the Puritans. On the one hand, Jewett disagrees with the Reformers, arguing that the Sabbath command is related to the Lord's Day.³⁶ He writes, "By making the Sabbath commandment merely a type and shadow, by reducing the Lord's Day to an expedient custom, the Reformers, we contend, erred on the side of Marcion; they failed to do justice to the church's inheritance in Israel."³⁷ On the other hand, Jewett believes that the seventh-day position commits the opposite error of doing injustice to the discontinuity between the covenants.³⁸ Jewett also distances himself from the Puritan insistence "on the perpetuity of the fourth commandment."³⁹ He believes that the Christian Sabbath position cannot be sustained, for it is clear that the fourth commandment specifies the seventh day.

For Jewett, the Sabbath has been transformed in the new covenant by the resurrection. He finds continuity and discontinuity between the Sabbath and Sunday. Yes, there is a change of day; but, like the Sabbath, Sunday is a day of rest. Referring to Hebrews 3:7—4:11, Jewett argues that, similar to the old covenant community, we also have our day of rest as a sign of our present rest in Christ and our future final rest.[40] In this view, there is some continuity between the Sabbath and Sunday since the rest still remains,[41] so we cannot split entirely the Sabbath from the Lord's Day.[42]

No transformation of the Sabbath. A no-transformation position holds that the Lord's Day cannot be identified with the Sabbath. It argues that there is no continuing creation ordinance that binds all people to Sabbath observance. That is why when we come to the New Testament there is no mention of Jesus resting on the Sabbath and no mention of the fourth commandment applying to Christians.[43] This position argues that the New Testament makes no distinction between moral and ceremonial law and that Paul did not regard the fourth commandment to be binding on Christians.[44] There is, however, a day set apart for the church, and this is the first day of the week.[45]

D. A. Carson articulates a no-transformation Lord's Day position:

> First, we are not persuaded that the New Testament unambiguously develops a "transfer theology," according to which the Sabbath moves from the seventh day to the first day of the week. We are not persuaded that Sabbath keeping is presented in the Old Testament as the norm from the time of creation onward. . . . We are also not persuaded that Sunday observance arose only in the second century A.D. We think, however, that although Sunday worship arose in New Testament times, it was not perceived as a Christian *Sabbath*.[46]

This position sees the Sabbath as a unique covenant sign and institution for Israel that was never intended to be a universal ordinance.[47] Proponents argue that the Sabbath that belonged to Israel's covenant was abolished by Paul in the new covenant. The Mosaic Sabbath was a shadow of what was to come in the Messiah. Referring to Colossians 2:16–17, A. T. Lincoln writes, "That Paul without any qualification can relegate Sabbaths to shadows certainly indicates that he does not see them as binding and makes it extremely unlikely that he could have seen the Christian first day as a continuation of the Sabbath."[48] In this regard it is noted that Bacchiocchi "fails to explain why the Sabbath alone of these shadows should abide in the era of the new covenant."[49]

In addition, in Galatians 4:10, "Paul viewed any attempt to impose Sabbath keeping . . . upon Gentiles as wrong, and any tendency on the part of converts to submit to this coercion as a retrograde step."[50] Finally, in Romans 14:5, Paul affirms that the keeping of various days (including the Sabbath) is a matter of conscience, over which no one may pass judgment.[51] Thus, D. R. de Lacy finds it hard to accept that Sunday is to be identified as the Sunday-Sabbath, since Paul allowed the continued observance of the Sabbath.[52]

What about Hebrews 3:7—4:11? The no-transformation position views this passage not as speaking of resting on a weekly Sabbath or Sunday but rather of stressing the importance of believing the gospel, by which we enter that rest.[53] So Hebrews 3:7—4:11 does not have Sunday in view, and "if any literal day of rest is presupposed by the passage then it would certainly be the Jewish Sabbath rather than the first day of the week."[54] But even this assumption is doubtful since the writer of Hebrews stresses a radical break with the old covenant.[55] Our rest is fulfilled in Jesus. By believing the gospel we receive that rest and will enter his rest in the future. So the first day becomes a day of celebration of Jesus' work, not a day of rest. It is essentially a new day rather than a change of day. Overall, there is no transference in New Testament theology between Sabbath and Lord's Day[56] and no direct relationship between the Sabbath and Sunday.

No Day

The Reformers held that all days are alike and holy. They believed that the church should meet on a particular day for expediency.[57] Calvin's position provides a representative view. He saw the Sabbath as a foreshadow of spiritual rest.[58] New Testament passages such as Colossians 2:17, Galatians 4:10–11, and Romans 14:5 clearly teach, according to Calvin, that the Sabbath was a shadow and is now abolished.[59] The Lord's Day, though not mandated, is to be kept for good order in the church.[60] Calvin writes, "For because it was expedient to overthrow superstition, the day sacred to the Jews was set aside; because it was necessary to maintain decorum, order, and peace in the church, another was appointed for that purpose."[61] Although the Sabbath was abrogated, Calvin argued that it is still expedient to assemble on certain days. The church may observe a different day or sequence, though we should meet at least once a week.[62]

Although Calvin argued that Christians are not required to observe the Lord's Day, he still held to a Sabbath creation ordinance. Commenting on Genesis 2:2–3, he wrote, "First, therefore, God rested; then he blessed this rest, that in all ages it might be held sacred among men: or he dedicated every seventh day to rest, that his own example might be a perpetual rule."[63]

So, as in the case of Calvin, one can affirm a Sabbath creation ordinance and yet argue for a "no day" position. The reason is that though one may hold to a Sabbath ordinance, there can be differences regarding what principle is carried through. For Calvin, the principle in creation that continues is not one of a specific day but one of resting from sin.[64] It was possible for Calvin to hold a no day position and still hold to a creation ordinance, since the principle of resting from our works is kept.

From Calvin we see that one can hold to different principles from the same creation ordinance. In other words, differing positions can still hold to the theological basis (creation ordinance) of the Sabbath, yet end in opposite positions. This is similar to what we have seen in the gender debate. Complementarians differ from egalitarians in what principle applies from the creation ordinance of marriage. Is it headship or source?

RELEVANCE OF THE SABBATH DEBATE

Regarding the Sabbath's theological basis, the Old Testament establishes the Sabbath in God's example in creation, in the Decalogue, and in the everlasting covenant. It gives the Sabbath a theological basis in creation, redemption, and the eschaton (Genesis 2:1–3; Exodus 20:8–11; Deuteronomy 5:12–15; Isaiah 66:22–23). So Sabbath-keeping was a central practice under the old covenant and identified a devout Jew. Seventh-day and Sunday-Sabbath positions, though differing on what day to observe, seize this theological foundation and argue for the Sabbath's continuation.

The argument proceeds as follows: because the Sabbath is instituted in creation, it "belongs to the nature of things."[65] The Sabbath is established in God's example at creation and God's character expressed in the Ten Commandments. It is therefore permanent. Because few would argue that we should abolish the other nine commandments, the Sabbath continues in the new covenant. And considering that neither Jesus nor any other New Testament writer abolishes this creation ordinance or the Decalogue, the Sabbath remains. Finally, in view of the rest *still* to come for the people of God, the sign of the Sabbath must continue.

The strength of this argument lies in the theological foundation given to the Sabbath. There are similarities between this line of thinking and proslavery, which argued for the continuation of slavery from its theological basis. Defenders of slavery found no repeal by Jesus or Paul and therefore argued for the continuation of the institution of slavery. The Sabbath, however, is on a stronger theological foundation than slavery. So it is more difficult to avoid the conclusion of pro-Sabbath arguments than proslavery. For example, by stressing the creation ordinance and an unalterable Decalogue, it is harder to escape the seventh-day argument that the seventh day must be kept, since the seventh day is specifically mentioned both in the creation account and in the Ten Commandments. Given that there is no explicit transfer theology in the New Testament, and based on the criteria that the creation ordinance is permanent and the Decalogue unchangeable, what reasoning allows for a change to Sunday?[66]

Most of the church, however, rejects the seventh-day position and its absolute adherence to the Sabbath's theological foundation. On what basis is such a rejection made? There is no clear command in the New Testament changing the seventh day to the first day or even abolishing the Sabbath.[67] So why do we meet on the first day of the week? The church today bases its answer on a particular event, the resurrection: the central event in Christianity—the vindication of Jesus as the Son of God and the beginning of a radical transformation of the cosmos. The resurrection brings a remarkable change to the story of redemption, and it is Jesus rising on the first day of the week that provides the occasion for a new day of worship and celebration.

Depending on what view is held, the resurrection either transforms the Sabbath or abolishes it and ushers in a new day. The resurrection—like love, freedom, or the image of God—is an essential part of the continuing gospel narrative. It is one of the many eschatological realities brought about by the Spirit in increasing measure. Once this interpretive move is made, passages and themes on the Sabbath are now interpreted in that light.

Various passages. There are prescriptive passages (Colossians 2:14–17; Galatians 4:8–11; Romans 14:5–6) that assign the Sabbath to a shadow, to the elements of this world, and to a day no different from any other. There are also descriptive passages where Christians meet on the first day of the week (Acts 20:7–11; 1 Corinthians 16:1–2), plus the example of John receiving his vision on the "Lord's Day" (Revelation 1:10). As an aside, that Christians started meeting on the first day is part of the historical evidence for the resurrection.[68] Something extraordinary must have happened for the Sabbath to lose its central place.

Jesus and the Sabbath. Jesus did not issue a command abolishing the Sabbath, nor did he criticize the institution. But he did bring a surprising twist to the story of the Sabbath. The book of Numbers recounts the incident of a man caught gathering sticks on the Sabbath (Numbers 15:32–36). His punishment: the community stoned him to death. Presumably, if you valued your life you became vigilant about the Sabbath. It's no wonder that religious leaders instituted further laws to help people not break the Sabbath—not in a legalistic sense but out of a concern to live under God's covenant. So it is surprising, for example, to find Jesus with his disciples collecting grain on the Sabbath (Matthew 12:1–8). When confronted by the Pharisees, Jesus has an unexpected answer, one unlikely to satisfy his questioners: "The Son of Man is lord of the sabbath" (Matthew 12:8). Jesus claims supreme authority over the Sabbath; so, by implication, his interpretation of the Sabbath is the correct one. The Sabbath finds its fulfillment in him, so now he calls all people to find their *rest in him* (Matthew 11:28–30).

Ceremonial Laws and Legalism. The seventh-day and Sunday-Sabbath positions sometimes use arguments that contemporary New Testament scholarship finds problematic. For example, passages that apparently criticize the Sabbath are sometimes viewed as only a criticism of various ceremonial laws surrounding the Sabbath or as a criticism of legalistic interpretations of the Sabbath. In other words, these passages, according to some, do not address the Sabbath institution as such; they only deal with wrong interpretations or applications of the Sabbath (legalism), or they address other practices surrounding the Sabbath that have passed away in the new covenant (ceremonial laws). But this argument depends on making a sharp division between moral and ceremonial laws, something few devout Jews would have done.[69] In Jewish understanding, the so-called ceremonial laws *were moral* because God told them to keep them. In addition, ever since the work of E. P. Sanders,[70] scholars have been careful not to apply a blanket label of *legalism* on various debates in the New Testament. They have also have been careful not to read into New Testament times the more legalistic interpretations of rabbinic Judaism that arose after the destruction of the temple in AD 70.[71] This is not to say that there wasn't something amiss with the Pharisees, but to see their interactions with Jesus as simply legalism misses the radical change that Jesus made with the old covenant.

Now the three points above do not deny the theological basis for the Sabbath, and that is not my intention. But when a transformation dynamic based on freedom, equality, and love becomes more important, the New Testament is read in a different way, as we saw in the case of the proslavery texts. Likewise, once the church elevates the transforming reality of Christ's resurrection, passages and themes related to the Sabbath are interpreted differently.

In comparing the proslavery and pro-Sabbath positions, there is a similar pattern of using the theological basis to argue for the permanence of an institution while not giving full weight to central gospel themes, themes that the church considers more important—like love, freedom, or the resurrection.

THE SABBATH: A CHANGEABLE INSTITUTION

Many complementarians hold to the Sabbath as a creation ordinance and part of the Ten Commandments, which specifically mention the "seventh day,"[72] yet are not seventh-day proponents. They trace the principle of Sabbath observance to the Decalogue and the creation narratives. Therefore, they acknowledge that there has been a change in the Sabbath creation ordinance and Decalogue, even if they see it as a minor change. If our theology includes the idea of creation ordinances, we can conclude that the possibility exists in this present age for a creation ordinance to undergo a structural change. Granting, for the sake of argument, the complementarian view that male headship in marriage is also established in creation, it is possible for a modification to occur. According to a common complementarian position, we can represent the possibility as follows:

1. Sabbath ordinance (creation)
2. Fulfilled in Jesus, who is our rest. A structural change from seventh to first day.
3. Final rest (eschaton)

1. Marriage ordinance (creation)
2. Fulfilled in Jesus, who is our bridegroom. A possibility for change of structure.
3. Great marriage banquet (eschaton)

According to this position, both creation ordinances continue in this present age. Each will reach a final consummation in the eschaton. Both ordinances find fulfillment in Jesus, who is our rest and bridegroom. The Sabbath has undergone a structural change; therefore, it is reasonable to affirm the possibility of change in marriage. This is granting many things to a complementarian position. My point is that even within a complementarian framework there is conceptual space for many complementarians to consider changing male headship.[73] One of the shifts needed, however, is for eschatology (the study of last things) rather than protology (the study of first things) to determine the church's direction.

Complementarians who hold to a change from Sabbath to Sunday agree that there is no explicit command to do so. J. Douma grants that there is no specific verse in the New Testament teaching a transfer of Sabbath to Lord's Day, but such a transfer has biblical warrant under the guidance of the Spirit.[74] For Douma, the change was not merely an ecclesiastical ordinance but an application of the gospel of redemption. So once again, as with abolitionism, interpretations and changes are justified by appealing to the gospel and to the leading of the Spirit. Therefore, some practices do not have direct warrant in the New Testament but are an inference or a result of New Testament teaching. In this case, according to a Christian Sabbath or a transference position, the outcome was a change in the structure of the fourth commandment and the creation ordinance. According to a no-transference position (held by some complementarians), the new covenant abolished the Sabbath, which shows even more markedly that what had a substantial theological basis may be overturned.

We have seen in our discussion of slavery that complementarians attempt to dismiss the implications of slavery by arguing that the institution was not established in creation or by a permanent moral command. Yet in approaching the Sabbath, which according to many complementarians is grounded in creation and the Ten Commandments, they allow for a change. The Sabbath is another example where complementarians and feminists agree that supposedly permanent institutions may be provisional. The Sabbath debate shows that an institution with a compelling theological basis can be transformed or even abolished. This does not mean, of course, that the church rejected biblical teaching in a cavalier fashion. But changes were made, and they were made apart from explicit texts.

The debate also illustrates, as with slavery, how the church came to modify or discard an institution with a strong theological foundation. It is a change or rejection based on an event—Jesus' resurrection—that is used as a transformational hermeneutical principle. Accordingly, how the church argues for such alterations is multifaceted. The reasons for a change or rejection are not immediately apparent and they are not based on some choice text. In each case, the proslavery and pro-Sabbath positions, with their theological foundations, are the simpler positions. The opposing views have a greater challenge to argue their position and explain a modification or abolition.

This change to the Sabbath has further implications for our topic, because it is clear that the Sabbath is more firmly entrenched theologically in the Old Testament than is complementarianism. The Sabbath is explicitly taught in the creation account of Genesis 2:2–3, whereas female subordination has to be inferred from parts of the story, such as Adam being created first and later naming his wife. The Sabbath is established in the Ten Commandments, whereas female submission is not.[75] And considering the rest of the Old Testament, we find the Sabbath clearly taught, whereas the submission of wives is not.

A few passages may mitigate this claim. (1) The curse in Genesis 3:16 is that a husband shall rule over his wife. Most complementarians, however, agree that this statement, as being part of the curse, is a harsh ruling—a punishment for disobedience.[76] (2) In Esther 1:22 Ahasuerus sends an edict throughout Persia commanding men to rule over their households. Few will argue, however, that such a command from a pagan king constitutes an enduring command. (3) Proverbs 12:4 describes a wife as her husband's crown. Such a metaphor is to be understood at least in comparison with wisdom being a crown (Proverbs 4:9), which is one of the numerous similarities the book makes between wisdom and the virtuous woman. (4) In Isaiah 3:12 it is lamented that in times of judgment women rule over the people. We should see such a statement, though applicable in its context, in the light of passages like Lamentations 5:8 where people in a time of punishment grieve that slaves rule over the land.

Yes, women were submissive in the Old Testament (1 Peter 3:5) and under the authority of their fathers or husbands (Numbers 30). But there were few, if any, explicit commands for them to submit. The relevant point is that according to the Old Testament the theological basis of the Sabbath far outweighs any basis for female submission. The Sabbath is permanently embedded in creation, the Ten Commandments, Israel's redemption from Egypt, the covenant, and the new heavens and earth (Isaiah 66:22–23). Keeping the Sabbath was a central duty of Israelites under the covenant and was to continue to the end of time. Nevertheless, most Christians agree with a substantial change or even an abolishment of the Sabbath.

Dual Practices and Transitions

The Sabbath-Lord's Day debate also lends itself to considering the possibility that many practices were in transition during the New Testament period. Some old and new covenant practices continued to be permitted alongside each other, such as baptism with circumcision and Sabbath with Lord's Day. Paul can require circumcision in one instance and vehemently oppose it in another. Timothy is circumcised (Acts 16:1–3) yet Titus is not (Galatians 2:3). Both men and women are baptized in the new covenant (Acts 8:12). Paul did not condemn Sabbath-keeping (Romans 14:5–6). Yet Christians, including Paul, are found meeting on the Lord's Day (Acts 20:7–11; 1 Corinthians 16:1–2).

Is it possible that there were dual practices regarding women in the New Testament, so that, depending on the circumstances, some were allowed leadership roles and others were not? Any position should take account of this prospect. Given the evidence in the New Testament of some women having leadership roles, one possibility is that leadership roles for women were not initially problematic because the church met in houses where women had strong roles. But as the church came under outside scrutiny, the leadership of women had to be regulated.

For another transition concerning women in the New Testament, consider an observation from N. T. Wright. He notes that, on the one hand, the resurrection narratives in the Gospels, which are based on an early oral tradition, all mention women as the primary witnesses to the empty tomb. But, on the other hand, in the extensive treatment of the resurrection in 1 Corinthians 15, where Paul recounts the tradition he received, these women are nowhere to be found.[77] It is well known that women, like slaves, were not considered to be reliable witnesses. So for Wright, by the time Paul writes 1 Corinthians 15 the tradition has removed women from gospel proclamation because having women as the primary witnesses to the empty tomb was "apologetically embarrassing."[78]

Complementarians argue that biblical egalitarians are inconsistent by claiming, on the one hand, that Paul requires male leadership in the church but, on the other hand, arguing that Paul allowed women to assume any role.[79] Here we need to note two things. First, as we have seen in chapter one, some egalitarians do not argue that Paul required male leadership. Second, those who hold such a position are consistent if we grant that in the New Testament dual practices were allowed or that there was a transition where women were sometimes allowed in leadership and sometimes prohibited.

Moreover, the inconsistency argument may be reversed. Complementarians regularly appeal to the *universality* of patriarchy, but in giving a reason why the subordination of women in the New Testament is not just cultural they argue that the Greco-Roman culture allowed for female deities and female priests. Thus, Paul prohibited women from leadership in a culture that allowed female leadership. Complementarians conclude that this gives weight to their view that women are not allowed in leadership because of creation, *not culture*. Is it consistent, however, to argue that all cultures are patriarchal, yet, based on the New Testament culture, women could have assumed any role but were not allowed?

CONCLUSION

The majority of the church accepts that the Sabbath has been transformed or abolished. For many, an institution that once defined the people of God and had a compelling theological basis is gone. So the Sabbath is not a creation ordinance continuing in perpetuity. Israelites wrote these creation narratives in the context of ancient Near East creation myths, and they reflect Israel's laws and culture. And even if these passages reflect an earlier tradition, they don't go back to a literal six-day creation (see the next chapter). All too often the requirements for subordination found in slavery, apartheid, or marriage have been fixed as creation ordinances—so that it is the nature of slaves, Africans, or women to be submissive. These become inflexible, adamantine interpretations, because God ordained these social structures. There is no room for change. Violate these structures of subordination and you are going against creation and God. The Sabbath, however, was radically changed or abolished by the church—and without direct textual warrant. This remarkable change is explained by the resurrection of the Son of God on the first day of the week.

Concerning the Sabbath and gender debates, both involve New Testament texts in which people debate the extent of the transformation. Take, for example, Colossians 2:14–17 and Galatians 3:28. It is debated whether Colossians 2:14–17 teaches an abrogation of the Sabbath institution or only deals with so-called ceremonial elements surrounding the institution. Similarly, does Galatians 3:28 eliminate male headship? Everyone agrees that there is at least some transformation from old to new covenant regarding the place of women. In the new covenant, men, women, slaves, and young are prophets, priests, and kings, in contrast to ancient Israel where old, free men generally filled these roles. Both men and women receive the sign of baptism (Acts 8:12). The Spirit is poured out on both men and women (Joel 2:29; Acts 2:18). There is at least some change in female positions. The question remains as to how far this transformation goes.

CHAPTER 4

Origins, Sex, and Evolution

We now come to our third dialogue partner—evolutionary theory. After looking at the debates over slavery and the Sabbath, we have seen how people argue for their theological position and how different approaches can come to remarkably different conclusions. The topic of human origins, sex, and evolution is another debate from which we can glean helpful material to expand our discussion. But why add a controversial topic to an already heated debate? There are at least three reasons:

1. A discussion on sex and gender, and in particular on, What is the relevance of Jesus' maleness? raises another question: Why is anyone male? And this is a question of considerable interest to science as well as theology.
2. In the debate over gender roles, as in slavery and the Sabbath, the arguments invariably go back to creation and to the origin of our species. This question of origins is also of great interest to both theology and science. As we will see, science can help us add layers of meaning, further our understanding, and rule out some interpretations. This is one of the benefits of engaging in an interdisciplinary discussion.

3. A key concern in the gender debate revolves around hierarchy, particularly the hierarchies of male over female and the popular association of male body size and strength with power and leadership. And this raises other questions, such as, What is the origin of hierarchies in nature and the differences between the sexes? Can science help us to answer these questions?

As noted in the introduction, we are proceeding on the basis that theology should be interdisciplinary and engage in conversation with outside disciplines. This leaves us with a few options. We could plow straight in and immediately address scientific studies related to human origins, the origin of sex, the formation of hierarchies, and the differences between the sexes. The risk, however, is to lose some readers who may be unfamiliar with the scientific basis for the entire discussion. It may also lose readers who would like reasons for accepting this scientific evidence. Thus, because an important part of our discussion includes the topic of evolution and its implications, it will be helpful at this stage to provide a brief overview as to why we should accept the overall theory. This will lay out, in a brief way, the scientific basis for the material that we will cover in the rest of the chapter. The summary will provide a helpful context for the subsequent discussion.

WHY ACCEPT EVOLUTION?

The word *evolution* usually refers to biological evolution, which describes the change of organisms over time,[1] but it is also used to describe the development of the universe. We will provide an overview of both.

Charles Darwin

Any list of evidence should include the work of this famous English naturalist. Evolution had been proposed before Darwin, from ancient Greek philosophers to one of the great eighteenth-century intellectuals, Erasmus Darwin (Charles' grandfather), in his work *Zoonomia*

(1794–1796). Charles Darwin, however, is rightly given the central place in the establishment of the theory of evolution. Darwin's theory finds its origin in his almost five-year voyage around the world on the HMS *Beagle*, a remarkable voyage that Darwin regarded as the most important and influential event in his life. His book *The Voyage of the Beagle* (1845) journals his travels and is still worth reading today as one of the great travel documents. We can only be impressed by Darwin's eye for detail, curiosity, broad knowledge and interests, and physical capability to cover the ground he did. During this journey he made countless meticulous observations on variations of species and different geological formations, collected plenty of specimens, dissected others, and unearthed fossils. All this work would eventually come to fruition.

Some twenty-three years after his return Darwin published his *On the Origin of Species* (1859), laying out the theory that living organisms evolved from a common ancestor through a process he called natural selection. This process of natural selection starts with the struggle for existence—there is always limited food and other resources, and organisms usually produce more offspring than can survive.[2] In a particular environment (or change of environment), organisms may inherit traits that give them a better chance to survive and reproduce, whereas organisms with deleterious traits die out.[3] Over time these changes add up, until the species is different from its ancestor. This is evolution by natural selection. Darwin left out a discussion on humankind in *On the Origin of Species*; but he did tackle this topic later in his other famous book, *The Descent of Man, and Selection in Relation to Sex* (1871), where he argued for the evolution of humankind and for his theory of sexual selection—how many behaviors and anatomical features arise through competition for mates, such as a bright plumage to impress and horns for fighting.[4]

Darwin's theory has secured its place as one of the greatest scientific theories of all time. It is hard to underestimate its importance for a multitude of scientific disciplines. Since Darwin first planted the seed, evidence for evolution has grown and flowered far beyond what he had at his disposal and beyond what he could have imagined.

Paleontology

The evidence from the fossil record demonstrates the change of species over time, and over the last twenty years substantial evidence has piled up.[5] The geologist and paleontologist Donald Prothero documents some of these recent discoveries and other evidence from the fossil record in his book *Evolution: What the Fossils Say and Why It Matters*.[6] Prothero lays out the vast fossil evidence demonstrating evolution over time, from the earliest and simplest forms of bacterial fossils some 3.5 billion years old to the diverse hominid[7] fossils that detail human evolution over the past 7 million years.

One example from the fossil record that paleontologists often use to illustrate the predictive and explanatory power of evolutionary theory is whales. The general evolutionary movement is from sea life to amphibians to land dwellers to eventually the dominance of mammals. So when we find mammals (whales) in the sea, we expect to find ancestors of whales that once lived on land. Paleontologists have confirmed this with the recent discoveries of many transitional forms like *Ambulocetus* (walking whale) that show the development of whales from four-legged hoofed mammals.[8] So it is no surprise to find in modern whales the vestigial remains of hip and thigh bones inside their bodies—a testimony to their past. This is only one example from a multitude. The fossil evidence is so remarkable and extensive that Prothero concludes that the fossil record is the strongest evidence we have for evolution.[9]

Genetics and Genomics

By the middle of the twentieth century evolutionary theory had developed into the neo-Darwinian synthesis. Part of this synthesis was the joining of Darwin's theory to genetic discoveries—which trace to the work of Gregor Mendel (1822–1884)—that DNA held the secret of how inherited traits, including mutations, are passed to descendants. Darwin lacked the benefit of knowing the laws of heredity and the existence of DNA. Science added more evidence to evolutionary theory and filled a gap in Darwin's theory of natural selection, that is, how genes and mutations in our genetic code produce change.

Just as significant are the results from the Human Genome Project that has recently mapped the 3.1 billion letters of human DNA. Francis Collins, head of the project, notes that "the study of genomes leads inexorably to the conclusion that we humans share a common ancestor with other living things."[10] Through an analysis of DNA, we can trace our evolutionary relationships to other living organisms: from our closest living relative, the chimpanzee (with whom we share 98.7 percent identical DNA),[11] through dogs, mice, flies, and worms. By comparing the genomes of different species and based on similarities of DNA, we can now construct an evolutionary tree of life—a tree that is remarkably similar to the fossil record.[12]

Daniel Fairbanks provides an illustration of how this works.[13] Imagine photocopying a page of a book and giving it to a friend. When you copied your page, any dust specks on your copier would also be transferred to the paper. Now say your friend makes another copy and gives it to her friend. This copy will also pick up dust specks on her copier and transfer them to the paper. With each additional copy the original specks are preserved and new ones are added. Even if thousands of copies are made, we could reconstruct the process and the relationships between each copy based on the marks on each page. This is analogous to organisms that copy their DNA and pass it on. DNA has millions of these "marks"; thus, geneticists can now look at this DNA and reconstruct the evolutionary relationship between organisms.

Here we have what some call a convergence of evidence,[14] where multiple scientific disciplines, such as genetics and paleontology, have independently come to the same conclusion: that evolution happened. Consider whales again. DNA analysis can show that their closest living relative is the hippopotamus.[15] Or for another example, paleontologists have long argued, based on evidence from the fossil record, that birds evolved from small theropod dinosaurs; and they have noted that most predatory dinosaurs had some kind of feathers that were used for insulation and not flying.[16] This evidence is confirmed and strengthened by a different scientific field: the genetic findings that birds have suppressed genes for teeth,[17] providing further testimony to their remote ancestry. Such findings, together with genetics adding other mechanisms for evolution (beyond natural selection) that now include genetic drift,[18] have all significantly increased the evidence for and our understanding of evolution.

Evolutionary Development

Evolutionary theory has undergone considerable development from Darwin's original theory, to the neo-Darwinian synthesis, through to the new science of evolutionary development, known informally as *evo-devo*. Evo-devo is now able to explain *how* different animal forms come about, how large-scale changes in animal design arise. Sean Carroll, a molecular biologist at the forefront of evo-devo research, writes, "For more than a century, biologists had assumed that different types of animals were genetically constructed in completely different ways."[19] This assumption made sense based on the remarkable differences in appearance between different species—a worm looks different from a mouse or a human. So it was believed that the development of humans was quite different from the development of, say, tigers or fruit flies. But as Carroll explains, evo-devo started with the unexpected discovery that particular genes in fruit flies that govern their body design had exact counterparts in other animals, including worms, mice, and humans.[20] These genes are the developmental or master genes, such as the Hox or Pax-6 genes, that form a basic tool kit from which different animals develop. Remarkably, this genetic tool kit was in place over 500 million years ago.[21]

The discovery of these master regulatory genes showed biologists how new and different animals can use the same genetic building blocks to evolve different shapes, body parts, and larger forms. Animals are not constructed in vastly different ways; their differences come by genes turning on or off in the course of the animals' development. Macro changes in design are made using the same tool kit but with a few changes in genetic switches.[22] So macro and micro changes to an organism are quite similar in how they come about.

Carroll provides a swath of examples of how animals evolved by "teaching very old genes new tricks,"[23] how species usually do not start from scratch to form body parts but tinker with what is available.[24] For example, insect wings developed from a gill branch of crustaceans,[25] or the development of eyes as diverse as found in flatworms to flies to those found in vertebrates are all controlled by the common master Pax-6 gene.[26] Carroll concludes, "The discovery of the ancient genetic tool kit is irrefutable evidence of the descent and modification of animals, including humans, from a simple common ancestor."[27]

Comparative Anatomy

In *Your Inner Fish*, anatomist and paleontologist Neil Shubin compares the anatomy of the human body to its ancient evolutionary past and particularly to fish.[28] Shubin and his colleagues found the fossil *Tiktaalik*, the beautiful intermediate fossil between fish and land animals. As described by Shubin, *Tiktaalik* had "part fin, part limb" and "a shoulder, elbow, and wrist composed of the same bones as an upper arm, forearm, and wrist in a human" and was capable of pushups.[29] This is only one striking comparison. There are numerous other signs in the human body pointing to our fish ancestry, including the convoluted routes taken by our arteries, nerves, and veins.[30] For example, our cranial nerves have "oddly redundant functions and torturous paths"[31] that only make sense when we see that we are modified fish.[32]

Other fascinating examples that Shubin provides include hiccups, which has its origin in our amphibian past. Shubin describes how amphibians need to draw water over their gills but at the same time prevent the water from entering their lungs, which they do by closing a flap (glottis) that closes their breathing tube.[33] A similar pattern is found in our hiccup: a rapid intake of air followed by the closing of the glottis.[34] Another example is hernias, which are a problem because of our evolutionary past.[35] Shubin describes how fish have their gonads located near their "chest," but mammals do not. Our gonads start in a similar position to fish, but during human development gonads descend; and in males this long path creates a weakness in the body wall, making them particularly susceptible to hernias.

These examples illustrate the general conclusion reached by comparative anatomy—that the human body is the modification of previous designs. As we saw under evo-devo, nature does not start from scratch but uses what is already available. This tinkering comes with a cost, so the route from a fish to a mammal has tradeoffs.[36]

To comparative anatomy we could also add embryology (for example, the fish-like gills and tail found in early human embryo development[37]) and vestigial structures (for example, humans still have suppressed genes for tails, and sometimes people are born with a complete tail—"with fully developed vertebrae, muscles, and other features of animal tails"[38]). It is no surprise that biologists like to quote the geneticist Theodosius Dobzhansky: "Nothing in biology makes sense except in the light of evolution."

Cosmology

Modern cosmology has also revolutionized our understanding. A hundred years ago we did not know of the existence of other galaxies, and we thought the universe was static and eternal. In the 1920s the astronomer Edwin Hubble made two great discoveries. First, he determined that faint and fuzzy patches, which astronomers thought to be nebulae, were in fact galaxies. This meant that our universe was incredibly vast and that our galaxy was one among a multitude. The number of galaxies has turned up to be over 400 billion[39]—an estimate that will likely rise with new discoveries. Second, Hubble discovered that our universe was expanding like an inflating balloon. He discovered what is now known as Hubble's law: the further a galaxy is away from us, the faster it is receding from us. All but the closest galaxies are racing away from us. This new evidence killed the view that the universe was static.

Couple Hubble's findings with the discovery in 1965 of cosmic background radiation (radiation left over from the beginning of our universe) and the Big Bang model became the standard model for cosmologists.[40] Today there are plenty of debates over problems and details regarding this model. There are also surprising developments such as the discovery a decade ago that the expansion of the universe is speeding up. There are even arguments for a different model to account for problems with the standard model. One new model, described by physicists Paul Steinhardt and Neil Turok in *Endless Universe: Beyond the Big Bang*,[41] is a cyclic model, based on string theory, which involves two universes located on different branes[42] that collide about every trillion years. For our purposes, however, no matter the precise details or the exact model, the scientific consensus is that the development of our universe is evolutionary to the core. From the formation of the first nuclei and elements, to the stars, solar systems, galaxies, and superclusters—all have evolved.

Take, for example, the formation of various elements. Cosmologists argue that after the Big Bang occurred about 13.7 billion years ago the first elements to be formed were the lighter ones such as hydrogen, helium, and lithium. But where did the heavier elements that we depend on, like carbon and oxygen, come from? They were formed through evolutionary development—the life and death of stars. As they age, massive stars produce elements like oxygen, carbon, and iron. But most elements heavier than iron are produced in supernovae—the death-explosions of massive stars. Astrophysicist Neil deGrasse Tyson calls this the "most underappreciated discovery of the twentieth century"[43]—that supernovae produced most of our heavy elements. These explosions burn brighter than an entire galaxy and scatter these elements into interstellar space. The dust is then incorporated into future stars and planets.

So the formation of elements took incredible amounts of time. Following the Big Bang, cosmologists estimate that it took about 200 million years before the first stars formed and even longer for these stars to live, die, collapse in on themselves, and explode. Carbon-based life forms have an almost incomprehensibly ancient history. As many are fond to point out, we are made of stardust. The conclusion of cosmology is that the development of our universe is evolutionary—our earth, solar system, galaxy, and universe all bear the marks not of an instantaneous creation but of a long evolutionary development.

Geology

Some of the first scientific evidence of the immense age of our planet came through the work of James Hutton (1726–1797). Hutton, the father of modern geology, has been called "the man who found time."[44] Prior to his work, most believed the earth was comparatively young—measured in thousands of years. Studying layers of sedimentary rocks on the coast of Scotland led Hutton to one of the most remarkable conclusions in science. He reasoned that the layers in the sediments were a result of a repeating process: rivers erode the land and deposit layers of silt in the sea. Over time these layers are buried, compressed, and then eventually turn to rock. The rocks are eventually lifted out of the sea by geological forces, and the whole process starts again.[45]

The question naturally arose, How long had all this taken? Hutton's conclusion was that the earth was ancient beyond imagining. It was "unknowably old."[46] Hutton had discovered geological time. Stephen Jay Gould wrote of Hutton, "He burst the boundaries of time, thereby establishing geology's most distinctive and transforming contribution to human thought—Deep Time."[47]

Similar enormous time scales are required for the movement of tectonic plates (now a widely held theory, though dating back just to the 1960s). Moving only a few inches a year, these plates, over millions of years, have transformed the earth and raised mountains from the seabed—explaining, for example, why rocks near the top of Mount Everest contain fossilized seashells.[48]

Hutton didn't provide an estimate of the age of the earth because there was no available method or apparatus to aid him. Today, with radiometric dating, geochemists say that they are able to date accurately various rocks such as meteorites that put our earth and solar system at about 4.6 billion years old.[49] As we move along the timeline, we find the oldest fossils of living things in 3.5-billion-year-old rocks.[50] And as we progress further a definite pattern emerges: the fossil record changes over time. Digging through these rocks, we have never found a *T. rex* in 500-million-year-old rocks or a trilobite in 50-million-year-old rocks. The order of fossils in rocks is further evidence for evolutionary development, and geologists were aware of this fact even before Darwin's theory. As Prothero notes, "The succession of fossils through time was established by devoutly Christian geologists *decades before* Darwin published his ideas about evolution."[51] Geology is one more example of a scientific field providing independent confirmation that our earth, and life on it, evolved.

This is just a sampling of scientific fields. We could add other disciplines, such as anthropology and biogeography, or add fields arising from evolutionary theory, including evolutionary psychology (how our evolutionary past affects our thinking and behavior), evolutionary linguistics (the origin and development of language), and evolutionary epistemology (constructing theories of knowledge based on our evolved cognition). That evolution happened is clear to nearly all scientists. Even the consensus from one scientific field would be enough to establish a theory, but in this case we have vast evidence and similar conclusions from multiple and independent fields.

Before continuing, we should comment on two concerns that some readers may have. The first relates to the idea that scientific theories change over time, and the second relates to the Intelligent Design movement. First, since science has changed its views in the past, isn't it possible that in the future evolutionary theory will be discarded for something else? Yes, that is possible; and if it happens, scientists, theologians, and everyone else will have to adapt again. Science has modified, expanded, and discarded theories.[52] Thomas Huxley's aphorism, "The great tragedy of science—the slaying of a beautiful hypothesis by an ugly fact," is always lurking in the background (although evolution is not a hypothesis but a well-established theory). The nature of science is to be self-correcting in light of new discoveries. The possibility that further evidence could overturn a theory always exists, and most scientists would like nothing better than to discover the next revolutionary theory.

In addition, there are plenty of areas in evolutionary theory that biologists fight over. But to hope that this one fact[53]—that evolution occurred—will be overturned is wishful thinking, like hoping that science will declare heliocentricity or gravity to be wrong or nonexistent. Although scientists agree that theories may change, they also hold that there is progression in knowledge—that "science is cumulative in the advance of its understanding,"[54] and through science we are coming to a better understanding of our world and universe.[55] We should take some things as well established.

The conclusion of science—that the evolution of life and of the universe happened and continues today—is neither a minority opinion nor is it from the cutting edge of science. It is the determination from over 150 years of research across multiple fields. The views on the evolution of the universe and of life are not, for example, like string theory, a relatively new endeavor based on complicated physics and mathematics—a theory that has reached no agreed on conclusions and where some question whether it is proper science.[56]

Evolution is more akin to the theory and fact of gravity. When Einstein developed a new way to understand gravity (as the warping of space-time), he reshaped the Newtonian theory of gravity as an attracting force between two bodies. Einstein's theory, however, did not remove the existence of gravity; and we still remain firmly attached to our world. Different theories about gravity or evolution may arise, but the reality remains. We have seen how evolutionary theory has changed from Darwin to the neo-Darwinian synthesis to evo-devo. Changes to the theory, however, have only served to confirm further that evolution happened.

Second, some readers may have concerns about the Intelligent Design (ID) movement.[57] Does it undermine evolutionary theory? Proponents of ID argue, for example, there are features in biological life that are so complex, with related parts all dependent on each other—like the bacterial flagellum or the blood-clotting mechanism—that to take away any one of these parts causes the whole system to stop working. With each part so dependent on the other, these complex forms could not have arisen naturally, one part at a time.[58] For ID, there are complexities of design or information that could not have arisen through natural selection.[59] Some things are irreducibly complex, and by looking at them we can detect snippets of intelligence. Because these complex features could not have arisen naturally, ID proponents argue that an intelligent designer must have been directly involved in creating the complexity.

As the debate over ID has progressed, it is clear that ID has not gained acceptance in the scientific community. The scientific community has two main objections: (1) ID is not science, and (2) the specific claims made by ID (for example, their arguments against evolution) are false. Concerns expressed by some scientists include these discussed briefly below.

Science by Definition Excludes the Supernatural. Science does not use the supernatural as an explanation for the areas that it studies. Science proceeds by way of methodological naturalism—it looks for natural explanations for natural phenomena. So scientists never insert a miracle or some input from God into their equations, formulas, hypotheses, or theories. So for scientists, when ID invokes the supernatural, it is not science, for it is untestable[60] and unfalsifiable. This does not mean that science rules out the supernatural, but that it has a particular focus and method. Based on its method, science makes no judgment about God one way or the other.

There are plenty of questions and areas that science doesn't focus on, questions like, What is the ultimate meaning of life? Is there any overall purpose? What is evil? What happens after death? What is the origin and goal of our quests for knowledge, purpose, or love—for truth, beauty, or goodness? Contemporary science doesn't answer these questions. It is outside the capabilities of the scientific method to discover or comment on ultimate explanations, such as the existence or works of God. To do so is to make a category mistake—to confuse science with theology. The only way around this is to redefine science and change the rules by which science operates.

Science Thrives on the Unexplained. The unknown provides impetus and challenge. Scientists become the most imaginative on the unsolved and thrive on what Richard Feynman calls "the pleasure of finding the thing out, the kick in the discovery."[61] To postulate an intelligent designer at the precise point where science is very interested is asking for trouble. To say "Here is something too complex to have formed naturally" only goads scientists to find natural explanations for what ID says are irreducibly complex. Kenneth Miller notes, "We are now far enough along in the development of science to appreciate that its track record suggests that ultimately it will find natural causes for natural phenomena."[62]

Based on this track record, many scientists have "faith" that science may well provide an explanation for the origin of life (how life came from nonlife) and for the anthropic principle (providing a theory for why the physical constants in the universe appear so finely tuned for the existence of life as we know it), and some even hope to explain the emergence of consciousness. We need to emphasize, however, that this does not mean that the explanations science provides are the *only* explanations, or that these explanations encompass *all* of knowledge, or that science will *definitely* answer these questions. So theology can still provide its own explanations for the remarkable emergence of life or consciousness or for the fine-tuning of the universe. But we should expect that science will continue to succeed; and we should be wary of saying, while looking at the natural world, "This is something for which science will never have any explanation." What seems impossible to us today may be elementary science in the next century or millennium.

Biological Life *Is* Incredibly Complex. There are indications, however, that even the specific examples that ID claims are irreducibly complex are reducible to simpler forms—forms that may have had a different function in the past. Miller provides examples of how the bacterial flagellum or the mechanism for blood clotting are not irreducibly complex.[63] For instance, blood clotting, according to Miller, "evolved from genes and proteins that originally served different purposes,"[64] so it "is a remarkable demonstration of the way in which evolution duplicates and then remodels existing genes to produce novel functions."[65] Through evolutionary processes more complex forms develop, and they sometimes develop from parts that originally had completely different functions—what is called exaptation—where a feature that had one function is co-opted for a different use, such as feathers that were once used for insulation or ornamentation and then adapted for flight.[66]

ID Fails to Supply an Alternative Scientific Theory.[67] Miller notes the absence of scientific research and suggests that ID's "goal of producing a significant amount of scientific work has apparently been abandoned."[68] For scientists, it is insufficient only to disagree with a theory you don't like. You also need to provide an alternative, a solution, or an explanation that makes better sense of the evidence. ID has still not provided a testable hypothesis that others in the scientific community can examine. If ID is not science, however, then it is evident why it cannot come up with a scientific theory.

In 2005, the question of whether or not ID is science came to a head in US federal court in the famous trial at Dover, Pennsylvania.[69] The trial developed after the Dover school board added the teaching of ID to the high school biology curriculum. Both the defense and plaintiffs asked for a ruling on whether ID was science, and the judge, John E. Jones, concluded that ID was not science.[70] The conclusion of most scientists and even a US court is that ID is fundamentally a religious argument and not science. Our concern here is not to discuss the theological difficulties that arise from ID but whether ID confutes evolution. For our purposes, ID has not provided acceptable evidence to the scientific community that weakens any part of evolutionary theory.[71]

So Why Should We Accept Evolution?

Below are five reasons (there are more) for us to consider concerning science and theology.

1. **Evolution Has Convincing Evidence.** The majority of scientists today accept evolution as a well-established theory. They argue that the evidence for evolution is overwhelmingly convincing.
2. **Good Theology Is Relational.** In this context, being relational means communicating in our time and culture in a plausible way. This does not mean that we should latch on to every newfangled hypothesis, but to rule out or ignore what is clear to experts in multiple scientific disciplines inhibits some tasks and goals of theology: faithful understanding, engaging the gospel in our present-day context, and being in relationship with contemporary people.
3. **We Have Much to Gain.** By incorporating science into our worldview, we have much to gain, including wisdom, insight, and a wider understanding of our universe. Science is neither a threat to the survival of Christianity nor the only way to knowledge. It is not a discipline that consigns Christianity to the realm of primitive superstition. John Polkinghorne and John Haught have argued that one benefit of engaging in science is that we add levels of explanation or layers of meaning to our understanding.[72] Science and theology can learn from each other, provided we are not looking for a fight or a quick harmonization. Inviting insight from various scientific fields keeps us from a blinkered approach that limits our vision and wonder of the world. Every academic field faces the danger of reductionism, where we are tempted to expand our limited area of specialization to encompass all knowledge or to elevate our discipline to a dictatorial position.

Diverse fields such as science, theology, and music have all had adherents claiming that their field is the highest form of pursuit. Theology was once heralded as the "queen of the sciences"; now some consider theology an invalid academic discipline. For some today, scientists are the high priests and science is the great arbiter of truth. In the nineteenth century, many saw art and music as the pinnacle of life, where "the artist walked in heaven: he was the chosen vessel through which God transmitted divine fire," the priest who brought truth and ministered to all people.[73] An interdisciplinary conversation can engender humility. In addition, science can help place constraints on theology by encouraging our thinking toward the concrete and away from nebulous abstractions (just as active ministry in the church can help theologians stay practical). And when theologians face a multitude of different possible interpretations, science may provide additional insight that favors one view over another.

So why do we include scientific discussions on origins, sex, and hierarchies in our study? Because there are different levels of explanation. Because the topics of sex, gender, and origins raise questions that theology cannot answer alone. Because we need each other.

4. **We Would Miss Interdisciplinary Dialogue.** One of the most exciting and productive developments in contemporary theology is the interdisciplinary dialogue with science. Developments in science are helping to reconfigure and reform some theological ideas that are problematic, worn out, or no longer make sense. For example, theories of relativity, quantum mechanics, chaos, evolution, and developments in neuroscience are providing theology with important and profitable lines of inquiry, such as opening up new discussions on humanity, the character of God, Christology,

evil, freedom, the future, creation, and the relatedness of all things. Theology—once formulated under a mechanistic worldview that considered space and time as absolute and that emphasized the substance of things—is now being reformed by a relational, open worldview where space-time is malleable and where the emphasis is on the relatedness of all things.

5. **Rejecting Science Creates an Unnecessary Obstacle.** To ignore or reject science is to snub a friend and perhaps to make an enemy. And making a foe of science pushes people away from science and leads beyond cognitive dissonance to a cognitive cadenza, for scarcely a week goes by without us hearing about a discovery that has implications for the evolutionary development of life or the universe. It creates an unnecessary obstacle for Christians who are taught, for example, that a particular interpretation of the early Genesis narratives is the only way to read the text, so they feel they have to choose between the Bible and science. And once evidence from science becomes overwhelming, they reject Christianity.[74]

Ignoring or rejecting science also creates an easy and legitimate target for atheists. Though it is fashionable to critique the new atheism and its disgust of religion, we should feel the weight of their concerns. Two of their criticisms relate to our topic: that Christianity has a history of terrible treatment of women and that Christianity inhibits free enquiry and scientific progress. Apart from whether it is a good idea to defend metaphysical theism, in our response to atheism we should readily acknowledge that many times the church has been complicit in supporting slavery, oppressing women, and opposing science.

THE ORIGINS OF HUMANKIND AND SEX

Darwin concluded his *Descent of Man* with these words: "Man with all his noble qualities, with sympathy which feels for the most debased, with benevolence which extends not only to other men but to the humblest living creature, with his god-like intellect which has penetrated into the movements and constitution of the solar system—with all these exalted powers—Man still bears in his bodily frame the indelible stamp of his lowly origin."[75]

From the fossil record and genetic studies,[76] most scientists claim that humankind arose in Africa. Our history with other hominids is a tree with many branches[77]—from the earliest of our family *Sahelanthropus tchadensis*, nicknamed "Toumai," from 6–7 million years ago,[78] to the australopithecines (the best known being "Lucy"), through to our genus *Homo* that includes a wide variety, such as *Homo habilis, ergaster, erectus, heidelbergensis, neanderthalensis*,[79] and *sapiens*. This long development in our history has included changes in brain size (increasing), jaw and teeth (reduction in size), locomotion (bipedality), loss of body hair, and social and cultural developments, including the development of language.[80]

Although debate continues over the precise order and classification of hominid fossils, there is no evidence from paleontology or archaeology that humankind suddenly appeared through an instant creation.[81] Population geneticists arrive at a similar conclusion: that modern humans are descended from about ten thousand people who lived between one hundred thousand and one hundred and fifty thousand years ago.[82] In our ancestral population there was never less than a few thousand individuals.[83] And going back further, geneticists have tied our evolutionary development to a common ancestor with chimpanzees.

Taking the evidence from areas such as our DNA, comparative anatomy, and the fossil record leads scientists to one conclusion: humankind evolved. And with the decoding of the human genome we now have better evidence for our evolution than for most other species.[84] We are inextricably tied to this universe—our humanity is tied to more than twenty other hominids; our genes demonstrate our evolutionary development from a common ancestor; even the essential elements in our bodies, like carbon, show the past evolutionary development of the universe. Embedded in our bodies is a multimillion-year-old, in fact a multibillion-year-old, history. Darwin was right: embedded in our bodies are the marks of our lowly origin.

Another question of origins that interests us is the question "Why sex?" When scientists are asked, "What remains to be discovered?" or "What hasn't science figured out?" usually one of the answers pertains to the origin of sex.[85] Even given the wild interest that humans have in sex, the existence of sex is still an enigma. This leads Richard Dawkins to say, "If you think you understand sex, you don't understand sex."[86]

Why do we need males anyway? Why don't females just clone themselves and give their offspring 100 percent of their genes?[87] Yet most species reproduce sexually, so there must be good reasons for sex. In sexual reproduction each parent supplies half of the offspring's DNA. What is the advantage of sex, when there is a 50 percent cost? Plus the growth rate is cut in half, since only females produce offspring.[88] Add to this that males often contribute significantly less in terms of raising offspring—and you have a considerable cost.[89]

Given this significant cost, Mark Ridley writes, "The problem of explaining sex is to find a compensating advantage of sexual reproduction that is large enough to make up for its cost."[90] Are there good reasons for keeping males around? Apparently so, although these reasons are debated. When the geneticist John Maynard Smith, who devoted much of his life work to the question of sex, was asked whether we need a new theory on sex, his reply was, "No. We have the answers. We cannot agree on them, that is all."[91]

There are two main theories on the existence and benefit of sex—theories that may not be mutually exclusive. One theory is that sexual reproduction helps to remove deleterious mutations.[92] Biologists such as Maynard Smith and Ridley have illustrated this by comparing two cars that have different things wrong with them.[93] One car may have faulty brakes, the other a broken ignition. You could make one roadworthy car by swapping components. Instead of two broken cars you now have one that works, and that is an improvement. According to this theory, sexual reproduction helps purge harmful errors from the genetic code. But for the theory to work the rate of harmful mutations has to be high enough for sexual reproduction to give an advantage, and there has to be a particular relationship between the "fitness of an organism and the number of deleterious mutations it contains."[94] Whether this is the case is still inconclusive.

The second idea is an elegant theory favored by many—aptly named the Red Queen theory[95]—that goes back to the biologist Leigh Van Halen, who was inspired by Alice's meeting of the Red Queen in *Through the Looking Glass*. The Red Queen is a woman who runs hard, but she remains in the same place because everything else is also running. In Alice's world, when you run, you get somewhere. In the Queen's world, you need to run just to stay in the same place. She is a metaphor for how evolution is a race: everything else is running, and you can never stop running lest your competitors overtake you. Competitors, such as predators, parasites, viruses, and bacteria, are all evolving; and if you don't keep up, you die. This is where one benefit of sexual reproduction comes in: it generates variety and diversity. It helps you keep up with your competition, especially with those that are rapidly evolving, such as parasites.[96] In the short term, sexual reproduction gives each new generation resistance to the attacks of parasites who quickly evolve abilities to sneak through defenses.

This diversity through sex also gives species long-term benefits. Biologist Joan Roughgarden writes, "The benefit of sex is survival over evolutionary time. Lacking sex, clonal species are evolutionary dead ends. On an evolutionary time scale, almost all clonal species are recently derived from sexual ancestors."[97] According to Roughgarden, sexual reproduction "rebalances the genetic portfolio of a species,"[98] maintaining its genetic diversity—like a rainbow of many colors.

The sexually reproducing species can survive long-term in changing environments because of its diversity.

We expect that science will eventually solve the "Why sex?" question. But even when solved, it would be reductionistic to say that this answer will encompass all that can be said about sex. Science can provide some layers of meaning; theology can provide others. Science and theology, however, are not completely separate areas of pursuit. At first glance we may think that science can only tell us about the barren mechanics of sex among humans (facts), while theology speaks to the ethical, relational, and deeper meaning of sex (values). On second glance there is overlap, and such rigid divisions break down. For example, theology may appeal to the early Genesis narratives to connect sex with companionship, fruitfulness, love, beauty, delight, intimacy, and marriage (Genesis 2:18–25; 4:1). It may include how our alienation from God has corrupted our sexual relationships (Genesis 3)—how by not listening to God we now trust other things, such as sex, to give us what only a vital relationship with God can provide. But from science we see that sex is more than simply reproduction. Humans engage in sex many more times than needed for conception. They also have sex during pregnancy, and they engage in sex after menopause. This leads some scientists to conclude that sex among humans is "more often to create and to maintain relationships."[99]

Science can also illuminate how particular practices such as monogamy enhance survival, given that human offspring require long-term care. Or evolutionary theory can illuminate why humans struggle with lust. We have taken over the planet as the dominant species and are descended from a long line of reproductive winners—ancestors who loved sex. But this can take us only so far, and no one suggests reading off morality from our favorite primate, be it the patriarchal, war-making chimpanzees or the sex-loving bonobos. All that to say, this does not deny the considerable differences between science and theology, but illustrates how we can interweave ideas to provide a broader understanding.

HIERARCHIES AND REPRODUCTIVE STRATEGIES

The theory of evolution encourages us to think differently about hierarchies. Science by no means rules out hierarchies, and nature provides plenty of examples of hierarchical ordering and emergent complexity. Neither does theology rule out hierarchies.[100] Scientists and theologians will continue to speak of some things as having more importance or value. In our discussion, however, some scholars assign hierarchies to the *unchanging nature* of things—specifically that it is the nature of men to lead and the nature of women to submit. Some also link leadership and authority to men's larger bodies, greater strength, and deeper voice.[101] As we will see, evolutionary theory questions the plausibility and validity of these formulations.

The classical and medieval "great chain of being" has held considerable influence in Western thought.[102] This was a hierarchical ordering of being, a linear chain that set the place of each thing in the universe. God was at the top; underneath were angels, then divinely appointed kings, and continuing all the way down to the bottom. Animals were below humans, fish were below birds, rocks below plants. At the lowest of all animals, of course, were snakes. Everything and everyone had their place, and your position was fixed. Even within humanity there was hierarchical ordering: kings above serfs, husbands above wives. It was a *chain*—not a ladder one could climb. To try to change your position was to go against your nature and to usurp your ordained place in the universe. And in this great chain there were no vacancies.

Evolutionary theory undermined this closed, fixed, static hierarchical ordering of being. Instead of a closed system, we find plenty of vacancies in the story of life. Of all the species that have ever lived, over 99 percent are extinct.[103] Instead of things fixed in their being, we find a blurring of lines—including the movement from nonlife to life and the development of *Homo sapiens* from prior species. Instead of life arranged in a static hierarchy, we find temporal hierarchies. Even from his Victorian culture, Darwin spoke of the provisional nature of hierarchies. In light of evolution, it is hard to maintain that "superiority" is static or innate—for all we need is a change in the environment and what was once superior can quickly become a liability.

Instead of the great chain of being, the metaphor for evolution is a bush or a tree with many branches. Life is dynamically interconnected, and continuity exists between all of creation and us. Humans are not the "superior" species endowed with the right to treat the "inferior" creation as they please. Of course, theologians affirm the value and purpose of humankind as imagers of God. But human nature is also part of the evolutionary process, and knowing our relatedness and dependence on the rest of creation can only strengthen Christian treatment and concern for the world.

Do the differences between men and women indicate an unchangeable structure of male leadership and female subordination? Is there a tie between leadership and male body size or strength? Some explanations for the differences between women and men go back to Darwin's theory of sexual selection.[104] Take, for example, the different reproductive strategies of men and women. Women have a high investment in reproduction: they have a limited number of eggs, they spend nine months pregnant and a few years nursing, and childbirth is still one of the highest causes of death among women worldwide. With this considerable amount of energy and commitment, we expect women to be more selective in regard to reproduction. Men, in contrast, have virtually unlimited sperm; and even if they are attentive fathers, they still invest far less in reproduction. We expect men to be less selective.

Michael Shermer summarizes a study by psychologists Russell Clark and Elaine Hatfield, in which an attractive college student posed three questions to fellow single college students of the opposite sex:

1. "Would you go out on a date with me tonight?"
2. "Would you go back to my apartment with me tonight?"
3. "Would you sleep with me tonight?"

The results were revealing. For women, 50 percent agreed to the date, 6 percent agreed to return to the apartment, and not a single one of them agreed to have sex. By contrast, for men, 50 percent agreed to the date, 69 percent agreed to the apartment, and 75 percent agreed to the sex![105]

For most, this illustration comes as little surprise. And the principle applies to other species as well. The sex that invests more in reproduction and caring for offspring is more selective about mating. The other sex tends to compete for mates—through fighting or elaborate displays. Males usually have ornamentation, such as a mane or antlers. The classic example is the extravagant male peacock's tail. Although there are exceptions, females are selective and males are competitive: fighting with other males for access to females, territory, food, and other resources. So males tend to be larger and more aggressive than females. We can see the association of size and aggression with reproductive strategies in two other areas.

First, there is a tendency for sexual dimorphism (a difference in size between the sexes) to increase with polygamy.[106] Species where the male is much larger tend to be polygamous.[107] This is understandable, because the larger the male the better he can control access to females and win fights with other males. For example, gorillas are polygamous. One male, about twice the weight of a female, guards and controls a harem of females. Richard Dawkins provides an example of extreme polygamy found in elephant seals, in which only 4 percent of the male population were involved in 88 percent of all copulations.[108] The result: a male can weigh up to 3.7 tons—over four times that of a female—and fighting between males is "among the fiercest in the animal kingdom."[109] Dawkins says that the slight sexual dimorphism in humans suggests a mild polygamous past.[110]

Second, there are exceptions in some species, whereby the usual sex roles are reversed. Exceptions include some birds, such as the Wattled Jacana and Wilson's Phalarope.[111] Called "sex-role-reversal polyandry,"[112] the male bird incubates the eggs and cares for the young while the female seeks to control a harem of males. Unsurprisingly, the females are larger, more colorful, and more aggressive than the males—as they fight and compete for mates. Another example is found in some species of pipefish, where females are polyandrous and compete with other females for a harem of males.[113] These females are also larger and more brightly colored than males. These exceptions confirm the rule that size, strength, and aggression are largely dependent on which sex competes for mates and which sex invests the most in their young.

STRENGTH, LEADERSHIP, AND A ONE-TON GORILLA

What are some other specifics that our dialogue with science can help us with regarding our topic? Consider two examples: one is a popular assumption—the connection between male size/strength and leadership; the other is a biblical text that is essential, central, and foundational to a complementarian position, a one-ton gorilla—the passage in 1 Timothy 2:9–15.

Regarding the first example, we sometimes find it argued in literature although it is more of a popular assumption and sentiment. Douglas Spanner says, "God reveals himself in masculine terms, not because he is male, but because men possess greater authority, for example, in terms of physical strength and voice."[114] As another example, David Knox writes,

> Considered individually as members of society at large, both men and women reflect the divine attributes of authority, power and creativity. Both have authority and dignity, both have power, and both have creative initiative. But considered in their relationship, that is to say in the polarity of the sexes, the male displays greater authority (if only in the depth of his voice), greater power (if only in the strength of his biceps) and clearly his sole physiological initiative in procreation, that is, in creative initiative and causality.[115]

The popular assumption goes something like this: males are generally bigger and stronger than females. This means males have more power, which gives them authority, which better suits them for leadership. Strength = power = authority = leadership. This should be an easy formulation to refute, for the two stories of life and gospel give no credence to such leaps in reasoning. From what we have seen, there are good reasons to view male size and strength related to reproductive strategies. These strategies have an ancient history and relate to competition with other males and access to females. Hence, human males are usually more aggressive and violent (prison populations are mostly male), and they sometimes pursue positions of power and status for sexual advantage and for access to resources like money. But this in no way makes males better suited for leadership.

In addition, the way *power* and *leadership* are construed in this formulation are opposite to the gospel story. In the kingdom of God, it is the weak who are strong, the last are first, the powerful are laid low, and leadership is a way of service. The association between male size/strength and leadership only morphs into a wretched view of leadership that more closely resembles King Kong than King Jesus.

Regarding the second example, the passage in 1 Timothy 2:9–15 is like a tooth drilled too many times, filled with theological amalgam, and now bored to the nerve. The passage includes these words, "I permit no woman to teach or to have authority over a man. . . . For Adam was formed first, then Eve" (1 Timothy 2:12–13). At this point in our discussion, we are only considering this passage in light of our dialogue with science. We will return to it later when we look at other theological issues surrounding such texts.

How can we apply the insights of science to our debate and to this text in particular? To be clear, we are not using science to rewrite the rules for doing theology; science does not trump theology. Nor are we attempting to fuse them together or to make a theological point directly from science.

Scholars have proposed various helpful metaphors to illustrate the interaction of science and theology, such as a duet (van Huyssteen)[116] or as lovers (Shults).[117] Here is another metaphor for doing theology in light of modern science. Think of theology as an attempt to paint a beautiful landscape in oils. Similar to a theologian's depiction of God, a painting is not the landscape itself but a portrayal and interpretation of it. Our theological community and tradition supply us with a limited palette and with rules governing how to paint. These rules may include the use of perspective, light, color, or brushstrokes (rules that may be broken from time to time).

How does science interact and help us? Consider that modern science gives us many additional colors for our palette, but in the process it takes a few colors away. So science doesn't change the rules by which we do theology, neither does it become the basis or overarching framework for doing theology, nor does it become theology itself.[118] But contemporary science modifies our palette. So as we set out to paint we now have a multitude of additional colors, some that we may wonder how we managed without—like a cerulean blue or a phthalo green—but in exchange a few of our original colors have been taken away. Perhaps they were even our favorites, but once we get used to the new palette we don't miss them. We find that we can now create far more hues and subtle shades than before. In the end, the painting more clearly depicts reality and is more pleasing and beautiful than one produced with the older palette.

So to translate: to argue that this was an actual historical event—"For Adam was formed first, then Eve" (1 Timothy 2:13)—is a color no longer available to us to paint with. However we interpret this passage today, the foundation on which the complementarian interpretation is built is no longer plausible. Male and female evolved together, and the two sexes have a history that far precedes our species. Our survey of evolutionary theory has shown that the origin of our species does not go back to two individuals created directly by God, or to a supposed androgynous being that God fashioned into two distinct sexes. Humankind evolved, and male is not first. In the early twenty-first century, any attempt to make the story of Adam and Eve a literal event will involve so many qualifications that it will only result in a shadow of that ancient narrative—ironically sucking the life out of the text that one intends to preserve.

What happens to an interpretation established on a view that is no longer plausible? Or as someone asked, "What happens when the plain sense of Scripture no longer makes sense?" The quick answer is this: Christianity adapts. Most have made at least some changes in interpreting and applying this passage, such as allowing women to wear braided hair, gold, pearls, and expensive clothes (1 Timothy 2:9). Most no longer believe that women are more easily deceived (1 Timothy 2:14). And Christianity will adapt again. When the foundation for an argument no longer makes sense, the strength and persuasive power of that interpreted text is undermined. We saw this happen with the slavery texts, which once seemed so clear to some. Assumptions such as "slaves are inferior" gave power to proslavery interpretations. But once these assumptions evaporated, their favorite texts could no longer carry the theological weight of their position.

A TALE OF TWO STORIES: THE GOSPEL AND EVOLUTION

Scientists as well as theologians sometimes greet a new scientific theory with incredulity or even disdain. "Repugnant . . . it leaves me cold," said the great astrophysicist Arthur Eddington. It "irritates me," said Einstein. "I would like to reject it," said astrophysicist Philip Morrison. It "cannot really be true" said the cosmologist Allan Sandage—when they heard about the new theory of the Big Bang.[119] We know that Darwin anticipated the trouble his theory would cause for religious believers. But he also expected opposition from his scientific colleagues, as he noted near the end of *Origin of Species*, "Although I am fully convinced of the truth of the views given in this volume . . . I by no means expect to convince experienced naturalists whose minds are stocked with a multitude of facts all viewed, during a long course of years, from a point of view directly opposite to mine."[120]

Theologians also sometimes have difficulties with new scientific theories, perhaps even more so because they not only have to reformulate their scientific understanding but also their theology. For instance, the change from the Ptolemaic (geocentric) to the Copernican (heliocentric) view raised the ire of some in the church, as exemplified by the famous trial of Galileo. Some reasons for the conflict are easy to find. As we would expect, the Bible is enmeshed in the thought forms of the day, such as a three-tiered view of the cosmos, with heaven located above, Sheol (the dwelling of the dead) below, and the earth immovable and fixed on foundations. But when thought categories change, such as a cosmological shift in understanding, inevitable questions arise.

If the earth rotates on its axis and revolves around the sun, where is heaven now? What about God who reigns *above* and has the earth as his footstool? Or what about Jesus who *ascended* into heaven? Where is God now? What about humanity's place in the universe? Are we unique and valuable if God has not fixed us at the center with everything else revolving around us? What happens if God did not directly create us? Where are we now?

With these questions comes the fear that to surrender the biblical or Ptolemaic cosmological view would be to surrender the truth of the gospel. And it is such fears that can keep interpretations of the biblical text glued to an outdated worldview—interpretations that then become isolated from the present world and are no longer perceived by most as good news.

Sometimes a change in view may not be such a great hurdle after all. Today people of faith still say, "You [God] knit me together in my mother's womb" (Psalm 139:13), even though we have a far better understanding, compared to the psalmist, of the physical and developmental processes involved. Similarly, we still hold that people are in the image of God, even though there was evolutionary development. Even a literal six-day, six-thousand-years-ago creationist agrees that everyone alive today came about through a process—a fusing of their parents' gametes, followed by growth and development, in the womb. Evolution just takes this developmental process back further.[121]

As we hold that God is creator (even though evolution is true), we hold that all people are in God's image (even though a process was involved). So we still do theology from the Genesis narratives and affirm the inspiration of these texts, even though we look through a different lens, so to speak—one of evolutionary theory rather than ancient Near East creation mythologies. For example, even though Adam was not the first immediately created human, this does not destroy the theology of the narrative that speaks of God as creator and humankind as fallen and in need of redemption and renewal.

Eventually, most Christians come to accept the new view and reformulate their interpretations. With such shifts it may seem that the mountains are giving way and that one's faith is undone. But God remains faithful and loving. The Spirit is still present and empowering. Jesus is still Lord and Savior. Humans are still in the image of God . . . and Christianity adapts. A casual observer may conclude that Christianity, chameleon-like, is either camouflaging its true intentions or simply changing to fit into its surroundings. On closer examination, Christianity is remaining true to the gospel, which is inherently a narrative—a developing story of God's inbreaking into creation. It is this continuing story that gives Christianity its ability to remain good news through the changing millennia.

We can view both the gospel and evolution as stories. One is the story of God's redemption and renewal of the cosmos; the other is the story of the natural development of life. Recent developments in biblical studies, theology, and practical theology have all placed increasing emphasis on "story."[122] One narrative emphasis that many have found helpful is the work of N. T. Wright. Much of Wright's prodigious writing is encapsulated and driven by a narrative framework, as seen in major works such as *The New Testament and the People of God*[123] and *Jesus and the Victory of God*,[124] and in topical treatments such as on biblical authority[125] or the question of evil.[126] According to Wright, human life is "grounded in and constituted by" stories,[127] so that humans perceive and relate to the world through story.[128] To illustrate how Wright uses narrative, take four diverse examples (italics are his):

1. When discussing the topic of evil: Wright says of the Old Testament, "It's written *to tell the story of what God has done, is doing and will do about evil.*"[129]
2. On Jesus: Jesus, in his teaching, retold Israel's story but emphasized "*a new moment in the same story.*"[130] Jesus is the one who brought Israel's story to its climax[131] by embodying the story that "promised YHWH's return to Zion."[132]
3. On Paul: The apostle Paul, like other Jews of his time, considered himself to be an actor "*within* a real-life narrative,"[133] and Paul's thinking was fundamentally narrative in structure.[134] "As Paul's own writings make abundantly clear, what we find in Scripture is above all a *narrative*: the great story of God and the world, and of God's people as the people of God *for* that world."[135]
4. On biblical authority: Here Wright makes his well-known division of the biblical story into a play of five acts—Creation, Fall, Israel, Jesus, and the New Testament writing and beyond.[136] Wright uses this structure to argue for a view of mediated biblical authority (the authority of God mediated through the Scriptures), where we live in the fifth act of the play—where we should act in continuity with the previous foundational acts but also have the freedom to improvise and move the play forward.[137]

Wright's work provides us with plenty of good reasons to accept the gospel as story. His metaphor of a play is also useful for our discussion. Whether or not we adopt the exact outline proposed by Wright, it is helpful to stress that there is a foundational gospel narrative and a *continuation* of that narrative of which we are a part. This meshes with our overview of the slavery debate where we saw a development in the church's understanding of the gospel. Again, this development was possible because the gospel is an ongoing narrative. Although descriptions of the gospel will always be elusive (because the gospel is a developing story), we may see the gospel as a story—a developing narrative about God's faithfulness, love, righteousness, truth, and salvation—primarily seen in Jesus Christ and the Spirit's continuing work. And as far as our discussions on slavery and Sabbath have led us, this story includes the preeminence of particular features—love, freedom, justice, resurrection, and the image of God—a story that is life-changing, world-transforming, and cosmic-renewing. It is one amazing story.

What is less well known are the discoveries in science that the universe's development is narrative in character—a story of development that is still in process. John Haught expresses it well:

> One of the most surprising scientific discoveries of the past century and a half is that the universe is an unfolding story. The sense that the universe is still in the process of coming into being began to emerge faintly several hundred years ago when Tycho Brahe and Galileo Galilei produced visual evidence that the heavens are not changeless. Today, however, developments in geology, evolutionary biology, and cosmology have left no doubt: the whole of nature, not just earth and human history, has an essentially narrative character."[138]

Evolution in its broad sense—as the development of the cosmos and life on earth—is a story; and like any good story it has its twists and turns, villains and victims, dead ends and fruitful avenues. There is conflict, drama, tragedy, hope, life, death, sex, and surprising developments.[139] Surprises such as the Permian extinction (250 million years ago and the largest extinction ever) or the Cretaceous extinction of the dinosaurs (65 million years ago) interrupt the normal flow of the story. These catastrophes, however, set in motion remarkable developments, such as the rise of mammals after the extinction of dinosaurs—a path leading eventually to *Homo sapiens*, with even more surprising developments, such as the emergence of consciousness, language, and the capability to relate to God. We have emerged after the passage of deep time, after a long process that has seen the rise and fall of over 99 percent of species that have ever lived.

This story of life reconfigures time, space, and matter. We orbit a normal star, out on the edge of a spiral galaxy containing over 200 billion stars—a galaxy among 400 billion others. And added to these nearly unimaginable numbers are the distances that separate us. It takes us about three days to get to the Moon and about six months to get to Mars; NASA's New Horizons spacecraft, launched in 2006, will take eight and a half years for its journey to Pluto; and traveling to the nearest star, Proxima Centauri, based on Voyager 1 speeds, would take about 73,000 years.[140] Even the nearest galaxy to us, Andromeda, which is one of the furthest objects we can see with the naked eye, is about 2.5 million light years away. We are seeing this galaxy as it was before our genus *Homo* walked the earth. This is another amazing story.

How do we relate the good news of God's inbreaking of our world with the multitude of discoveries of modern science? No doubt it is difficult to relate these two stories together, and I do not want to minimize the challenge that comes to Christian theology in light of evolution. But viewing them both as narratives can help considerably in relating them together. Before we face some of the difficulties, let's look at some examples of resonance between these two stories and see how these similarities can further our discussion.

Story Resonance

Some have rightly spoken of God as a storyteller.[141] And as the creator of both stories, God the storyteller provides the basis for resonance between the stories of life and gospel. It turns out that there are many similarities between these two stories. Life and gospel are not instantly created, plopped down from above, fully formed, and ready to go. The gospel is no systematic theology, neatly packaged and timeless, untainted by cultural interference or the messiness of life, and handed down by God from above.

The gospel story starts small with one man, Abraham, called by God to be a blessing to all nations; moves to the least of all the nations, Israel; progresses to the New Testament church where not many were wise, powerful, or of noble birth (1 Corinthians 1:26)—and it continues to develop. And life is also given as much time as it needs to emerge and develop, which turns out to be immense. Both stories have humble beginnings. Most of our planet's vast life history has consisted of single-celled organisms, and humanity did not appear instantly. God is not in a hurry, and without coercion God has given the loving gift of vast time and space to this creation for its development.

These are stories in development. Both are going to change in the future. Both stress the relatedness and connectedness of life. And as each story develops, both of them affirm God's love and embrace of process and diversity. Evolution has generated a remarkable diversity of life, as each species has found and explored its niche or biological space. The story goes that the noted biologist J. B. S. Haldane was once asked what he could infer about the Creator from studying creation. Haldane's reply was, "An inordinate fondness for beetles." The evolutionary process has produced, in Darwin's famous phrase, "endless forms most beautiful."[1432] The story of life is a wonderful celebration and embrace of diversity.

The gospel story is also diversity-affirming, from Jesus' willingness to interact with both religious leaders and the outcasts of society, to the inclusion of the Gentiles, to Revelation's scene of "a great multitude that no one could count, from every nation, from all tribes and peoples and languages" (Revelation 7:9). Some people have the curious tendency to view the church's diversity as intrinsically problematic, or even to select their own manifestation of diversity as the pinnacle to which all others should aspire. In light of these two stories, however, it is tempting to think that the church diversifies and fills niches just like species, as each group is free to explore and find its "kingdom space," sometimes becoming so diverse and separate from their ancestor that they can no longer interbreed (ecumenically speaking).

Another similarity is our full life and blood inclusion in both stories, not as people only reading about it, but living it, participating and contributing to the further development of each story. This also adds to our discussion. Part of our contribution to the gospel story is to recognize and live out the *life avenues* and not the *dead ends* of this narrative. In other words, and in terms of our discussion, does this continuing gospel story include slavery? Or the Sabbath? Does it include patriarchy? What trajectories of the story continue? What themes are essential?

This question of the story line is evident in the New Testament itself. So John the Baptist asks of Jesus, "Are you the one who is to come, or are we to wait for another?" (Luke 7:20). John's question relates to his expectations of the story's direction: Wasn't the Messiah going to defeat our enemies? And how much of Paul's teaching emphasized the new direction of the story and enfolding this story around Jesus? Not all parts of the story are of equal importance, and Paul marginalizes some sections once considered central: The Abrahamic covenant is now more important than the Sinaitic; the Torah is not the all-encompassing reality that will bring the kingdom.

For that matter, what about the temple, sacrifices, and promised land? Or the Old Testament accounts of genocide, its casual view of rape, or its endorsement of slavery? Are these actions and beliefs part of the continuing narrative that we should adopt? For sure, without a developing gospel narrative we are stuck—trapped in a world that is not good news for us. Yes, the Old Testament is an essential part of the story (unlike Marcion's outright rejection), but we place it in the context of a larger and developing story. As we saw with slavery, a static view that allows no development wreaks havoc with good, true, beautiful, and just applications. With proslavery, the failure to distinguish between particular content of Scripture and the developing gospel narrative led to supporting an unjust and evil institution. The only way for Christianity to thrive as good news is through the unfolding and developing narrative of the gospel story.

For another example of what can occur with a loss of a continuing narrative, N. T. Wright notes what happened to Judaism after the destruction of the temple in AD 70 and the banning of all Jews from Jerusalem, together with the end of the Jewish nation, in AD 135. He writes, "The events of AD 70 and 135 had the effect precisely of bringing to a full and grinding stop the implicit narrative which second-Temple Jews had been living in, thereby generating a new form of normative Judaism which would find its primary expression in terms not of story but of dehistoricized law-exposition."[143] To this we would add that, today, a loss of the gospel as a continuing narrative can easily lead to legalistic readings of Scripture—a search for rules or laws that are then used to define a community's identity and regulate behavior. This "law" then becomes an overarching structure, abstracted from the biblical material, disconnected from its place in the story, and substituted for the empowering Spirit of God. Legalism is a dark system with no continuing story.

Living *in* these two developing stories of life and gospel also means that it is impossible to figure out the exact ending. The plots are still unfolding, which allows for unexpected turns, radical twists in the tale, and surprise endings. The unfolding drama of these two stories encourages the recognition of possible changes to structures that may seem so inviolable, such as slavery, Sabbath, patriarchy, or immediate creation. In addition, this development has implications for eschatology. The Bible gives a few snippets of where the story is going—mainly in ancient apocalyptic language, which should give us double caution. What threads of the gospel story are going to continue? What will die out? What have we misunderstood? If great prophets like John the Baptist and other devout Jews missed the new directions Jesus was taking the story, will we be any different?

Having said this, how can we illustrate what this might look like, since surprises by definition are unexpected? For the sake of illustration, and a mild surprise, and because God has evident patient love of *process* as exemplified in our two stories of life and gospel, perhaps we will find the final Day of Judgment is not a quick event but a long process of truth and reconciliation, of which the Truth and Reconciliation Commission in South Africa was a reflection. This surprise would emphasize and expand the strong gospel thread of *restorative* justice, where, among many other things, God gives victims the opportunity to talk and be heard, perpetrators have the opportunity to hear about the terrible impact of their behavior on victims, and victims have an opportunity to forgive. Are not the hints we have about the end just hors d'oeuvres for a grand continuation of both stories of life and gospel?

The dialogue with science connects us to *this* cosmos—this story of unimaginable depth of space, time, and fruitfulness. It emphasizes our embodiment and integral relationship to this world and other creatures. It connects us to this reality, not some eschatology that imagines our future disembodied from this renewed cosmos. It is *this* creation that God has allowed to develop and grow and has given the gift of time and space. The gospel story is renewing *this* creation, so these two stories are inextricably entwined.

Story Dissonance

But what about the dissonance between these two stories? Do the conflicts cause an intractable problem for theology? And more specifically, do they undermine our dialogue with science in the above sections? Not if we view these "difficulties" in their proper context. As we have seen, scholars have proposed different helpful metaphors to illustrate the interaction between theology and science, like a duet or lovers. In a piano-cello duet, if one player speeds up the other will adapt. In a marriage, inevitable conflict does not signal the end of the relationship but an opportunity for deeper intimacy. Why should inevitable problems dissolve an otherwise productive, good, and beautiful relationship? What are some of these difficulties? Putting them in the form of questions . . .

- Wasn't there an originally perfect creation? And what about the fall of humanity? Are we still sinners in need of redemption? Didn't Jesus answer Adam's sin (Romans 5:12–21)? Or for some, what about double imputation—the imputation of Adam's sin

to his descendants and the imputation of Christ's righteousness to his people?
- What about death before this fall? Wasn't death the punishment and result of a historical fall? How can something as terrible as death be natural?
- What about the origin of evil?
- How does God relate to the world if the cosmos has evolved?
- If humanity evolved, are we still in the image of God? Are we different from animals, and do we have a soul? Given these unimaginably long eons of time, are we unique, important, valuable, and moral?
- If we turn back the evolutionary clock and run things again, isn't it highly unlikely that we would be here? So again, are we unique and destined by God? Is our uniqueness simply an appearance, because we have overtaken or eliminated our close relatives, such as *Homo neanderthalensis*, *erectus*, and *floresiensis*?

Looking at this list, we need to say at least two things. First, we need to say that theology has always faced difficulties and problems in its interaction with its own cultural context. This is nothing new. The concerns listed above are simply new difficulties that many people face today. To be sure, some theologies will have a harder time than others. We may imagine that those with a more Irenaean view of the development of creation, or a view of God that is more relational and less controlling, will struggle less. In addition, like theologians of today, theologians of yesterday by no means solved all problems and they created quite a few of their own. Earlier theology, for example, had to face the question of coherence over how a perfect and pristine creation could even fall, or the question of justice over the imputation of one person's sin and guilt (Adam) to all people. Any cursory examination of church history will show that the church has continually reconfigured its interpretations in light of its culture. Some examples include Anselm's atonement theory (against the medieval concept of honor), or God as first cause of all things (against the mechanistic view of Newtonian science).

So what can we do with today's difficulties and cultural context? One option is to close the blinds, turn out the lights, and under candlelight pretend that we are back in the seventeenth century. Another is to go outside, take a breath of fresh air, and deal with it.

Second, we need to say that although considerable theological work remains, compelling material is already available that directly relates to some of these difficulties or even reconfigures the questions. Here are a few examples. In *Alone in the World? Human Uniqueness in Science and Theology*,[144] van Huyssteen's remarkable work shows how a thorough interaction with the insights from paleoanthropology can help theology better understand and expound what it means to be in the image of God—including keeping theology's talk of human uniqueness concrete, holistic, and embodied.

In *Life's Solution: Inevitable Humans in a Lonely Universe*,[145] paleobiologist Simon Conway Morris argues that even if the evolutionary clock was turned back and run again, something like humans would emerge. This is because there are limited options available to species as they explore biological space. (Hence, we don't find a giraffe with wheels instead of legs).[146] Because we live in a constrained universe, "all evolutionary possibilities in a given 'space' will inevitably be 'discovered.'"[147] Through this evolutionary convergence the emergence of sentient beings is inevitable.[148]

In *Christology and Science*, Shults uses insights from contemporary science—such as evolutionary biology, cultural anthropology, and relativity—to reconfigure and reform our understanding of Jesus' identity (incarnation), agency (atonement), and presence (*parousia*).[149] Shults' overall innovative project of reforming theology shows how theological formulations wedded to outdated philosophical and scientific categories only cripples theology—becoming repugnant, incoherent, or implausible, and no longer perceived as good news by contemporary people.

Conflicts between the two stories of gospel and evolution are a challenge, but when placed in their proper context these difficulties can help the development of both theology and science. We may find that the so-called difficulties morph into an interplay of delightful harmony. To illustrate briefly how we may approach one of these difficulties, consider the question of death.

Stories of Death

The stories of life and gospel intersect and diverge on the topic of death. From science we know that death is part of nature and that death existed for millions, even billions, of years before the arrival of humans. From theology we know that death is a curse, a "sting" because of sin, and that in the future God will destroy death. These two views on death are not mutually exclusive[150] or contradictory, and they can help each other.

On the one hand, science can help theology accept that death is the natural end of human life and see some benefits arising from death. The results of death are not all terrible. Death and the evolutionary development of life are integrally connected. Death allows for change, development, and new life. Death prevents overpopulation—it gives room for others. So even as we die, we make room for our children, provide opportunities and resources for others, and allow for innovation. For instance, imagine an academic world where no one retired or died and scholars still held to what they argued in their doctoral dissertations written four hundred years ago. It is rare to find senior academics turn from what they have argued for thirty years.[151] My point is that death provides opportunities for others; it allows for change, innovation, and novelty.

Now as we consider death in this light we may go back to the gospel story and find threads that emphasize the productiveness or positive results of death. For example, speaking of his impending death, we read Jesus' words in John's Gospel: "Unless a grain of wheat falls into the earth and dies, it remains just a single grain; but if it dies, it bears much fruit" (John 12:24); "No one has greater love than this, to lay down one's life for one's friends" (John 15:13). By giving up his life, Jesus accepts the evolutionary process that includes death. Or we could examine the three essential pillars of the Christian life—faith, hope, and love—and find that each includes a death of one's beliefs, desires, and actions. To trust God is to face the death of false beliefs. To hope is to die to the desire for present fulfillment. To love includes dying, for it means giving up our lives for the sake of others. To repent is to turn around and die to a wrong way of traveling. The Christian life of discipleship is thus an imitation of Jesus: a call to take up one's cross daily (Matthew 16:24; Mark 8:34; Luke 9:23). So this way of death is a means to love, life, and renewal; and this produces a resonance with science.

On the other hand, theology can help scientists look beyond their field and see that death is not the end of all things. When science looks into the distant future, it sees death. When theology looks to the future, it sees life. The story from science has no happy conclusion. When science looks to the future, death stares back. In the near future, is an asteroid going to blot out life on earth? This is a possibility. Hence, the recent interest in tracking near-Earth objects, such as the asteroid Apophis (aptly named after the Egyptian god of darkness and dissolution) that has a low probability of hitting our planet in 2036 (less than 1 in 45,000).[152] Perhaps we will figure out ways to avoid impacts.

But further into the future, in about 5 billion years, as the sun depletes the remainder of its fuel it will expand into a red giant, enveloping the orbits of the inner rocky planets, including the earth—evaporating our oceans and atmosphere, leaving a superhot charred husk. Perhaps by that time we will have found another habitable planet (and never mind that the average lifespan of a mammalian species is *only* about 2 million years). But then, in about 7 billion years, the galaxy Andromeda will crash into our Milky Way.[153] This also doesn't sound promising, but the distances between stars are so considerable that we may survive this as well, even as we form into a super galaxy. Yet even if we survive these events death is coming, as the latest evidence suggests that the universe will not end in a fiery crunch but continue to expand as everything runs down and moves to an absolute cold, dark, and featureless uniformity.[154] The end is not fire but ice—or as T. S. Eliot put it, "This is the way the world ends / Not with a bang but a whimper." One way or another, the end will come.

The interaction between science and theology runs both ways. There is more we can say about death than what science provides. Theology is interested in unpacking other sides to death, such as death as a curse; death as a terrible severing of loving relationships; death as a "sting" because of sin; death as an alienation from God ("in the day that you eat of it you shall die"—Genesis 2:17); how the powers of this world co-opt death for their instrument of fear, oppression, and destruction; and how death is not the end of the story—as the last enemy it will be defeated.

In particular, theology can help scientists avoid a narrow and idolatrous scientistic conclusion that death is God—that death is the all-embracing final word, the Omega. Many scientists, however, are not scientistic but instead are aware of the limits of science, that there are levels of explanation beyond what their discipline provides.[155] Because of the arriving future, the "newness" of God inbreaking into this world, theology speaks of good news—for the real future is life. Science aids us in focusing our care on *this* creation. Theology aids science in saying that *life* is the future, and therefore this creation is worth saving.

CONCLUSION

Evolution, accepted as a fact by the scientific community, is a well-established theory with predictive and explanatory power. Today we do theology in this context. Similarly, the biblical writers wrote their narratives against their background: ancient Near East creation myths. To label the biblical writers as primitive or erroneous is silliness.[156] They communicated in the thought forms of their day. How else should we expect them to write? We should not be surprised to find a seven-day structure or mention of the sea monster Leviathan, which were part of those ancient mythological stories. The creation narratives do not look like evolution, but they do look like the creation mythology of the ancient Near East. Likewise, we should expect to find in the biblical narrative theological ideas wedded to slavery and patriarchal forms. But given what we know of the gospel, we anticipate this continuing story to critique these structures.

Our present-day context opens up new avenues for consideration. Our dialogue with science renders implausible the views of male superiority or authority—whether because of a male's size/strength or because a male was formed first. Our context encourages us to think differently about hierarchies and the differences between the sexes. The evolutionary process of creation undermines static views such as the idea of creation ordinances, where a structure is fixed forever. Or to express it differently: we now know that these creation ordinances include and use the notion of development and adaptation. We live in a dynamic world of changing nature, changing hierarchies, and changing creation.

Part of the task of theology today is to communicate the gospel story in an understandable and plausible way. Reformation is inevitable, for our cultural context is not about monsters and Marduk but about muons and mutations. This expansion and reconfiguration of our theology may be unsettling, but it is unavoidable given changing cultural contexts and given our relationship with God. We only have to think of Abraham, Job, Peter, or Paul, who all underwent considerable expansion and reforming of their understanding of God—finding that an encounter with the living God is always going to be both comforting and disruptive.

CHAPTER 5

Jesus' Maleness and Creation

We now have an abundance of different interpretations and views—on gender, slavery, Sabbath, and science—and it is time to draw them together and connect the gospel story to some questions surrounding the meaning of Jesus' maleness.

In many debates there are extreme positions in which, ironically, the polar positions end up agreeing with each other on central points. In the debate over slavery the polar views believed that the Bible affirmed slavery—hence the one group justified slavery and the other rejected Christianity. In the gender debate, one position argues that the Bible requires patriarchy; the other agrees and therefore spurns Christianity. On science, one group argues that the Bible requires that we hold to an immediate creation; the other agrees and thus rejects Christianity as primitive myth. This may be represented as follows:

Topic	Polar views	Agreement
SLAVERY	proslavery and ultra-abolitionists	The Bible teaches that slavery is moral.
GENDER	complementarians and post-Christian feminists	The Bible teaches and requires patriarchy.
SCIENCE	creationists and ultra-evolutionists	The Bible teaches and requires an immediate creation.

All these positions have a similar method for approaching and interpreting Scripture, yet they reach opposite conclusions. They have an uneasy symbiotic relationship, feeding off each other in more ways than one. The opposing position is lambasted as the source of many evils—be it feminism, evolution, or religion. Feminism is blamed for destroying families, churches, and society. Evolution is damned for the Holocaust. Religion "poisons everything." Some go so far as to reject the entire discipline of their opposition. Some creationists reject outright the findings of biology and some atheists completely reject theology. To dismiss an entire academic discipline is reckless, and is usually done by those with no recognized competence or expertise in the area being dismissed. And of course there is no incentive to study the rejected discipline. Why study it if it is useless? The heated rhetoric from both sides only serves to entrench and confirm their own respective positions, be it that evolution is atheistic, that religion is blind, or that Christianity is irredeemably patriarchal.

This explains why each Christian position (proslavery, complementarianism, creationism) regularly appeals to the slippery-slope argument—that is, if you reject our position you will end up like those who reject Christianity outright. For instance, it is argued that if you spurn patriarchy you will end up abandoning Christianity, for patriarchy is essential to Christianity. Or if you reject immediate creation, you will end up in atheism. If patriarchy is indispensable to Christianity and you consider patriarchy evil, the only option is to reject Christianity. This concern is a self-fulfilling prophecy, for it is precisely those who hold similar approaches to Scripture who may go to the opposite extreme, once they decide slavery, patriarchy, or immediate creation is immoral or untenable.

The opposing positions also have similar understandings of God. God as *Master* supports and justifies slavery—so slavery is approved by Christianity. God as *Father* supports and justifies patriarchy—so male rule is required by Christianity. God's existence or work can be decided by science—either by showing us that God can tinker with life and intelligently design or by showing us that there is no God.

DIFFERENT PERSPECTIVES, APPROACHES, EMPHASES, STRENGTHS, AND WEAKNESSES

We can also analyze the different views on the gender debate in terms of different perspectives or emphases. Some positions focus more on the text of Scripture, others more on the cultural context, and others on personal experience. This threefold difference of perspective or emphasis can be summarized as the difference between God's word, God's world, and God's image, or between orthodoxy, orthopraxy, orthopathy (right thinking, right practice, and right experience). Some have called it "text, soul, culture"[1] or "normative, situational, existential."[2] For our discussion we will just call this threefold difference Scripture, culture, and experience.

Considering the various positions, generally speaking, it may be said that complementarians start with and focus on specific texts of Scripture, biblical egalitarians on the cultural context (ancient and modern), and Christian[3] and post-Christian feminists on women's experience. Of course, any theological formulation will have a particular emphasis, but to the extent that each position excludes the other reality we may anticipate imbalances or weaknesses. We will first look at some of the weaknesses and then the strengths of each position.

We saw in our discussion on slavery that the complementarian position, generally speaking, has neglected cultural and experiential factors. There is a narrow focus on particular texts, and complementarians often disconnect their discussion from culture and experience. They imply or state that some biblical passages or themes are *beyond* culture, and they inadequately deal with the inhumane treatment, torture, and ridicule of women throughout history to the present day. Without significantly challenging the appalling history of the church in its treatment of women, the position leaves itself open to the criticism that it does not speak to our world or our experience. Given this lack, complementarianism finds itself at variance with the modern world. It faces the danger that its communication of the gospel is unnecessarily offensive to the world.

In claiming to begin and end with Scripture, complementarians give the impression that their experience or cultural context does not influence their interpretation. In this regard, Christian and post-Christian feminists are more self-aware: by claiming to begin with experience they acknowledge the impossibility of interpretation without involving one's life, race, class, sex, and culture. Complementarians also recognize that "there is a growing consensus within the Church that rejects male government."[4] They acknowledge that the church is increasingly abandoning their position.

In addition, one finds statements like those that the complementarian Thomas Schreiner made to a friend adopting an egalitarian view of 1 Timothy 2:9–15: "I would like to believe the position you hold. But it seems as if you have to leap over the evidence of the text to espouse such a position."[5] Here is tacit admission that the interpretation of some complementarians runs contrary to their *own* experience and context. This identical struggle was apparent in proslavery, as seen in the statement by the proslavery advocate Hopkins: "If it were a matter to be determined by my personal sympathies, tastes, or feelings, I should be as ready as any man to condemn the institution of slavery; for all my prejudices of education, habit, and social position stand entirely opposed to it."[6] Such struggles with a sense of justice and moral intuition are good indicators of problematic interpretations of the biblical text.

Biblical egalitarians have a particular focus on the situation or culture (both ancient and modern). Given this focus, we find "creative" interpretations of Scripture. A few egalitarians, like Jewett and Mollenkott,[7] have a dichotomous view of Scripture and of Paul himself—the view that Paul at times taught out of his patriarchal socialization but in other places taught out of his gospel understanding.[8] The notion that there was confusion or contradiction in Paul's thinking is unsatisfactory, and few egalitarians have adopted this as a viable position.

We find a less radical split regarding Paul's thinking in Richard Longenecker's approach, in which Paul, even in the same passage, can argue for subordination from creation and for equality from redemption. Longenecker writes, "At the heart of the problem as it exists in the Church is the question of how we correlate the theological categories of creation and redemption. Where the former is stressed, subordination and submission are usually emphasized—sometimes even silence; where the latter is stressed, freedom, mutuality, and equality are usually emphasized. What Paul attempted to do in working out his theology was to keep both categories united—though, I would insist, with an emphasis on redemption."[9]

However valuable it is to stress redemption rather than creation, the argument has little traction when appealing to the biblical text. We saw that slavery is given a theological basis in the work of Christ—that is, *redemption* (1 Peter 2:18–21). The Sabbath is given a theological basis in creation (Genesis 2:2–3; Exodus 20:8–11) and redemption (Deuteronomy 5:12–15). In fact, regarding our debate, Paul not only bases role differentiation in creation (1 Timothy 2:13) but also in redemption (Ephesians 5:22–33). There is a tendency among biblical egalitarians to interpret texts in a manner that either excuses or reduces their patriarchal character: Paul was wrong (Jewett, Mollenkott); 1 Corinthians 14:34–35 is an interpolation and unauthentic (Fee);[10] some associate subordination with creation and equality with redemption (Longenecker), and others give complex cultural explanations for alternative readings of the text.[11] Although biblical egalitarians have attempted to provide alternative interpretations of 1 Timothy 2:11–15,[12] it is telling that the majority of positions believe that patriarchal texts such as these are indeed patriarchal—that is, they teach and require male headship. Complementarians hold this, and so do Christian feminists, although they argue for an alternative normative tradition. Post-Christian feminists argue that these texts are patriarchal. In addition, even some biblical egalitarians, like Jewett, agree.

By starting with and emphasizing women's experience, Christian feminists and post-Christian feminists sometimes argue for views that are hard to reconcile with the biblical text and the continuing gospel story. (Of course, post-Christian feminists are not looking to reconcile any of their thinking with Scripture or the gospel.) For some, not only is patriarchy a problem but also a host of traditional attributes of God, such as his omnipotence, freedom, underived existence, providence, and lordship.[13] In constructing a "theology after Auschwitz," sometimes the call is to go beyond a belief in the presence of God.

In addition, in their legitimate quest to remove dualisms between spirit and matter and male and female (where one is inferior and the other superior), Christian feminists often challenge the dualisms of good and evil, light and darkness, and divinity and humanity.[14] With such dismissals, wrestling with the biblical text is often absent, or there is a lack of compelling reasons given for why we should read the text differently. Post-Christian feminists like Hampson reach a position where God is excluded and nothing can interrupt the causal nexus of history.[15] Hampson agrees, however, that the church is not going to part with its text.[16] The church collectively is not going to give up believing, for example, that God is good and present in our world.

Apart from these weaknesses, complementarians and feminists have unique strengths. In earlier chapters we noted that the strength of complementarianism is its theological basis and the strength of feminism is its transformation dynamic. Complementarians have a firm position, arguing that God has established a created order and that as long as the first creation continues this order remains. Their strength lies in texts such as 1 Timothy 2:11–15, where Paul appeals to creation and the pre-fall situation. Their focus on specific texts is also a strength, for it encourages the church to wrestle with its Scripture.

As the complementarian position is firm, so is the feminist position, in different areas. The focus on broader gospel themes, such as the image of God, love, freedom, and the impartiality of God, has significant weight. The emphasis feminists place on culture and experience is another strength, as it enables them to speak more compassionately to this world and to take significant account of the culture in which the Scriptures were written.

Both sides have different emphases, and the strength of the one is the weakness of the other. As suggested in our discussion on slavery and the Sabbath, each position is correct in its respective strengths. Similar to proslavery and pro-Sabbath positions, the complementarian position has a clear, firm, and strong theological basis. Feminists should recognize this. On the other hand, feminists have a strong basis when appealing to broader gospel themes. Complementarians should recognize this.

So we affirm that complementarians are correct regarding the theological basis—that patriarchy is connected to theological themes such as creation, redemption, and the names of God—and that feminists are correct regarding the transformation dynamic—that we are all in the image of God, called to love and to be free, and that God is impartial. This is nothing less than accepting the strengths of each position. On the one hand, Christian and post-Christian feminists, as well as some biblical egalitarians, agree that texts like 1 Timothy 2:11–15 assign permanent subordinate roles to women based on creation, and so they concede that there is a theological basis. On the other hand, complementarians agree that God does not show favoritism and that all people are in the image of God, and so they acknowledge the truth of the transformation dynamic. In the case of slavery, the transformation dynamic showed that proslavery was contrary to the gospel and the Spirit. A question that remains for us is if this theological basis permanently establishes patriarchy or if there is sufficient weight to the transformation dynamic to overturn male rule. To express it another way, is complementarianism contrary to the gospel story?

The Weight of the Gospel Story's Transformation Dynamic

From our chapters on slavery, Sabbath, and science we can summarize a few points:

- Feminists use a hermeneutic that emphasizes the transformation dynamic of the gospel story, and complementarians use this same hermeneutic to argue that slavery is wrong.
- The idea of creation ordinances, where a structure is fixed forever, is undermined by considering the Sabbath debate and the evolutionary process of creation. Creation is still in process and all things are caught up in this development.

- Just because patriarchy, slavery, and the Sabbath have a theological basis does not mean they are permanent. We saw a remarkable change with slavery and the Sabbath. In the Old Testament, the Sabbath had a stronger theological basis than the submission of women or slavery. For most in the church today, the Sabbath has undergone a considerable modification or has been abolished.
- Our interaction with science renders implausible the view of male authority—either because of size/strength or because male was formed first. We saw that the story of life gives no support for male being first or head. We will now consider whether male rule has support from the gospel story.
- Even the complementarian position has undergone transformation. Complementarians have modified the church's traditional teaching regarding the inferior status of women, and many now limit male headship to church and family, thus conceding that, concerning gender roles, even some *post*-New Testament transformation is necessary. And some complementarians grant that the commands in Ephesians 5:31–33 and 1 Timothy 2:12–13 could be transposed by "weighty hermeneutical considerations."[17]

Proslavery, pro-Sabbath, pro-male leadership, and pro-creation positions all claim to have the clear texts and the plain interpretation on their sides. There is some validity to this claim. All these positions have a theological basis, and that basis is persuasive to some. The error of both the proslavery and pro-Sabbath positions, however, was to presume and argue that the theological basis permanently established their institutions. Complementarians argue that their position is clear and permanent. Have they made a similar error? As seen in the debate over slavery and the Sabbath, the position that goes counter to the theological basis needs more explanation in arguing for a change. Nevertheless, with slavery and Sabbath, what appeared to be established commands and institutions can and should be abolished. So, what is the weight of this gospel transformation dynamic, which includes the gospel themes of equality, love, and the impartiality of God?[18]

If the transformation dynamic in the gospel story is of sufficient weight, we expect to find in the complementarian position irreconcilable difficulties or contradictions relating to this dynamic. If not, we anticipate the position to remain consistent with the overarching principles. In the case of slavery, the principles of love, freedom, and equality (image of God) ultimately condemned slavery and opposed what some people thought of slaves—that they were "equal but subordinate," suited to their position, needed protection, and that God had permanently consigned them to servitude.

Creation and Recreation in the Image of God: The Equality of All

A fundamental element of the gospel transformation dynamic is the image of God and its implied egalitarian principle. It is unnecessary to discuss the various possible meanings of the image of God or chart its development through church history. Neither is it necessary to get into a discussion of whether *equality* is only an Enlightenment concept. We are concerned about the gospel story and are working on the assumption that the principles derived from the image of God give all humans (female and male) equal dignity and value and place them as caring rulers over creation. All positions agree with this, including complementarians, who include an *equal* in their "equal but subordinate" scheme. No one holds that one group of humans is superior—like Orwellian pigs, more equal than others.

Historically, the church has argued that women are denied leadership because they are inferior. Apart from its clear error, this position has a simple consistency: women are unable to lead because, by nature, they are less capable than men. Today, all Christian positions affirm that women and men are created in the image of God and that neither is inferior. Complementarians affirm the full equality and leadership capability of women, but this equality is qualified by subordination of role. There is an *equal but subordinate* construction.

What is the basis for this subordination of women? Some complementarians, like Packer, argue that the subordinate role of women is grounded in their nature, so to depart from these roles is to put strain on the "nature of both men and women."[19] Elisabeth Elliot speaks of surrender as the essence of femininity.[20] And Piper and Grudem argue that subordination is grounded in the heart of mature femininity.[21] The nature of women establishes their subordinate role. Complementarians divide over whether to apply this subordination universally, the majority limiting subordination of women to church and family.

Considering those who apply this subordination solely to church and family, we expect that for them subordination is not grounded in the nature of women. If women are subordinate by nature, we anticipate a universal application, since this would apply to every woman and in all situations. Nevertheless, those who limit the subordination of women to church and family regularly ground subordination in the nature of women. Knight applies role differentiation to church and family but also speaks about leadership as a characteristic of maleness,[22] and he sees subordination as the ontological and ordained role of women.[23] Waltke argues that church and family is to maintain male authority, yet he appeals to Goldberg's thesis (from his book *Why Men Rule*) on the *universality* of male rule.[24]

Similarly, Dorothy Patterson argues that subordination only applies to church and family; and in this context a woman's subordination, like Christ's, is *not* by nature, but voluntary.[25] Nevertheless, she agrees with Packer about the strain put on men and women if these roles are reversed, and she believes that these *ontological* understandings are foundational.[26] Furthermore, she asks the question, "How is the woman's *nature* [italics mine] affected by the Fall?"[27] Her answer is that women now have corrupted subordination. Although limiting the application to church and family, Patterson regularly speaks of a biblical theology of *womanhood*.

Knox argues in a similar manner: "But turning from the general social life, where men and women are equal, to those relationships of men and women in which the polarity of the sexes has significance, namely marriage and the home, we see both in *nature* [italics mine] and in Scripture distinctions which are never confused. Here the roles of male and female are quite distinct, cannot be reversed or interchanged and are not the same."[28] Knox goes on to say that God is spoken of as masculine and incarnates as a male because "he displays the male attributes par excellence."[29] In speaking about the role of women and men in the church, Brown also speaks about an order of being[30] and about created differences that cannot be changed.[31]

For one final example, Schreiner argues, "Women are equal to men in essence and in being; there is no ontological distinction, and yet they have a different function or role in church and family."[32] He claims:

> God's order of creation is mirrored in the nature of men and women. Satan approached the woman first not only because of the order of creation but also because of the different inclinations present in Adam and Eve. . . . Women are less prone than men to see the importance of doctrinal formulations, especially when it comes to the issue of identifying heresy and making a stand for the truth. . . . What concerns [Paul] are the consequences of allowing women in the authoritative teaching office, for their gentler and kinder nature inhibits them from excluding people for doctrinal error.[33]

Although assigning a different function in church and family, Schreiner still writes, "There is a direct link between women appropriating leadership and the loss of femininity."[34]

So complementarians routinely establish the distinctions in church and family based on a woman's nature. In the end, nature, being, or ontology is the basis for a woman's subordinate position. This is a significant problem, as addressed in the five points below.

1. **Why Limit What Is True by Nature to Only Church and Family?** If all women are equal but subordinate, why restrict the application? Either subordination is grounded

in nature and therefore applies universally, or it is not established in nature and therefore cannot refer to ontology. Complementarians regularly appeal to Goldberg's thesis, but why refer to this if you are limiting the application to church and family? Moreover, Goldberg argues that although males will predominate in hierarchical positions, there will "be an eradication of one-sex occupations."[35] This is precisely the point complementarians will not concede.

Complementarians also regularly refer to the homosexuality debate. One reason for their concern appears to lie in this very issue: the subordination of women is grounded in nature, and therefore for someone to deny male headship is to minimize the distinctions between the sexes and thus open the door to homosexuality. Their apprehension arises from basing women's subordination in ontology.

All positions agree that there are plenty of differences between the sexes.[36] Differences are not the essential issue, unless one of these differences is women's subordination. In the earliest stages, feminists were understandably hesitant to speak about differences between the sexes, for fear that those differences would be used to keep women subordinate. Today, most agree that there are numerous social, psychological, and physiological differences between the sexes. We can say many positive things about the differences between the sexes. The differences between the sexes are not under debate, except if one of these differences is one of leadership and submission.

2. **If the Subordination of Women Is Established in Nature, Then It Is Not Only a Subordination of Role.** It becomes a characteristic of being female, for subordination is inextricably connected with a woman's being. Significantly, complementarians not only find subordination of women in Genesis 2 but also in Genesis 1:26–27, a passage they use to

establish the *equality* of the sexes. Raymond Ortlund writes, "There is a paradox in the creation account. While Genesis 1 teaches the equality of the sexes as God's image-bearers and vice-rulers on the earth, Genesis 2 adds another, complex dimension to Biblical manhood and womanhood. The paradox is this: God created male and female in His image equally, but He also made the male the head and the female the helper."[37] Yet Ortlund goes on to argue for male headship in Genesis 1:26–27, where "man" is used generically.[38]

Similarly, Dorothy Patterson argues for equality from Genesis 1 and complementarity from Genesis 2,[39] although she also finds the foundation for headship in Genesis 1:27.[40] In other words, the passage used to establish equality is also used to establish subordination. Questions now arise as to whether complementarians hold to a subordination only of role or function. The question also arises as to how men, who by nature are to lead, can ever submit to any woman. How can a man obey the general commands of submission (e.g., Romans 13:1, 5; 1 Corinthians 16:16; Ephesians 5:21; James 3:17; 1 Peter 2:13; 5:5) if by nature he is to lead but he is relating to a woman in authority or to one who is older? Finally, if the subordination of women is grounded in nature, why claim that women are capable of leading?

Groothuis has noted a problem with this formulation.

"What determines the fittingness of male authority and female subordination? Nothing less than the "underlying nature" of the male and the female. A man is fit to lead by virtue of his male nature. A woman, by virtue of her female nature, is not. Yet, traditionalists insist, a woman is perfectly competent to lead a man; nonetheless, for her to do so is for her to act in opposition to her true nature. It seems that a woman is, by nature, at the same time fit to lead and unfit to lead. She has the natural ability to do so, yet it is somehow unnatural for her to do so."[41]

To establish female subordination in nature leads to the tension noted by Groothuis: that women are able to lead, yet commanded not to lead; yet again, it is against their nature to lead.

3. **The "Equal but Subordinate" Scheme Is Understood and Argued as Equal in *Being* and Subordinate in *Relation*.** In regard to their being or substance, women are equal to men; but they are subordinate in their function or relation. This bifurcation between ontology and function, between substance and relation, made sense under an Aristotelian worldview where a sharp distinction is made between substance and relations and where substance is primary and unchanging. According to this worldview, who you are *is* the stuff or substance you are made of. Substance is what is real, and relations are secondary. So, under this framework you can speak of *being apart* from your relations, and relations do not change who you are.

Contemporary theology has rightly reacted against this Aristotelian worldview by emphasizing that your *relations* define who you are. For example, Torrance speaks of an "ontorelational" understanding of God or of God as a "communion constituting Being."[42] Zizioulas speaks of "being as communion" and communion as an "ontological category."[43] And Shults notes that people are no longer understood today as isolated individuals—that we find our being in our relations to others, that our persons are formed and shaped by our interaction with others.[44] Relationships or communion *is* being. As a person, you are a being-in-relation-to-others, so your relationships define you as a person. Humans are not isolated individuals but are constituted by their relations to others. Today, it is implausible to separate being and relation, ontology and function. Being and relation are like a Möbius strip—a strip of paper given one twist and joined at the ends, making an object with one side—both move into the other and cannot be separated. Speak about one and you speak about the other. If you are subordinate by nature, that is who you are—subordinate. If you are subordinate in relation, that is who you are—subordinate. The "equal but subordinate" scheme is a distinction with no difference.

4. **What Will Happen in the Consummation?** If female subordination and male leadership are by nature, it follows that this structure is an eternal structure, unless one argues that in the consummation there is a considerable change of being/relation. In addition, as seen in chapter one, complementarians do not stop at creation to secure their position, but establish it in the Trinity. How then can male headship be established in male nature and the being of God and yet only be applicable in this present age? If it is by nature, and grounded in God's Trinitarian nature, how can there be a change at the consummation? As we saw in our discussion on slavery, most complementarians, however, maintain that the structure of the present age will be abolished. But it is difficult to justify such a change if the present structure is based in ontology—male, female, and divine.

Nevertheless, in agreeing that the current situation of male headship will be abolished in the consummation, complementarians have in principle conceded that leadership is not inherent to maleness. More consistently, Letham argues that male headship is grounded in creation and in the nature of God; and so he says, "Consequently, there are grounds for assuming that this relation of order within equality will remain permanently as man images God throughout eternity."[45] In the consummation, however, there is neither marriage nor giving in marriage (Matthew 22:30; Mark 12:25; Luke

20:35). The church will be perfected and unified under one head, who is Christ (Ephesians 1:10; Revelation 21:1–27). If these structures remain, we can imagine a Sadducean dilemma: "In the resurrection, a woman who had seven husbands—to whom does she submit?"

5. **Does the "Equal but Subordinate" Construction Degrade the Worth of Women?** In other words, does assigning a subordinate role to women detract in any way from their dignity and value? When questioned about the worth of women, Ortlund provides a typical complementarian reply: "*There is no necessary relation between personal role and personal worth.* Feminism denies this principle. Feminism insists that personal role and personal worth must go together, so that a limitation in role reduces or threatens personal worth. But why? What logic is there in such a claim? Why must my position dictate my significance? The world may reason that way. But doesn't the gospel teach us that our glory, our worth, is measured by our personal conformity to Christ?"[46]

Paige Patterson agrees, saying, "Equally obvious is it that role assignments and submission to various authorities are demanded in Scripture with no essential estimate of worth or value implied for the one in authority or the one who is subordinate."[47] Similarly, Frame argues that subordination does not impinge on a woman's worth or ability to image God, for men are also placed under authority. Jesus placed himself under authority, and in submission we reveal God.[48] And for one more example, Litfin argues, "Submission of wives to husbands is no more logically inconsistent with ontological equality than is the submission of citizens to elected officials. The one may be more palatable to the contemporary Western mind than the other, but neither one is more logical than the other."[49]

For complementarians, subordination does not imply inferiority, because all are called to subordinate positions—under civil leaders, church leaders, and parents. Such calling, however, does not imply any superiority of the civil government, church leadership, or parents. In addition, it is argued that this subordination of women in church and family is voluntary, not coerced.[50]

By responding in this manner complementarians have minimized the problem facing them. We may use their argument to justify the subordination of a race, nationality, or class—slaves, Africans, or untouchables—by saying that their subordination does not detract from their capacity to image God, for everyone is under authority, including Jesus. We could argue that in their subordination they image God, so it is a position of high value; that there is no necessary connection between their role and personal worth; and that it is voluntary in the sense that God does not coerce their subordination.

The problem, though, is the *legislation*. People, of course, are not equal in many ways because we have differing abilities, positions, and work. The essential point, however, relates to legislation based on gender, race, class, or nationality. The debate is not whether we image God in submission or in rule. The question is whether this subordination based on gender contradicts the principle of all being in the image of God. Complementarians have not answered the dilemma that faces them: Does *legislated* role (based on gender) and personal worth go together?

It is true that one's role does not dictate worth. To be a president or a janitor does not dictate worth—that is, the janitor is not worth less than a president. He is not inferior or expendable. The point that is frequently glossed over is whether *requiring* a person to be a janitor would be *indicative* of his worth. Why would we mandate such an action? It implies that some intrinsic characteristic makes that person better suited for servanthood—a quality that suits the requirement of service. To reply, for example, that citizens of equal worth still have to submit to the government is to ignore the issue at stake. This is because citizens are *permitted* to be in government leadership. On this basis, the requiring of submission of children is understandable; for although they image God, by virtue of their youthful nature they are unwise and in need of instruction and leading (cf. parental teaching in Proverbs). The crucial point does not concern authority structures, different roles, or different capabilities, but whether leadership is permitted or denied based on gender. The crux of the matter is not the requirement to submit, but the requirement to submit based on being, so that by nature you are confined to being led.

The slavery debate demonstrated that although equality was affirmed in principle, in practice the slave was considered suited to his or her position. With slavery, the problem was not subordination as such, but subordination based on being. Such argumentation for slaves is now considered racist. Smith writes, "In short, racism from the Christian standpoint is a response that violates the equalitarian principle implied in the biblical doctrine of the *imago Dei*. If, for example, a person regards another race as an inferior member of the human family and seeks to deny it an equal opportunity for growth and participation in the common life, he is a racist. Racism is two-directional in its evil expression. On the one hand, it impeaches the impartiality of God and, on the other, it breeds social discord."[51]

Everyone agrees with this because we no longer believe that other races are inferior in being. Why then do complementarians disagree with applying this reasoning to our debate? An "equal but subordinate" construction, if applied to a race, class, or culture, would be rejected as discriminatory. The reason is clear. What we have said about personal worth and required subordination *clearly* conflicts with the egalitarian principle, unless one already believes that women are subordinate by nature. Complementarians do not apply such reasoning, because if they did apply it to gender the sexual differences inherent to creation would be minimized. In their position, differing race, class, or culture is not founded in nature, but the subordination of women is.

The reason why complementarians fail to see the relevance of statements like Smith's is that they maintain that women's subordination is inherent to their nature. So although holding in principle to equality, they view women as suited to subordination. This is apparent in the manner of their answer to the problem of personal worth and required subordination. Because women are *suited* to this position, there is no problem in *assigning* them this position. In other words, complementarians can claim that women are not worth less because of their position, since foundational to their view is that it is women's nature to be subordinate.

In the slavery debate, the gospel transformation dynamic exposed fundamental incompatibilities that existed between proslavery and the gospel. Likewise, this dynamic, and in particular the egalitarian principle implied by the image of God, may be used to show that the complementarian position is contrary to the gospel story. Complementarianism runs counter to this story because it breaks the egalitarian principle. Although complementarians say that women are equal, their position runs contrary to this claim, for in the end women are suited to subordination.

An application of the gospel theme of *image of God* to all humanity indicates that there is sufficient weight to the transformation dynamic to overturn male headship. In other words, it demonstrates that the theological basis of complementarianism does not permanently establish patriarchy. It shows that the gospel story does not ultimately establish these commands in the nature of men and women. So although the New Testament gives various commands to men and women a theological basis, this basis is open to transformation.

Gospel Love

The law of love and the Golden Rule are essential to the gospel transformation dynamic. The existence of slavery and the treatment of slaves violated this gospel jewel. But what about the gender debate? Although we could use *love*, like the image of God, to show further incompatibilities in complementarianism, we want to look at another way of using these gospel themes, by showing how they can be applied to bring about transformation—even within a complementarian system.

In our discussion of slavery we saw that both proslavery and complementarianism incorporate love into their system. Though they consider love to be fully compatible with their position, complementarians do not believe that love transforms complementarianism. Proslavery advocates likewise believed the same. Abolitionists argued, however, that a rigorous application of Paul's commands to masters and slaves in a passage like Ephesians 6:5–9 would abolish slavery. In other words, if what Paul commanded was consistently applied, the institution of slavery would be abolished.

So what about Paul's commands to husbands and wives in Ephesians? We have no disagreement with complementarians, who argue that love does not undermine, unlike slavery, the institution of marriage.[52] Our question is whether love can change the structure *within* marriage. We are interested in the outcome when the commands Paul lays down in Ephesians 5:22–33 are thoroughly applied. Complementarians stress the irreversibility of roles, based on the comparison between Christ and the church. What is frequently glossed over is that this reasoning could also be used against the abolitionist use of Ephesians 6:5–9, where Paul describes irreversible roles for master and slave, especially by speaking of God as Master (Ephesians 6:9). Nonetheless, our concern is not so much whether Paul gives different commands to husbands and wives (just as he gave different commands to slaves and masters); our concern is in regard to their practical outworking.

For the sake of argument, we will grant the complementarian interpretation of this passage: that Paul is giving different commands to husbands and wives, as the husband is compared with Christ and the wife with the church. We will also concede their position that the mutual submission of Ephesians 5:21 does not override what Paul states subsequently. Once again, this is nothing less than accepting the theological basis of complementarianism.

How do complementarians define headship and submission in this passage? Knight writes: "Paul's direct command to husbands is to 'love your wives, just as Christ loved the church and gave himself up for her' (verse 25). This is clearly how the apostle demands that the husband exercise his leadership in everything as the head over his wife. . . . In his leadership role as head, he seeks to lead by giving of himself to his wife in ways analogous to how Christ gave Himself to His bride."[53]

Clearly Paul is not stating that, as head, the husband is like Christ in every respect, which would be idolatrous. Paul qualifies and limits the extent of the analogy. He defines what he means by headship: it is a matter of love, not rule.[54] Complementarians agree that this love of the husband is "a giving of oneself for the benefit of the other."[55] So to unpack the meaning, the husband, as head, is to love like Jesus. He is called to completely give himself. It is a calling to die. In dying, he gives up his *life*, which presumably includes his desires, ambitions, control, interests, reputation, and pleasure. It is a call to an all-embracing (verses 28–29) and ministerial (verses 26–27) love for his wife. It is a continual love with the goal to serve another.

How do complementarians view a wife's submission? Dorothy Patterson describes submission as the abandoning of one's rights, desires, and energies.[56] It "denotes humility, selflessness, helpfulness, respect, and honor."[57] This biblical submission is defined by the example of Christ, who "never considered Himself, His rights, and His will (John 5:30)."[58] The wife is called to submit as the church submits to Christ. This submission is also all-embracing (Ephesians 5:24) and ministerial, since in being submissive she is being a *helper*. The wife yields her will for the good of her husband. It is a giving of her life, including her desires, ambitions, control, interests, reputation, and pleasure. In fact, complementarians emphasize that this submission follows the example of Jesus' love in giving up his life.[59]

Significantly, Jesus is the model for the husband as well as the wife. What then is the difference, when the commands are practically applied? Complementarians will claim there still is a difference in that the husband *initiates* this love—though one wonders at this point whether the distinction is vacuous, as both give up their lives and both are initiating and responding. Piper and Grudem acknowledge, "Husbands and wives will often yield their own preferences to make each other happy. That is the way love is."[60] And Foh writes, "Because the wife's submission to her husband is an expression of the mutual submission of all Christians to one another, it is easy not to distinguish it from the command to the husband to love his wife, which is also an expression of mutual submission. In practice the two duties resemble each other."[61]

Practically speaking, in this passage *love* and *submit* become synonymous. That the two will coalesce is understandable, since at the heart of the gospel story is loving submission or submissive love. For example, Philippians 2:6–8 describes the submission and love involved in Jesus giving up his life. Jesus therefore becomes a model for our submission and love (Philippians 2:3–5).

When thinking about love, complementarians redefine or modify their view of leadership. This is a corrective to their overall approach. In fact, the entire structure of male leadership versus female submission sets up a fatal dichotomy for understanding gospel leadership. By ripping submission from leadership they cut a pound of flesh from the heart of leadership. As seen in the kenotic life of Jesus, subordination or submission is an essential part of good leadership. And in this light, if women are by nature subordinate, are they not better suited for Christian leadership? Just as the story of life gave no credence for male leadership, so the gospel story gives no justification to separate leadership from submission.

With the joining of love and submission, the understanding and application of a key complementarian text undergoes transformation. This is the position advocated by Andrew Lincoln. His commentary on Ephesians adopts a complementarian understanding of the text—that is, Paul is teaching complementary roles of husbands loving and wives submitting.[62] In terms of our discussion, this is nothing less than accepting the theological basis for complementarianism. Nevertheless, when considering the practical outworking, Lincoln argues:

> Instead of assigning love to the husband and submission to the wife, a contemporary appropriation of Ephesians will build on this passage's own introductory exhortation (v. 21)

and see a mutual loving submission as the way in which the unity of the marriage relationship is demonstrated. Indeed, Ephesians itself elsewhere asks both love (cf. 5:2) and submission (cf. 4:2) of all. Both wife and husband can look to Christ as the model for the sacrificial kind of love required (cf. 5:2). In this way, submission and love can be seen as two sides of the same coin—selfless service of one's marriage partner.[63]

Richard Hays comes to the same conclusion regarding this passage. "Although the symbolic world of Ephesians remains patriarchal, we see the beginnings of a remarkable hermeneutical revision of patriarchy through the story of the cross."[64]

There is sharp disagreement over Ephesians 5:21–33, yet in practice the positions are closer than often acknowledged or realized. We have argued, based on the gospel theme of love (and an overall *complementarian interpretation* of the passage), that marriage undergoes a transformation, becoming a mutually loving and submissive relationship. Marriage, then, is a relationship where both partners lay down their lives for the love and good of the other. As love and submission become synonymous, the so-called irreversible roles lose their force. Love transforms a key complementarian text. Similar to the image of God, the enduring reality of love adds significant weight to the gospel transformation dynamic—again, enough weight to overturn patriarchy.

Gospel Transformation

The story of the gospel emphasizes particular realities, such as the image of God, love, freedom, justice, humility, resurrection, and the impartiality of God. These themes are primary and essential. If they are undermined the heart of the narrative stops beating, and the gospel story collapses, for it is no longer good news. At this point in our discussion, we can now emphasize different language to describe these themes or realities. Although *gospel principles* made sense in the context of nineteenth-century discussions on slavery, for us today *principles* may sound rather static—that is, as *timeless principles* that conflict with the dynamic gospel story. Furthermore, these gospel principles may be construed as another theological basis. Our emphasis on the gospel as story encourages us to use different language. What is determinative is not so much static principles derived from the Bible but new realities or events that are working themselves out in light of the eschatological Christ-event. As the church embodies the gospel, it recognizes the transforming *life avenues* of this gospel story.

Our emphasis on this gospel transformation dynamic raises some other areas for consideration.

Clear and Specific Texts. The church rarely decides or resolves issues by an appeal to specific texts. The great debates are not solved by coming to an agreement on the meaning of Scripture. For example, the Salem witch trials ended not because the judges changed their minds about how Scripture supposedly demonstrated the existence and capabilities of witches, but because public opinion changed. Abolitionism in the United States was decided not by biblical argument but by the American Civil War and a constitutional amendment. I believe the same will happen with evolution. Biblical exegesis will not be the deciding factor, but the overwhelming scientific evidence will become evident to most and opinions will change. Evolution will become ubiquitous and the assumptions that made particular texts seem so inviolable will transform or disappear. Likewise, we should expect that the gender debate will not be decided through biblical argument. Even now it appears that the textual argument from all sides has run its course.

This is not to disparage debate over Scripture or the vital work done by historians, exegetes, or theologians, but to recognize that other factors usually decide the outcome of a debate. This means that even the "clear texts" of proslavery, pro-Sabbath, pro-creationism, and pro-patriarchy are, *in the end*, indecisive and peripheral. In addition, the stress on "clear texts" by these positions has questionable assumptions and is usually accompanied by a naive view of "Scripture interprets Scripture." As we have seen illustrated in examining these debates, there is always the question of which Scripture interprets which? Or more to the point, which interpretation (by which interpreter) of which Scripture interprets which interpretation of Scripture? The "Scripture alone" approach only serves to isolate further the interpreter from today's world, other communities, and our experience.

It is even tempting to say that in light of our four debates—slavery, Sabbath, evolution, and gender—that the "unclear" texts interpreted the "clear." But that would also assume that the debates are simply over various texts, which they are not. We have decided none of these issues by a simple appeal to various texts. But to emphasize: our discussion relates to the *interpretation* of Scripture—how we *use* Scripture—and does not undermine God's inspiration of Scripture. We expect that Paul and others, as people of their time, believed many things related to the ancient world; and we expect that God would speak in terms of their understanding. But this does not lock us into their worldview. As we saw with slavery, Paul was not an abolitionist and did not consider abolishing the institution of slavery, but this does not glue us to a proslavery position.

Our discussion does not require giving up a high view of the Bible, but rather involves questioning a particular way of interpreting and using the Bible. It is arguing for an interpretative approach that is an interplay of gospel, Scripture, and community—under the Spirit of God—where the church's decisions are based on what seems "good to the Holy Spirit and to us" (Acts 15:28), where the *life avenues* of the gospel story are recognized and decided by the church community as it engages with its text and gospel and keeps in step with the Spirit of God. This method of interpretation is clearly demonstrated and powerfully reflected in the pages of Scripture itself—in the Jew-Gentile debate.[65]

The large and considerable problem facing the early church revolved around the Gentiles. Were the Gentiles *as Gentiles* to be fully included into the people of God? When the issue comes to a head the Jerusalem council, recounted in Acts 15, shows how the church dealt with this difficulty. When Peter speaks, he does not appeal to specific Old Testament texts to justify including the Gentiles. He explains, rather, what God is doing through the Spirit. Similarly, Paul and Barnabas speak of the work of God among the Gentiles. Even when James concludes and quotes a passage from Amos, he is not using it as a proof text. (The Hebrew text is nationalistic, and James' quotation from the Septuagint has some remarkable differences from the Hebrew.) Instead, it is a rereading of Scripture in the light of the good news of Jesus. In fact, the *clear* texts of the Old Testament excluded Gentiles *as Gentiles*, and following these texts would have led the church in the opposite and wrong direction.

This debate shows the earliest Christians, including some who would contribute to the formation of the New Testament, arriving at a new understanding of God's purposes and Scripture in ways similar to what we have recommended. Thus, even in the early church, interpretation was driven by eschatology—a future opened up by Jesus and the Spirit's work—and not protology. It was not a harkening back to the ways things were but rather recognizing what God was now doing in Jesus. This approach eventually led to the relativization and redefinition of the Torah in the light of the Christ-event.

What happens to these "clear texts" once an issue reaches broad consensus? They lose their persuasive power. No one feels the weight of proslavery texts today; we simply read them differently. What will happen to foundational texts such as 1 Timothy 2:11–15 if the whole church eventually rejects patriarchy? This Maginot line of complementarian thought will be bypassed, outmaneuvered by the gospel story, leaving behind a relic of a now implausible and rejected position.

The focus on particular texts, joined with a narrow "Scripture interprets Scripture" approach and a neglect of the gospel transformation dynamic, has severe limitations. With the major areas of slavery, gender, and evolution, this approach has not only failed to solve satisfactorily the issue under discussion, it has led precisely in the wrong direction. The progression of these debates has increasingly exposed this interpretive method as one unable to serve the church today. The method may have survived the slavery debate (although no one uses it anymore to argue for slavery), it barely survives the gender debate, and it staggers under the weight of modern science.

The Transformation of Identity. The real battle is not over texts but identity. The four debates—slavery, Sabbath, gender, evolution—all have questions of *identity* at their core. Who am I? What about those I relate to? What is my place in this world?

- Are we superior?—to slaves, women, or other species?
- Are we inferior or subordinate?—to masters, men, or other species?
- Are we at the center of things?—of the universe, of life in this world?
- Are we God's chosen?—so must we keep the Sabbath to mark our identity?

Tied into questions of identity are questions of purpose, meaning, and morality—and ultimately questions about God. Who is God? There is the correct realization and an understandable fear that if we change our views of ourselves, our view of God will change. Because we image God, and, as Calvin famously noted, our knowledge of God and of ourselves are integrally connected,[66] any reformation of views about ourselves will surely change our view of God.

These debates all undermine the hierarchy of being, our place in the world, and our sense of importance. Each involves a humbling. And with each debate, the crisis has worsened: if the slavery debate felt like a village-destroying tsunami, the gender debate feels like a city-destroying nuclear bomb, and the evolution debate feels like a planet-destroying asteroid—capable of wiping out life as we know it.[67]

Nevertheless, what will be lost if patriarchy disappears? And what would be gained? For example, if conservative churches and seminaries allowed women into leadership and teaching positions, would it really be such a wide-ranging disaster?

- Would women lead worse than men?
- Would women reveal God less than men?
- Would their teaching or preaching be a sorry state compared to that of men?
- Would churches lose male members?
- Would it bring less—or more—balance and insight to leadership decisions?
- Would it bring less—or more—beauty?
- Would it exemplify principles of justice, love, freedom, and God's impartiality?
- Or would it undermine male identity and a particular interpretive method?

How are we to define our identity? Is it through our sex, race, class, nation, or species? Is it through securing a central place in time and space? Or is it through the gospel story, as we *identify* ourselves with Jesus, placing our trust in him, and live under the Spirit, who *defines* us as children of God in a new community. As the gospel story secures our identity, it will surely also reform and renew our understanding of God as Master, Father, and Creator.

Truth and Justice. Given the theological basis of slavery and patriarchy, and given the gospel transformation dynamic, it is unsurprising to find Christians at the forefront of both the proslavery and abolitionist movements. The same goes for the gender debate.[68] But given our place in the church's history, we are not left in the dark as to which approach best serves the quest for truth and justice. The church opposes slavery, and everyone uses some form of the gospel transformation dynamic to maintain that slavery is immoral. The majority of the church rejects the seventh-day arguments that are based on the Sabbath's theological basis. Even with evolution, I am convinced that a consensus will come because of the increasing and overwhelming evidence from multiple disciplines. For sure, it will be a long process for theology to incorporate insights from the theories of evolution, quantum mechanics, chaos, or relativity.

In the case of slavery, the view that held to the supposed clear texts held the immoral position. The proslavery method of interpretation justified and propagated evil and oppression. This needs to be clear in case anyone argues that the gospel transformation dynamic is an uncontrollable fission reaction surely to explode in a multitude of immoralities and irradiate the church. The church, under the Spirit and with its understanding of the gospel story, now transposes these key proslavery texts. This Spirit-energized gospel story will continue to show us what is loving and just, even as we struggle to understand what is true and right. Our example is Jesus, who, for example, is found on the Sabbath loving and healing the crippled woman (Luke 13:10–17) and the man with the withered hand (Mark 3:1–6)—doing what was right on the Sabbath, even though Jesus' opponents argued that the *just* position was to keep the rules of the Sabbath. In the end, the view we should accept is the one that is just, loving, and impartial—the one that affirms and is in accordance with the truth of the continuing gospel narrative.

CONCLUSION

We conclude that the gospel transformation dynamic—which includes love, freedom, the impartiality of God, justice, and that all people are made in God's image—gives many reasons for abolishing the "equal but subordinate" scheme as it is applied to women. These *life avenues* of the gospel can be found even within key complementarian texts, and when applied bring about the transformation of patriarchy. This is nothing less than an inbreaking of the "new creation" in Christ.

We can now turn to applying our discussion specifically to the maleness of Jesus. In the introduction we raised three broad questions: What would happen to our understanding of the character of God, the gospel, or of creation if God were embodied as female? So far we have been considering questions related to creation; in the remainder of the book we will focus our attention on topics related to the character of God and the gospel.

So again to ask the question regarding creation: Was God embodied as a male only because of the ancient patriarchal culture or because of God-ordained culture (including role distinctions of male headship and female submission)? In other words, is Jesus' maleness an accommodation to a patriarchal society consisting of only culturally defined role distinctions, or is it related to God-established roles and a created order that includes male leadership up to this present age? To put the question another way, was the ancient patriarchal culture provisional or permanent? If it was provisional, then the male incarnation was more of a cultural accommodation, because a woman in that culture was not allowed to teach or have authority. Some aspects would still be revelational, such as God demonstrating opposition to patriarchy through the incarnation. If, however, the patriarchal culture was God-ordained, the male incarnation moves more to the revelational side. A male incarnation was necessary because a woman is commanded by God not to teach or have authority. As a male, Jesus then reveals the authority and lordship of God reflecting the created order. As a male, Jesus follows the headship given to Adam at creation and the way Israel and the church were established. Some aspects of the male incarnation would still be cultural, like culturally defined male roles, clothes, and traditions.

So is Jesus' maleness connected to

1. a creation ordinance of male headship, established by God at creation and continuing through the New Testament and later church period up until the consummation?
2. a cultural accommodation to a sinful (in contrast to God-established) patriarchal society?
3. the overall theological basis that is given to patriarchy in the Bible—*but* open for transformation?

The first option is the complementarian position, where Jesus' maleness is connected to a God-ordained patriarchal culture. The second option is a common feminist position, where Jesus' maleness is God's accommodation to a sinful patriarchal culture. The third option grants the theological basis of male headship but allows for and requires a transformation of this structure.

Although I have sympathy for position two, my argument has led in the direction of option three. This option accepts the theological basis of the complementarian position and rejects attempts to work around it. It also incorporates the substantial transformation dynamic of the feminist position. There is a theological basis, but there is also transformation. The result is that we may view Jesus' maleness as related to the overall theological basis given to patriarchy, which includes the creation narratives, the Old Testament cultus, and the various types, as well as the Old and New Testament authority structures. These patriarchal structures, however, are open to transformation; and, as such, they are not of the nature of things—where nature is considered static and unchanging. Since they are open to transformation, there is much to be said for Jesus' maleness critiquing patriarchy. As a male, he provides the finest example of love and submission. Jesus led a life that is good news for all, a life that provided the basis for a continuing story that has sufficiently developed to expose patriarchy as a dead end.

CHAPTER 6

Jesus' Maleness and His Sonship

There are still some other questions raised in the introduction that we need to address. Does the maleness of Jesus reveal anything about God's character? And if so, what? Is Jesus' maleness foundational for the gospel? "Can a male savior save women?"[1] Do men represent or image Jesus better than women? May we speak of a *Daughter* as well as a Son?

Again, how can we go about answering these questions? As seen in chapter one, the discussion and arguments roam far and wide, leaping across multiple issues and topics. We need a framework to consider the life of Jesus and his revelation of God, a structure that unpacks and shows the basis of the gospel. Then we will be able to see in what ways Jesus' maleness is connected to this gospel basis and his revelation of God. In order to bring coherence to the material and to provide an opportunity to interact with these questions, we will use the sonship of Jesus as this framework, as an organizing motif for much of our remaining discussion. This will enable us to address our questions as well as to interact with related concerns.

For this chapter we have chosen the biblical text as our overall dialogue partner. Here we will look at the biblical material to see how Jesus' sonship is described and established. In subsequent chapters we will unpack the implications of this sonship for our topic.

THE SONSHIP OF JESUS

We start with the general agreement that Jesus was a male and that the New Testament refers to Jesus as Son. But what does *Son* mean? Our first line of discussion is an overview of Jesus' sonship and the multitude of differing features to that sonship.

Firstborn Son and Heir

We see in the Old Testament that the firstborn son had special privileges and responsibilities and received the birthright. M. J. Selman notes that these privileges may have included a larger inheritance (Genesis 25:5–6; Deuteronomy 21:15–17), a paternal blessing (Genesis 27:27–29), a position of family leadership (Genesis 42:37), and an honored place at the table (Genesis 43:33).[2] There was a unique relationship between father and firstborn son that may be seen, for instance, in the lives of the patriarchs. Abraham had a special love for Isaac (his firstborn from Sarah),[3] including a concern for Isaac's wife (Genesis 24:1–9); and at his death Abraham left all he owned to Isaac (Genesis 25:5). Isaac gave special attention to his firstborn, Esau (Genesis 25:28). Jacob devoted himself to the firstborn of his beloved wife Rachel (Genesis 37:3). There clearly existed a special relationship between the father and firstborn son, hence Joseph's concern and objection when Jacob blessed the younger Ephraim ahead of the firstborn Manasseh (Genesis 48:17–20).

According to the Old Testament, the firstborn male animal and human belonged to God (Exodus 13:2, 12–13; 22:29; 34:19; Numbers 8:17; Deuteronomy 15:19). This was a sign of Israel's redemption from Egypt (Exodus13:12–16). The special position of the firstborn became analogous to Israel's relationship with God (Exodus 4:22; Hosea 11:1; Jeremiah 31:9). Matthew, when portraying the life of Jesus as a recapitulation of Israel's history, extends the analogy of son to Jesus (Matthew 2:13–15). Though Mary's firstborn (Matthew 1:25; Luke 2:7), Jesus is also God's firstborn Son (Psalm 89:27; Hebrews 1:6). Jesus fulfills the position of which David was a type (Psalm 89:27). As that fulfillment,

Jesus is the true Israel and the true firstborn Son. In the New Testament, the analogy of firstborn is further applied to the resurrection, where Jesus was the *first* raised from the dead (Romans 8:29; Colossians 1:18; Revelation 1:5). It is also developed into a title for the Son (Colossians 1:15), meaning one who is superior or preeminent. As firstborn Son, he is the creator of all.

Therefore, as firstborn, Jesus' sonship includes the ideas of being preeminent, being the first raised from the dead, belonging to God, having a special relationship with God, and being a sign of redemption.

Consideration of the analogy of firstborn leads us to the related idea of heir. There are numerous connections between being a son and an heir. In Psalm 2:8, the son is encouraged to "Ask of me, and I will make the nations your heritage, and the ends of the earth your possession." As Son, Jesus is heir of all things (Hebrews 1:2). He can be called firstborn (Hebrews 1:6) because he is the appointed heir.[4] He is the son-heir whom the tenants kill in order to claim his inheritance (Matthew 21:38). A parallel thought is found in Galatians 4:7, where Paul connects sonship and heir. To be a slave, in contrast to a son, is to have no inheritance. So because we are related to Christ, all things are ours (1 Corinthians 3:21–23) because all things belong to the son-heir. To be *in Christ* is to be given all that belongs to Christ (Ephesians 1:3). Jesus as Son stresses that he is heir and that all things belong to him.

Incarnate Son

In his birth narrative, Luke places some emphasis on the connection between sonship and the incarnation. Leonhard Goppelt notes, "Luke based Jesus' divine sonship on his birth accomplished by the Spirit (Luke 1:32, 35)."[5] In Luke's theology, Jesus is a son who will be called the Son of the Most High (Luke 1:31–32). The reason for the title of Son is that the Spirit will be uniquely present in Jesus' birth. "The angel said to [Mary], 'The Holy Spirit will come upon you, and the power of the Most High will overshadow you; therefore the child to be born will be holy; he will be called Son of God'" (Luke 1:35). Through the work of the Spirit in the incarnation, Jesus will be called Son. Here is the true or real Son, in contrast and continuity to Luke's surprising conclusion to his genealogy that Adam is the "son of God" (Luke 3:38).[6] Jesus was the one born of God (1 John 5:18), and he was a son—that is, a male child (Revelation 12:5). Another feature of Jesus' sonship relates to the incarnation.

Son as Messianic King

In Luke's birth narrative, Jesus' sonship is also directly connected with kingship (Luke 1:32–33). God's promise to David was a son who would rule forever (2 Samuel 7:12–16). This king would not only be David's son by birth (v. 12) but also God's son by adoption (v. 14). The Old Testament taught that the messianic king would come from the seed of David (Isaiah 11:1, 10; Jeremiah 23:5–6; 30:9; 33:14–18; Ezekiel 34:23–24; 37:24–25). In other words, the coming king would also be a son. The New Testament confirms this fulfilled promise by stating that Jesus is the son of David (Romans 1:3). Matthew, by his multiple use of the title *son of David*, stresses Jesus' royal sonship. This title *son of David* defines the Messiah (Matthew 22:42), an identity even recognized by children (Matthew 21:15). Jesus, however, is not only David's son as his descendant. Referring to Psalm 110:1, Jesus asks the question, "David himself calls him Lord; so how can he be his son?" (Matthew 22:41–46; Mark 12:35–37; Luke 20:41–44). Here Jesus is not denying his Davidic descent, but emphasizing his true identity as King and Son. The Messiah is a fulfillment of whom David was a type and shadow—though his kingdom is not of this world, as seen in Jesus' interaction with Pilate (John 18:33–37).

The connection between sonship and kingship can further be seen in the titles *Son of God* and *Son of Man*, which have royal connotations. Psalm 2 speaks of the king who is adopted as the son of God. At the king's enthronement he is begotten—that is, adopted as son. This anointed one is king (vv. 2–6) and son (v. 7; cf. Ps. 89:26–27). In Psalm 82, the rulers are identified as gods and sons (v. 6). And Nathanael's confession in John 1:49 connects *Son of God* and kingship. Thus, the title *Son of God* applies especially to the king, who represented the people. As the anointed one, Jesus is the Son of God (Matthew 16:16; 26:63–64).

Similarly, the "Son of Man" figure in Daniel 7:13–14 (NIV), which most agree forms at least part of the background to New Testament usage, is a kingly figure. Daniel speaks of him as the one who will usher in the everlasting kingdom of God. Coming in the clouds, he is a heavenly king who will rule the earth. This imagery is adopted, for instance, in Matthew 16:28, which speaks of the coming of the Son of Man and his kingdom, and in Revelation 14:14, where the Son of Man is seated on the clouds. The Son of Man and the kingdom are integrally connected, so the coming of the Son is the coming of the kingdom.[7]

As the son of David, Son of God, and Son of Man, Jesus' sonship applies to kingship. He is the messianic king. So to speak of Jesus as Son is to accent his kingship.

Sonship and Humanity

On one level, the connection between sonship and humanity is obvious. To be a son is to be part of humanity. But can we say more? One possible way would be to connect sonship and humanity through the *Son of Man* title used of Jesus—though this would be like trying to run through a minefield, hoping not to get blown up before reaching our goal on the other side. Perhaps, however, we can stand safely on this side of the minefield and point to a possible goal that some have seen on the other side.

Dunn provides a helpful summary of this debate that has gone on for over a century and still has reached no consensus.[8] He outlines two broad options, not necessarily exclusive, for understanding the *Son of Man* title: a human figure or a heavenly figure. Considering only the first option, part of the background of the *Son of Man* title may include the notion of "human one." If it does include this idea of humanity, the title would be similar to the common Hebrew understanding that *son of man* means "human one," as seen in Ezekiel's prolific use (93 times) of *son of man* (NIV). Some scholars allow for this connection between Ezekiel's use and the *Son of Man*.[9]

Many agree that Ezekiel's meaning of *son of man* is "human one" and that the phrase particularly contrasts humanity with divine transcendence.[10] Ezekiel himself is called a son of man, denoting a human being,[11] which emphasizes Ezekiel's frail humanity as compared with God. A similar sense of *humanity* is found in Psalm 8:4 (cf. Hebrews 2:6) and Psalm 146:3 (refer to NIV on preceding three references). Some New Testament passages, such as Matthew 12:32, may even have this meaning.[12]

In this view, the apocalyptic Son of Man in Daniel 7:13 and the apocryphal books of 4 Ezra 13 and 1 Enoch 37–71 cannot account for all the New Testament uses, since a major aspect of the ministry of the Son of Man is his suffering (Matthew 8:20; 17:12; 26:2; Mark 8:31; 9:12; Luke 9:22, 58). This suffering Son of Man, however, does fit Ezekiel, who had a similar ministry of suffering (Ezekiel 2:6; 21:6, 12; 24:16 NIV) and prophetic lament (Ezekiel 2:10; 19:1; 27:2; 28:12; 32:2).

The connection between *son of man* and *humanity* may also be seen in Daniel 7:13–14, which, as we have previously mentioned, forms part of the background of Jesus' "Son of Man" sayings. The figure in Daniel 7:13 is *like* a human being, for he is *like* a son of man. Daniel 8:17 uses the phrase in this sense of "human one." Here is a human figure (possibly representing Israel)[13] in contrast to the beastly worldly kingdoms.

The title *Son of Man* is apparently a development from multiple backgrounds. These multiple backgrounds perhaps suited Jesus' intention not to make the overt claim to the messianic figure of Daniel 7:13–14.[14] There are reasons for including "human one" as part of the background and meaning of *Son of Man*. So apart from the obvious connection between sonship and humanity, we can also follow Moltmann and others who have incorporated the meaning of "true human being" into Jesus as the Son of Man.[15]

Baptism and Transfiguration

At Jesus' baptism and the outset of his public ministry, he is declared to be Son (Matthew 3:17; Mark 1:11; Luke 3:22; John 1:34). It is generally agreed that the Synoptic Gospels follow a similar pattern of alluding to Psalm 2:7 and Isaiah 42:1. By referring to Psalm 2:7, the Synoptics stress the messianic appointment of Jesus at his baptism. This appointment is confirmed by the coming of the Spirit (mentioned in all four Gospels). The descent of the Spirit is an anointing (Luke 4:18; Acts 10:37–38; cf. 1 Samuel 16:13; Isaiah 61:1) that sets Jesus apart and empowers him for his ministry. Thus, when challenged about his authority Jesus refers to his baptism (Matthew 21:25; Mark 11:30; Luke 20:4). His appeal to his baptism by John is understandable, for it was his messianic appointment—where the voice from heaven declared him to be the beloved Son and where the Holy Spirit descended on him.

In the church's concern to oppose adoptionism (Jesus was a mere man adopted by God as the divine Son), the significance of Jesus' baptism is downplayed. The reference to "beloved Son" in the baptismal narratives does indicate an already existing relationship. Nevertheless, the association with Psalm 2:7 shows that there is a development in Jesus' sonship. The quotation from Psalm 2:7 denotes a heightening of sonship. It is a progression of sonship that may become a problematic adoptionistic Christology if one is thinking in *substance* categories. The baptism of Jesus is at least a declaration of sonship. But it is more than that—it is a new stage in his identity as Son. It is a higher stage of sonship, a new stage of sonship in which Jesus is given the Spirit without measure, given authority, and anointed for service. As we shall see, in the progression of redemptive history there is a progression of Jesus' sonship, even to the resurrection and exaltation.

At the transfiguration we find a further identification of this sonship (Matthew 17:5; Mark 9:7; Luke 9:35; 2 Peter 1:17). The baptismal statement, "You are my Son, the Beloved" (Luke 3:22), is basically repeated as Jesus goes to the cross. The event reaffirms his sonship precisely when Jesus has explained the path of obedience that the Son will take. This leads us to a connection between sonship and obedience. By alluding to Isaiah 42:1, the Synoptics make the connection between sonship and servanthood, a connection between the Son and the Suffering Servant.

Obedient, Suffering, and Subordinate Son

Many have recognized the relationship between sonship and obedience.[16] Jesus is Son in his obedience to the will of the Father (Matthew 26:39). As Son, he follows the Father's example (John 5:19), does the Father's will, and completes the work given to him (John 4:34; 17:4). There is a nonreciprocal relationship with the initiation of the Father and the obedience of the Son. As a Son, he learned obedience (Hebrews 5:8). To be the Son is to be obedient. This obedience is ultimately obedience to death. So as Son he lives a life of suffering (Matthew 8:20; 17:12; 26:2; Mark 8:31; 9:12; Luke 9:22, 58). He lives this life of suffering because he is obedient, coming to do the will of the Father (Hebrews 10:9).

Immediately following Jesus' baptism, which he underwent as part of his obedience to fulfill all righteousness, Jesus was taken into the wilderness. Here he was tested as to his obedience as Son: "If you are the Son of God" (Luke 4:1–13; Matthew 4:1–11). It was a test to see if Jesus would fulfill his mandate as obedient Son to the Father.[17] The temptation was to deny his call to be Son—that is, obedient Son. It was a temptation to achieve his messianic kingly role by serving Satan (Matthew 4:8–9; Luke 4:5–7). Similarly, the taunt at the cross was, "If you are the Son of God, come down from the cross" (Matthew 27:40). This was a direct challenge to disavow his mandate as obedient Son by using his power to rescue himself.

In 1 Corinthians 15:24–28, Paul says that when the Son has brought all things under his dominion then the Son will be made subject to the

Father, so that God may be all in all. The Son's obedience continues to the end of redemptive history. This is the final redemptive work of the obedient Son, albeit future, that culminates his great work. It was once popular to make a division between ontology and function, so many understood this text to refer only to Jesus' function and not his being.[18] In connection with this verse, Cullmann wrote his well-known statement: "Here lies the key to all New Testament Christology. *It is only meaningful to speak of the Son in view of God's revelatory action, not in view of his being.*"[19] Perhaps with the subordinationist framework of the passage some felt it necessary to distinguish between Jesus' work and his being—to preserve his equality with God but allow for a subordination of role. For a variety of reasons it is unhelpful, even impossible, to separate ontology and function. Nonetheless, this passage lends itself to consider another aspect to Jesus' sonship: his subordination.

Jesus as Son is subordinate in three areas: *authority, knowledge,* and *glory*. Related to the Son's obedience is his subordination to the Father's authority. The Son is under the Father's authority and obeys him. The Son does have authority to teach (Matthew 7:29; Mark 1:22, 27), forgive sins (Matthew 9:6; Mark 2:10; Luke 5:24), judge (John 5:22; cf. Acts 17:31), and drive out demons (Mark 1:27), and he gives authority to the disciples (Matthew 10:1; Mark 3:15; Luke 9:1). Nevertheless, this authority is given to him by the Father (Daniel 7:14; Matthew 28:18; John 5:27; 17:2).

The Son is also subordinate in knowledge (Matthew 24:36; Mark 13:32; cf. Acts 1:7). Only the Father knows the day or hour. These times and dates the Father has set by his own authority. There are things that Jesus, in his subordinate state, did not know.

Finally, not only is authority given by the Father to the Son, but also glory (John 17:22, 24). Sonship relates to subordination in glory, since glory is given to the Son. So the Father is greater than the Son (John 14:28); and at the consummation, the Son will be subject to the Father (1 Corinthians 15:28).

Resurrection and Exaltation:
The Powerful Son and a Name above Angels

Romans 1:3–4 refers to Jesus Christ, "who was descended from David according to the flesh and was declared to be Son of God with power according to the spirit of holiness by resurrection from the dead." It is agreed that a two-nature interpretation has clouded this passage.[20] These verses do not speak of a human-divine nature scheme; rather, the contrast involved between verses 3 and 4 is two successive stages of Jesus' incarnate existence.[21] It is a difference between Jesus' incarnation (according to the flesh) and his resurrection (according to the Spirit). As to his incarnation he was a descendant of David, namely a son. Yet, Jesus' resurrection ushered in a new stage of his sonship.[22] The resurrection is the appointment[23] or enthronement of Jesus as the Son[24] where he becomes the Son of God with power. In his resurrection, Jesus is declared to the world to be the Son of God.

Similar to his baptism, the resurrection is a further heightening of Jesus' sonship. It is another new stage in his sonship. This interpretation is confirmed by Paul's application of Psalm 2:7 to the resurrection of Christ in Acts 13:33. The resurrection is a new state of sonship, in which Jesus is made alive by the Spirit (1 Peter 3:18) and with power. A parallel example may be observed in Acts 2:36, where Peter claims that God has made Jesus both Lord and Christ. We still hold that Jesus was Lord and Messiah prior to his resurrection and ascension. Peter, however, is emphasizing a new stage in the lordship of Christ. Similarly, regarding the resurrection, Jesus is now the *powerful* Son of God. We may speak of it as Jesus' greater adoption, similar to our greater adoption at our resurrection (Romans 8:23).

There is one final development in Jesus' sonship. The writer of Hebrews applies Psalm 2:7 not to the resurrection but to Jesus' exaltation to the right hand of God (Hebrews 1:3–5). After the Son secured salvation (Hebrews 1:3), he sat down at the right hand of God and received a better name than angels. This better name is "Son" (Hebrews 1:4–8). It is a name conferred at the exaltation, which confirms his superiority to angels and gives Jesus a new status. Given the profound message of Hebrews 1:1–8, we may say that this inheritance of the better name *Son* is of such a climatic character that, in comparison to his status before this moment, it seems as though he was barely a son.

The Son as Image, Priest, Prophet, and God Embodied

There is a clear parallel between Jesus' sonship and image. As the Genesis narrative links the image of God to kingship and ruling over creation (Genesis 1:27–28), it also connects image with sonship in Genesis 5:3, where Seth is described as being in Adam's image. Two New Testament passages (Colossians 1:13–15; Hebrews 1:3) explicitly connect Jesus' sonship and the image of God. Jesus as Son is the *character* of God (Hebrews 1:3). He is the expressed or exact representation of God—the radiance of his glory. Since the Son is in the image of God, he faithfully represents and reveals God. To see the Son is to see God (John 14:9), for he is the exact image of God.

As the writer of Hebrews connects sonship and image, he also connects sonship and priesthood. In Hebrews 1:3, it is the Son who has provided purification for sins. And the writer of Hebrews applies Psalm 2:7 to Christ's appointment as high priest (Hebrews 5:5). Commenting on Hebrews 5:5, William Lane writes, "A correlation between Christ's sonship and priesthood was implied in the exordium [introduction] to the sermon, when the priestly function of making 'purification for sins' is ascribed to the transcendent Son (1:3), but here it is asserted explicitly."[25] Jesus' sonship is integrally connected with his priestly redemptive work. The connection is one in which Jesus' sonship forms a foundation for priesthood (Hebrews 7:3)—for only as Son is he holy, blameless, and pure (Hebrews 7:26). Of course, in Hebrews 5–7 priesthood itself is transcended, as the writer overflows Old Testament categories and terminology.

We see the relationship between Jesus' sonship and prophetic ministry in Hebrews 1:1–14, where the writer speaks of the superior revelation, in contrast to angels, that has come in the last days through the Son. It is because of this superior revelation that we must pay more careful attention to the Son (Hebrews 2:1–4; cf. 10:28–29). Sonship is foundational for Jesus' prophetic ministry. No one knows the Father except the Son and vice versa (Matthew 11:27; Luke 10:22). This intimate and reciprocal knowledge is the basis for Jesus' ministry. As Son, he is at the Father's side, and therefore he is in the unique position to reveal and make known the Father (John 1:18).

Finally, Jesus' sonship indicates that he is God embodied. For this, we cannot make a blanket appeal to the title *Son of God*, for it does not usually refer to divinity but means "Messiah" (which didn't include the idea of divinity).[26] We can, however, find places in the New Testament where there is a movement beyond Messiah to Jesus as God embodied or to Jesus revealing a distinction in God—the eternal Son, Word, or Wisdom. Although it took time for the church to develop a doctrine of the Trinity, there are already high Christologies in the New Testament.[27] This is more clearly seen in sections in Paul, John's Gospel, and Hebrews. This moves our discussion to the question of eternal sonship.

THE ETERNAL SON

To speak of Jesus as the Son is to speak of him in a diverse and multifaceted way. Jesus is the firstborn Son who is preeminent, the heir of all things, and has a unique relationship to God. He is the first raised from the dead. As the Son-king, he is the promised messianic king, the son of David, who has God's authority and establishes God's eternal kingdom. As the Son-prophet, he is in the unique position to image, reveal, and represent God. As the Son-priest, he is holy and blameless, and so he can secure salvation for his people. Jesus is the obedient Son to his Father—even to the end of history, where he gives all things to the Father. As Son, he is God embodied. There is a progressive development and heightening of his sonship: from the incarnation, through baptism, resurrection, and to his exaltation.

The question now arises as to whether we may speak of an eternal Son. As suggested, there are passages where there is a movement toward viewing Jesus as God embodied or to Jesus revealing a distinction in God—the eternal Son. This is not to claim that we find in the New Testament a fully developed doctrine of the Trinity; such would only appear later on.

To make the point about the eternal Son, we will touch on a few select passages from John, Paul, and the book of Hebrews.[28]

John 3:16

God's love for the world is demonstrated precisely because God's unique Son is the object of God's giving. Conceivably, the proximate reference of the giving is the death of Jesus, and thus *Son* only has meaning post-incarnation. This is confirmed by the reference to his death and the "lifting up" in verse 14. Nevertheless, to confine the giving of the Son simply to his death undermines the significant point of verse 16, which is the supreme manifestation of God's love. By implication, there exists an intimate relationship of Father and Son prior to the giving and sending for the demonstration of love to be meaningful. The love in view is precisely in the giving (v. 16) and the sending (v. 17), by which light has come into this world of sin and rebellion (v. 19). To limit sonship to redemptive history weakens this ultimate demonstration of love (cf. 1 John 4:9–10). It appears that John presupposes that sonship exists before the incarnation.

John 17:1–26

In his prayer, Jesus addresses himself as "Son." The passage emphasizes that it is the Son who was sent into the world by the Father (vv. 3, 8, 18, 21, 23, 25). But is this sending only related to the relationship of Father and Son commencing at the incarnation? Two elements indicate an eternal aspect: the glory the Son had with the Father before the world began (v. 5) and the Father's love for the Son before the creation of the world (v. 24). The foundation of the sending lies in an eternal fellowship and relationship of Father and Son. Again, eternal sonship is presupposed.

Romans 8:3, 32; Galatians 4:4

Romans 8:3 concerns the *sending* of the Son for a particular purpose. The intent of sending the Son is to deal with sin. So God sends the Son to be found in the "likeness of sinful flesh." As in Galatians 4:4, it appears that this sonship is not constituted at the incarnation but is already in view. The Son is sent, born of a woman and born under the law. Concerning these passages, Wright notes Paul's innovation here that moves beyond Son as only Messiah to the sending of the Son—and tying this sending to the second-temple Jewish hope that God would send Wisdom or Word to God's people.[29]

Romans 8:32 refers to the "not sparing" or "giving up" of the Son. The phrase "did not withhold his own Son" takes us back to Genesis 22, where Abraham did not withhold his only son (see vv. 12 and 16). A number of commentators have indicated the allusion to the near-sacrifice of Isaac.[30] The stress on God's *own* Son has the same emphatic force as John's *unique* Son and the *beloved* Son of the baptism narratives. The persuasiveness of Paul's argument is related to God giving up the Son; God will "give us everything," for he has already given up his own Son. The promise of God's continuing love is based on the Father giving up his own Son. If we can only speak of sonship from the incarnation on, Paul's argument is weakened. Here again, we find an emerging understanding of a loving relationship of Father and Son existing prior to the incarnation.

Hebrews 1:1–14

In Hebrews 1:1–2, the writer describes the Son as the supreme revelation of God. We note the obvious parallelism:

Long ago	In these last days
God spoke to our ancestors	God has spoken to us
By the prophets	By a Son

At this point, is *Son* to be understood only from the incarnation onward? This is unlikely, given how the writer beautifully elaborates on the meaning of *Son*.[31] The same Son who is appointed heir of all things, and who has received the inheritance of a better name, is also the Son through whom God made the universe. The writer then goes on to describe the Son as the character or "exact imprint of God's very being" (v. 3), who sustains all things by his word (v. 3), provided purification for sins (v. 3), and sat down at the right hand of God (v. 3) with a name far superior to angels—that is, "Son" (vv. 4–8, 13). The passage concludes by identifying the Son as God (v. 8), creator (v. 10), and eternal (vv. 11–12).

The writer of Hebrews extends the meaning of Son far beyond the context of Jesus' life that began at the incarnation. The eternal Son is God—the one who sustains all things and through whom God made the universe. Here is the Son in his creative action, in his redemptive life, and in his final enthronement. Once again, we may speak of eternal sonship.

CONCLUSION

Son has a multitude and diverse range of meanings, and any Christology should take account of this diversity. As Robert Jenson has noted, *Son* is both a name and a story.[32] *Son* also has meaning prior to the incarnation. As we have seen, we should extend our understanding of sonship beyond Jesus' life on earth, for the life of Jesus revealed a distinction in God—the eternal Son, Father, and Spirit. And this eternal sonship provides the basis for the gospel. It is the Son whom the Father loves, gives, and sends into the world. It is the pure and holy Son who can be our high priest. It is the Son who knows the Father and so can reveal the Father to us. It is the eternal Son who is our messianic king.

The story of the Son does not end with the New Testament. There is a further development of understanding based on particular trajectories found in the New Testament. As the church moved beyond New Testament times it slowly developed the doctrine of the Trinity, whereby it tried to speak more fully about this uniquely Christian understanding of God. This process took several hundred years. The church now considers this development an *essential* part of the story, and there is no going back. So once again we find a development in the continuing gospel story. And the story continues today, as seen in the revival of interest in the Trinity in the twentieth and twenty-first centuries. We are still engaged in the unfolding gospel story as the Spirit leads us into all truth (John 16:13).

CHAPTER 7

What Have We Done with the Eternal Son?

In our discussion, we have arrived at two main emphases: (1) the multifaceted and numerous features of Jesus' sonship; and (2) the eternal Son. The question now before us relates to the meaning and implications of eternal sonship. Does the existence of the eternal Son mean that there had to be a male incarnation? If the eternal Son is the foundation for the gospel, does this exclude women from salvation? Is the eternal Son always subordinate, thus justifying an "equal but subordinate" scheme?

We will consider five different views or approaches to understanding the eternal Son. We have chosen views that relate directly to our topic, and we will see that the eternal Son has been molded into a multitude of different shapes and sizes. How has the concept of the eternal Son developed from the biblical material?

IS THE SON ETERNALLY GENERATED?

Behind the traditional doctrine of the Trinity as one essence and three persons lies an analogy of causation. The Father is the fountain or source of the Trinity. This is the historical position of the church as expressed in the Nicene Creed, that the Son is begotten of the Father, begotten not made. The precise meaning of this concept of eternal generation, originally formulated by Origen,[1] is unclear. J. N. D. Kelly notes that apart from the creed's clear denunciation of Arius, it is "much more difficult to determine its positive teaching."[2]

Even though the exact meaning of eternal generation is unclear, the concept is used to justify opposing positions. Both complementarian and Christian feminist positions use *Son* as an analogy, and use it in a particular way. Following classical christological categories, some biblical egalitarians (such as Jewett) and Christian feminists argue that the essential or univocal element of *Son* is that he is generated from the Father. So just as a father generates a son, we may speak of a mother generating a daughter. Jewett, for example, argues that the only univocal element in the Trinitarian name—Father, Son, and Spirit—is that the second and third persons originate, as persons, from the Father.[3] Therefore, it is legitimate to substitute a Mother-Daughter analogy, for it still retains the univocal element of the original analogy—namely, causation or origin. In doing so, we have left our conception of God unaltered and have shown that a male incarnation is unnecessary.

Some complementarians as well, however, argue for a necessary male incarnation based on eternal generation. They contend that since Jesus is the eternally begotten Son it is nonsensical to conceive of a female incarnation. Furthermore, complementarians use the doctrine of eternal generation to maintain that the Son is eternally subordinate in authority.[4] The eternal generation of the Son is employed to provide a basis for women's subordination yet full equality. They stress that this is the teaching of the church through its history and argue that biblical egalitarians, by denying a subordination of role to the Son, have departed from historic Christianity.[5]

A similar position was adopted by Karl Barth, who said that God "exists as a first and as a second, above and below, *a priori* and *a posteriori*."[6] For Barth, the doctrine of eternal generation provides the basis for the relationship between Father and Son,[7] a relationship where the Son is subordinate and obedient to the Father. Such a relationship gives justification for the subordinate but not inferior position of a wife to her husband.[8] We will address this eternal subordination of the Son in the following section. For the moment, we note the connection that is made between eternal generation, a male incarnation, and male priority.[9] Eternal generation is used to establish complementarianism permanently in the Trinity and to justify an "equal but subordinate" scheme.

Eternal generation is used by both positions to justify the necessity or nonnecessity of Jesus' maleness. Some of the ways in which this discussion is conceptualized and framed involves a problematic use of analogy. Is eternal generation the univocal aspect of *Son*? And when speaking about God, does univocality exist?

Even if generation were univocal, it would still be analogical, since no one would say the Son is *literally* begotten. Even so, we understand that by using *univocality* people mean that aspect or feature of a metaphor that may be extended to reveal truth. But more importantly, this approach inclines to a single-point approach to metaphor that is heavily reductionistic. It suggests that a metaphor may be extended in only one particular way. Yet language cannot be limited in this scientifically precise manner. A metaphor may be extended in some ways and not in others. A metaphor is open-ended, often incorporating many features at the same time, and its meaning cannot be reduced to an idea of univocality. In chapter six we outlined over a dozen different features of Jesus' sonship. To insist that the univocal aspect of *Son* is limited to causation or origin is unsatisfactory.

Furthermore, there are other difficulties with extending the analogy *Son* to imply causation, origin, or subordination in the eternal Trinity. We will now examine two further key areas where problems arise: (1) the textual basis, and (2) how it leads to further philosophical and theological problems.

Textual Basis

A number of verses are cited for the doctrine of eternal generation (2 Samuel 7:11–13; Psalm 2:7; Proverbs 8:23–24; Micah 5:2; John 3:16; 5:18, 26; 10:38; 14:11; 17:21; 2 Corinthians 1:3; Colossians 1:15; Hebrews 1:3).[10] An examination of these passages, however, has not established a doctrine of eternal generation or support for an analogy of causation. This lack of scriptural evidence was demonstrated as far back as Calvin. According to B. B. Warfield, Calvin opened up the way for the denial, or at least a neglect, of the doctrine of eternal generation, for he undermined the proof texts and left little biblical basis for the doctrine, except what could be inferred from the terms *Father* and *Son*.[11]

A couple of examples will suffice. We have already seen that Psalm 2:7 is applied in the New Testament to the baptism, resurrection, exaltation, and priesthood of the Son. As Son, Jesus fulfills this psalm in history. But there is no indication in the New Testament that Psalm 2:7 teaches or implies an eternal generation of the Son. Another example, John 5:26, reads, "For just as the Father has life in himself, so he has granted the Son also to have life in himself." In context, this verse has a different intention than generation, and rather concerns the resurrection (cf. verses 21, 28–29). Furthermore, a generation interpretation would imply that the Son was created—that is, given life—contrary to Jesus' claim that he *is* the life (John 11:25; 14:6). So Pannenberg echoes the conclusion of most by saying that there is little biblical basis for eternal generation.[12]

Apart from these passages, the doctrine has been derived from John's use of *monogenes* (unique) Son (John 1:14, 18; 3:16, 18; 1 John 4:9). Although the tendency in the past was to use this word to argue for eternal generation, few would argue this today. A general consensus is being reached that *monogenes* does not refer to an eternal generation,[13] but rather denotes the uniqueness of the Son. To derive *only begotten* from *mono* and *genes* is a root fallacy error, like trying to derive the meaning of *horsefly* from *horse* and *fly*.[14] In addition, eternal generation is a theological construct that endeavors to explain combined biblical teaching. To then turn around and derive such a theological concept from a single word amounts to a confusion of word and concept.[15] So most now conclude that John's use of *monogenes* refers to familial relations,[16] not to eternal generation.

Further Philosophical and Theological Problems

When reading in the Scriptures of a familiar analogy such as the "eye" or "ear" of the Lord, we understand that this tells us something about the character of God. Nevertheless, we don't use this to speak of God as having an all-seeing "super-eye." Though we do have a true understanding and knowledge of God, human attributes cannot be directly applied to God. While not holding to a super-eye, the church does teach the omniscience of God. We recognize that the human eye or ear is a dim reflection of the all-embracing knowledge of God.

Considering the infinite difference between God and humanity, does eternal generation confuse the divine and human? Just as it is absurd to conceive of God having a super-eye, so it is difficult to conceptualize God generating. Thus, Calvin states, "Indeed, it is foolish to imagine a continuous act of begetting, since it is clear that the three persons have subsisted in God from eternity."[17] Calvin had an obvious problem with the doctrine of eternal generation as it stood. Warfield observes, "Calvin seems to have found this conception difficult, if not meaningless."[18]

Calvin's position serves as a relevant illustration of the difficulties that arise when Trinitarian relationships are conceptualized in this manner and when the elements of causation, source, or origin are applied to the eternal Son. It also shows that the church has not been unified regarding this concept. As noted, some complementarians argue that egalitarians depart from a supposed monolithic teaching regarding Trinitarian relations—in particular, the subordination in role of the Son as implied by eternal generation. We need to say two things here: (1) It is not at all clear what was meant by eternal generation. Although subordination of role could be one conclusion, we could also argue that the *intention* of the church has always been to refute any form of subordinationism. (2) Eternal generation was denied by some in the early church,[19] was later modified by Calvin, and the concept is increasingly under attack.[20]

Calvin objected to the generation of the essence of the Son because of its implications of subordinationism, claiming that such a theology produced three unequal divine essences; compromised the one essence of God, hence the oneness of God; and denied justice to the Son as *autotheos* (God in Godself).[21] Such a position was, for Calvin, a denial of the aseity (underived being) of the Son. Yet, to mark the differentiation in the Trinity, Calvin held that the *person* of the Son was generated by the Father. He wrote, "Therefore we say that deity in an absolute sense exists of itself; whence likewise we confess that the Son since he is God, exists of himself, but not in respect of his Person; indeed, since he is the Son, we say that he exists from the Father. Thus his essence is without beginning; while the beginning of his person is God himself."[22]

Calvin's overriding concern was to do full justice to Christ as *autotheos*, the full and complete deity of the Son. So when considering classical formulations, especially the Nicene fathers, Calvin objected to some of these formulations. Again, complementarians, who claim that eternal generation teaches subordination *in role*, are not entirely correct. It was sometimes viewed as teaching a generation of *being*, hence Calvin's problem with the doctrine. Calvin was thus to revise the doctrine and consequently speak only about the generation of the person of the Son. In his position, Calvin defended the classic formula of "one essence, three persons." In keeping with this formula, Calvin preserves the one essence of God by denying the generation of the essence of the Son. Christ's full and complete deity is argued from the one essence of God. And Calvin safeguards the three distinct persons by appealing to the generation of the person of the Son.

Calvin, however, appears to be on even weaker grounds for such a distinction. Having undermined the biblical texts for the classical view on generation, he has left little basis for his position. In addition, is such a bifurcation of essence and person satisfactory or even possible?

Nevertheless, even if we don't follow Calvin in splitting person and essence, or arguing for distinctions in the Trinity based on causation and origin, we recognize and adopt his foundational concern: to hold to and argue for the eternal Son as God.

A modern example of using the analogy of origin or causation is seen in the work of Miroslav Volf. He raises the question, "Are the relations between divine persons not asymmetrical, nonegalitarian, hierarchical? Is not the Father first, the Son second, the Spirit third? So it would seem, if the Father is the 'origin,' if the Son is 'generated,' and if the Spirit 'proceeds.'"[23] While desiring an egalitarian society, Volf still wants to maintain the traditional formulation of the Father as source of divinity, but together with an egalitarian metaphysic. This leads him, following Moltmann, to postulate a distinction between the constitution and life of the Trinity. Volf writes:

> At the level of the *constitution* of the divine persons, the Father is the "first" because he is the source of divinity. Without such a source, it would be impossible to distinguish between the three persons; they would collapse into one undifferentiated divine nature. At the level of *relations*, the Son not only "comes from" and "goes to" the Father, but the Father has "given all things into his hands" and "glorifies the Son" (John 13:1ff.; 17:1). With respect to the immanent Trinity, these statements about the economic Trinity mean that in constituting the Son, the Father gives all divine power and all divine glory to the Son. As the source of divinity *the Father therefore constitutes the mutual relations between the persons as egalitarian rather than hierarchical*; all persons are equal in power and equal in glory. At the level of the life of the Trinity, the Father is not "the First," but "One among the Others."[24]

In his desire to have human egalitarian relationships, Volf makes a division in the Trinity between being and relation. On the level of being, the Father is source and first; yet in the area of relationship, the Trinity is egalitarian. A few pages later Volf notes that all three persons constitute each other. He writes that the "distinct persons are internally constituted by the indwelling of other persons in them. The personal identity of each is unthinkable without the presence of others in each; such presence of others is part and parcel of the identity of each."[25] Volf emphasizes the mutual indwelling or *perichoresis* of the Trinity. But once again, a distinction is made between being and person. On the level of being, the Father is the one who constitutes the Trinity; yet on the level of person, each member constitutes the other.

Nevertheless, Volf still has a Trinity that is hierarchical in being—an arrangement that complementarians use to justify their position. Furthermore, Volf's claim that failing to maintain the Father as the source of divinity would lead to a dissolving of distinctions in the Trinity is debatable. Calvin argued that such reasoning led to subordinationism. More recently, Pannenberg, who rejects Moltmann's distinction between a constitutional and relational level,[26] has echoed Calvin's concern at this point: "Any derivation of the plurality of Trinitarian persons from the essence of the one God, whether it be viewed as spirit or love, leads into the problems of either modalism on the one hand or subordinationism on the other."[27]

This suggests that applying causation or generation to the eternal Son is unsatisfactory today. Such formulations move us away from our understanding of the biblical material and the gospel story—and sometimes toward what van Huyssteen calls the twilight zone of abstraction.[28] This is not to oppose speaking of the "eternal Son," but to question the wisdom of applying, in our day, generation, causation, or origin to Trinitarian relationships. When some argue that the language of Father and Son suggests "both kinship and derivation,"[29] it is this derivation that is problematic. As we have seen, the language and story of sonship suggests many things; and "eternal generation" was not something we found in our overview of the biblical material regarding sonship. In addition, thinking in terms of *substance* categories and applying a *causation* analogy to the Trinity inevitably leads to some form of subordinationism.[30]

Speaking of "eternal Son" still maintains the differentiation in the Trinity. Eternal Son remains a name to describe the underived distinctive character/being/relation of the Son that differentiates the Son from the Father and the Spirit. The Trinitarian names, gospel story, and experience of the church preserve these distinctions. This eternal sonship is an affirmation against various forms of modalism (since the Son is distinct from the Father and the Spirit), a Trinitarianism that is only economic (since sonship is not limited to the incarnation onward), and subordinationism (since the eternal Son is God, *autotheos*, the Creator, the beginning and the end). This is nothing less than a contemporary exposition of the Nicene *homoousios* and Calvin's *autotheos*.

Eternal generation made sense to people long ago who sought to expound the meaning of *eternal Son* in their particular world and culture. Such a formulation also made more sense in a culture that understood a human father as the cause of life, as the one who generated, the one who implanted life in a mother—who was just a passive receptacle. It wasn't until 1826 that the embryologist Karl Ernst von Baer discovered the ovum, the female egg, which led to a revolution in our understanding of human reproduction. By connecting *eternal generation* to the substance or being of God—although the intention was to preserve the "sameness" of the Son with the Father—this formulation opened itself up to different forms of subordinationism, some of which are still found today. The analogy of causation caused other causation problems: How does the Spirit relate in the Trinity? Does the Spirit proceed from only the Father, or from the Father and Son? Is the Spirit subordinate to the Father, or to the Father and Son?

Today, no one reads the texts once used to justify eternal generation in that way. Our thought categories move us in other directions. Because we no longer live under the philosophical frameworks of substance and causation, we are free and encouraged to reformulate our understanding of the eternal Son.

IS THE SON ETERNALLY SUBORDINATE?

To provide support for their "equal but subordinate" scheme, complementarians appeal to the Trinitarian relationships, where they argue that the eternal Son is both equal and subordinate to the Father. From this they conclude that their view on the subordination of women does not negate the full equality of women, just as the Son's subordination does not minimize his full divine equality.

Grudem writes, "If the Son is not eternally subordinate to the Father in role, then the Father is not eternally 'Father' and the Son is not eternally 'Son.' This would mean that the Trinity has not eternally existed."[31] Letham makes a similar point—that a denial of this order of authority and obedience in the Trinity would end in modalism.[32] These statements may seem unusual to many readers, and despite such emphatic statements we wonder: Why define the distinctions between Father and Son in terms of subordination? Given our discussion on the multifaceted and multivalent nature of Jesus' sonship, complementarians take only one of these features (subordination) and apply it to the eternal Son. They look at Jesus' sonship, reduce it to one feature—namely, subordination—and then expand it to encompass the essential distinctions between Father and Son.

Moreover, in Grudem's discussion this subordination is also used to define the relationship of the Spirit in the Trinity. In other words, as subordination defines the distinctions between Father and Son, so it defines the distinctions between Father and Spirit, and Son and Spirit. We might wonder how this consistently relates together. For example, Grudem holds that the Father *and* the Son send the Spirit,[33] while also holding that the Son is eternally under the Father's authority. But doesn't the Son need his *own* authority in order to send the Spirit?

Grudem suggests that the Spirit relates to the Father and Son as children relate to their parents. Therefore, the Spirit remains under the authority of Father and Son, like children under the authority of their mother and father. As the mother is under the father's authority, so the

Son remains under the Father.[34] He notes that this illustration has no biblical warrant, and this lack is unsurprising. *Father* and *Son* is already an analogy between parent and child, which Grudem uses to distinguish the Son as eternally subordinate to the Father. To then explain the Spirit's distinction by moving *Son* to a position of parent is a conceptual contortion that introduces further confusion. Furthermore, the name *Holy Spirit*, in contrast to *Son*, is a name that has no familial or subordination connotations. It has no causation or gender associated with it. So why define the Spirit's distinction with categories derived from the Son?

But what about the Son? Not only do complementarians apply this one feature of Jesus' sonship (subordination in authority) to the eternal Son, they only apply one feature that is already a subset of a broader category of subordination. We saw in chapter six that Jesus' subordination consists of three aspects—namely, a subordination in authority, knowledge, and glory. Is it possible to limit subordination only to authority, and not also to knowledge and glory? It is difficult to separate these features from each other. For instance, the limitation of the Son's knowledge is related to the Father's authority (Matthew 24:36; Mark 13:32; Acts 1:7), where the Son does not know the times that have been set by the Father's own authority. Why not consistently apply all the subordination texts to the eternal Son?

Most, however, do not apply subordination in knowledge and glory to the eternal Son,[35] so why apply subordination in authority? It is clear that Jesus is given authority from God (Daniel 7:14; Matthew 28:18; John 5:27; 17:2). Nevertheless, in what context is Jesus given this authority? Primarily, it is Jesus as the Son-king who is given authority. He is the adopted messianic king of Psalm 2:8–9 (cf. Revelation 2:26–27) and the royal figure of Daniel 7:13–14 to whom God gives authority. As the Son of Man, he is given this authority (John 5:27)—authority to forgive sins (Matthew 9:6; Mark 2:10; Luke 5:24) and to judge (John 5:22; cf. Acts 17:31). As Son of Man, he is Lord over the Sabbath (Matthew 12:8; Mark 2:28; Luke 6:5). Significantly, the verse prior to the mention of the Father giving authority to the Son (John 5:27) speaks of the Father giving life to the Son (John 5:26). As most interpret this giving of life to apply to the resurrection—that is, to Jesus in the historical context—we argue for a similar understanding of this giving of authority. No one argues that the eternal Son was given life by the Father, and neither should we say that the eternal Son does not have authority, whether it is to forgive sins or to judge.

This authority is given to Jesus in a certain context and is particularly bestowed subsequent to the completion of his mandate. So there is even a development in this giving of authority. In Luke 4:6, the obedient Son of God is tempted to obtain the *authority* of the nations by worshiping Satan rather than by fulfilling his role as obedient Son. Thus, after completing his mission, full authority is given to the resurrected Son of God (Matthew 28:18; Ephesians 1:20–22).

It will be helpful at this stage to draw on our previous discussions and summarize why the "equal but subordinate" scheme as applied to the eternal Son is wrong. Each one is sufficient to subvert this formulation.

1. Jesus' subordination in authority is related to God giving Jesus this authority for his mission, and this giving of authority includes a development culminating with the resurrection and exaltation. With over a dozen features of Jesus' sonship, why apply this to the eternal Son, and why choose only one part of a broader notion of subordination that includes knowledge and glory?
2. We have seen that, for humans, being and relation are inseparable, thus the "equal but subordinate" construction is a distinction with no difference. The same goes for the Trinity. The Trinity is being-in-relation, so an eternal subordination in function or relation is a subordination of being. The so-called subordination of the Son is nothing less than an all-embracing subordination.
3. The "equal but subordinate" scheme, when applied to women or slaves, falls apart in light of the gospel story. Such a formulation runs contrary to the gospel transformation

dynamic. If for these reasons it is wrong to apply it to humanity, why then apply it to the Trinity, the author of the story?

4. The formulation is contrary to gospel realities. At the heart of mature love is submission. If there is mutual love in the eternal Trinity, then there is mutual subordination or submission. Similarly, when the gospel story emphasizes and transforms our understanding of justice (such as teaching the full inclusion of women), it conflicts with any metaphysical view of God that supports injustice.

5. If the eternal Son is eternally subordinate, how can Jesus reveal the authority and rule of God? As Son, however, he reveals God; and he reveals the authority of God, for he is God embodied. In him dwells the fullness of God (Colossians 1:19; 2:9). Jesus images God, and whoever has seen the Son has seen the Father (John 14:7–11). Furthermore, the position that denies full divine authority to the eternal Son appears to make the eternal Son less than God—that is, not having all the attributes of God, including God's authority and rule.

6. We can make an argument that the *intention* of the church, in its formulation of the Trinity, was to oppose any subordination of the eternal Son. The emphasis on the *sameness* of the Son and the Father, and on *eternal* generation, even though conceptualized in the categories of substance and causation, was intended to preserve that the eternal Son was God. Indications are that the church has tried to stay away from subordinationism when discussing the Trinity,[36] although some of its formulations like *eternal generation* lent support for later subordinationist tendencies.

7. What complicates this discussion is that Jesus reveals God, he reveals a distinction in God, *and* he reveals how we are to live before God. His life was one of entrusting and

submitting himself to his Father and relying on the powerful presence of the Spirit. So here the revelational significance is that we all (female and male) live subordinate or submissive lives, not only among ourselves but also under God the Father. In other words, Jesus' subordinate life is the pattern for our lives—an encouragement for us to entrust and submit ourselves to our heavenly Father and to keep in step with the Spirit.

8. We have seen that in order to give weight to their controversial "equal but subordinate" arrangement many complementarians[37] appeal to a particular view of the Trinity and apply it to human relationships. This may be summarized in four points:

1. Father:	authority and head
2. Son:	equal but subordinate in role to the Father
3. Man:	authority and head
4. Woman:	equal but subordinate in role to man

Points 3 and 4 are a reflection of points 1 and 2 respectively. These supposed Trinitarian relationships are a justification for complementarianism. As seen above, there are many reasons why this "equal but subordinate" formulation is wrong. In addition, should we even compare the relationships between men and women to the inter-Trinitarian relationships? Nevertheless, granting this formulation we note the following: Given point 3, Jesus, as a man, must have authority, because according to this scheme male is given authority, reflecting Trinitarian relationships and the created order. But given point 2, the Son does not have authority. So given point 2 and 4, why wasn't there a female incarnation? If the Son is eternally subordinate, according to this arrangement the Son should have been female. Why insist on a male incarnation? The more points 2 and 4 are emphasized, the more the conflict is exposed and a necessary male incarnation is undermined.

Here is the crux of the matter: complementarians emphasize the Son's eternal subordination to justify an "equal but subordinate" scheme, but at the same time they emphasize male authority and insist on a male incarnation. Their argument ends with two irreconcilable positions: (1) the Son is eternally subordinate, and (2) the Son is incarnated male, in a position of authority. Both, however, are crucial to the position.

IS THE SON ETERNALLY OBEDIENT?

We may extend this discussion by briefly commenting on a related understanding of the eternal Son. The subordination of the Son is directly related to, and almost synonymous with, the obedience of the Son. To speak of the obedient Son is to speak of the authority of the Father, an authority to which the Son subordinates himself and obeys. As complementarians apply subordination to the eternal Son, some scholars specifically apply obedience to the eternal Son. For example, John Thompson, reminiscent of Barth,[38] applies the obedience of Jesus to the eternal Son.

> The obedience of the incarnate Son reflects that of the Son in the eternal life of God. Were this not so, the obedience in the incarnate life up to and including the cross would not be possible. In going this lowly way of obedience to death Jesus is not following a capricious or arbitrary way but one which God the Father has chosen for him and which has its basis in the very being of God in the relation of Son to Father.[39]

Similar to the discussion on subordination, here it is argued that to deny eternal obedience is to be left with no basis for the obedience of Jesus on earth. Nevertheless, Thompson is selective about what he applies to the eternal Trinity. For example, he argues against the view that the Spirit, along with the Father, also generates the Son. Thompson disagrees by saying that the Spirit's begetting only applies to Jesus' humanity. Concerning the Spirit's begetting of Jesus, he writes, "To transfer this directly to the eternal Son and then say he was begotten of the Father through the Spirit is exegetically problematic and theologically speculative. It moves away, in an unhelpful way, from the main thrust of biblical revelation and our experience of salvation."⁴⁰

We agree, but why not apply the priority of the Spirit, found in particular texts, to the Trinity? There is a priority given to the Spirit in that Jesus was conceived by the Spirit (Matthew 1:20; Luke 1:35), anointed by the Spirit (Luke 4:18; Acts 10:37–38; cf. 1 Samuel 16:13; Isaiah 61:1), lived in the power of the Spirit (Isaiah 11:2; 61:1; Luke 4:1, 14, 18), offered himself over to death by the Spirit (Hebrews 9:14), and was resurrected by the Spirit (Romans 1:4; 8:11; cf. 1 Peter 3:18). If we are going to speak of the eternal obedience of the Son, why not also speak of the eternal priority of the Spirit over the Son? Why one and not the other?

We need not rehash the arguments covered in our discussion on subordination. But to speak of eternal obedience raises a question about the nature and context of this obedience. Is it even meaningful to speak of *obedience* in the eternal Trinity? In contrast, the obedience of the Son can be understood within the context of a sinful world. The Son's *obedience* is in the context of a world where *disobedience* is paramount (Romans 3:10–18) and where temptations to disobedience are universal (e.g., Galatians 6:1; James 1:14; 1 Peter 5:8; Revelation 2:10).

Furthermore, in the incarnation, the Son's humanity naturally recoils before suffering. In such circumstances, the Son's obedience is in marked contrast and understandable. It is in this context that the Son is obedient in resisting the temptations that come from suffering (Hebrews 2:18; 4:15). He learns obedience by what he suffered (Hebrews 5:8). It is in this world that the Son experiences what it means to obey and the power of temptations that comes to humanity in a suffering world. Thus, he is now one who is sympathetic (Hebrews 4:15) and merciful (Hebrews 2:17). For the writer of Hebrews, there is an unbreakable connection between temptation, suffering, and obedience; thus, the Son *learns obedience* through suffering and its temptations. Together, they lead to the perfecting of the Son (Hebrews 2:10; 5:9; 7:28).

IS THE SON FROM ABOVE OR FROM BELOW?

It is usually assumed by all positions in our debate that *Son* is an analogy and that this analogy does mean something. Complementarians and biblical egalitarians hold that *Son* is an analogy. Christian feminists have criticized complementarians for not holding consistently to their own view on analogy. Post-Christian feminists also believe that metaphors or symbols have truth content. One major area of disagreement is how we are to approach and understand this analogy. The tendency is to polarize this analogy, viewing the Son as either "from above" or "from below."

From Above

We saw in chapter one that many complementarians have an approach "from above." When it comes to the analogy of *Son*, there is the implication that at least some forms of revelation come to us devoid of cultural interference. Thus, considering the title *Son*, it is argued that there is no separation between what God is and what he reveals of himself. Bloesch and Kassian speak of *Son* as a catalogy. It is an analogy *sui generis*[41] (of its own kind, or unique).

Such formulations are extremely problematic, and some have addressed Bloesch's apparent confusion.[42] Our language is human and cultural, so to speak of a catalogy presupposes a vantage point outside our history and culture, from where we can see "clearly." It also seems to suppose a clear, unambiguous, and pristine text—untainted by interpretive methods or culture. Complementarians acknowledge, however, that God transcends sexuality and that sexuality may not be predicated of God. This admission that at least some features of the analogy of the Son cannot be applied to God acknowledges that there is no such thing as a catalogy.

In our discussion on slavery we saw that complementarians employed a different hermeneutic to argue against slavery. Here again, they adopt a different approach when it comes to this debate: other analogies in Scripture are treated as they relate to culture, but *Son* is considered to lie beyond culture. Complementarians usually take significant account of culture in other topics, but in our topic the tendency is to argue that this issue is beyond culture, or "from above," or that God ordained the patriarchal culture.

Such a method attempts to circumvent the difficult task of interpretation. What is the place of patriarchal culture? To say that God ordains and defines the culture solves the difficulty far too easily, and in their favor. For example, when considering the creation narrative, complementarians tend to see Genesis 1 and 2 as *prior to* culture. However, this "prior to" is often only applied to our topic. So in defending male headship, Waltke argues that God ordained Israel's culture.[43] Nevertheless, when considering another aspect of the same creation narrative, Waltke interprets this according to the Leviathan imagery of ancient Near East culture.[44] In other words, he significantly interacts with culture on the broader topic of creation, but does not when dealing with the narrower creation of male and female. In one area of the narrative, cultural factors are heavily weighed, and in another area they are not, for God ordained them.

Similarly, many complementarians, like Dorothy Patterson, argue that "Adam" is used in Genesis 1:26–27 for both men and women, thus justifying male headship.[45] But again, there is little interaction with the historical-cultural situation. The obvious points that the Pentateuch was written in a patriarchal culture, in a particular language, and with particular theological concerns are minimized. Even on the level of language, *Adam*, as a Hebrew word, is related to culture. Even the complementarian Carson notes some of the linguistic complexities usually glossed over in this type of argument.[46]

Because of taking account of culture, complementarians would not argue for a three-tiered, geocentric universe. They substantially interact with culture in other areas as well, so most have no difficulty, for example, recognizing that the creation account parallels ancient Near East creation myths,[47] or that the structure of Deuteronomy is comparable with Hittite suzerainty treaties,[48] or that Jesus spoke in parables whose content is specifically related to that society.[49] Nevertheless, in approaching our topic there is a tendency to remove culture and to speak of analogies like *Son* as coming "from above."

Because *Son* is a name from above there is little incentive to understand what it meant or why it was used in ancient culture. By adopting a "from above" approach, complementarians imply that the meaning of *Son* is transparent and unrelated to culture, that it is a divine name having no origin in human experience. This approach, in its extreme form, then becomes a search for these "truths from above"—a form of gold mining in which one ton of cultural ore has to be extracted and eventually discarded to get one ounce of "transcultural" gold, a "timeless truth" to be stored away in a theological Fort Knox and guarded by wary theologians.

From Below

As many complementarians approach this topic "from above," many feminists argue "from below." Biblical egalitarians like Jewett speak of the "need to struggle creatively with the basic language of theology, which has projected the masculinity of the theologian on the God of whom he speaks."[50] Christian feminists have made a similar point. Halkes writes, "The feminist protest against the image of God as Father was necessary because the dominant culture had developed this image according to its own ideal and had made it subservient to that."[51]

The tendency in feminist thinking is to say that *Son* is from below—that is, the analogy is *only* a reflection of patriarchal society. If complementarians move in the direction of "transcultural," feminists move in the direction of *only* cultural, where the analogy *Son* is only a reflection of a patriarchal society. If *Son* is an ideal created by men, what then are the options for speaking about God? Some examples: Chopp uses "Word" for God,[52] Schüssler Fiorenza uses "G*d,"[53] and Daly changes God to a verb.[54] A "from below" approach leads to alternative ways of speaking about God, though it sometimes moves toward more impersonal speech.

Opting for either end of the polarization—"from above" or "from below"—is fraught with difficulties. If it is from above, God's revelation entirely forms the culture, and *Son* has little or no relationship to culture. If it is from below, humanity entirely defines revelation, and *Son* has no revelatory meaning and tells us nothing about God. Rather, we should speak of God's revelation *within* history, and adopt neither an approach from above or below. If the analogy of *Son* is transcultural or only cultural, the question may be raised how either one of these serve our knowledge of God. If *Son* is transcultural, then it is severed from our humanity, world, and experience. If *Son* is only cultural, then it is just a Feuerbachian projection of the desires, ideals, and goals of men. We do, however, have a genuine knowledge of God. Israel knew God, the New Testament church knew God, and we know God. The danger is when we adopt ways of speaking that are a movement away from a personal, known, and knowable God.

DOES *SON* HAVE SEXUAL CONNOTATIONS?

Though all positions are careful to state that sexuality may not be predicated of God, there are many examples where different positions have sexualized the analogy of *Son*. The eternal Son is often given a sexual connotation, even though it is claimed that such an association is illegitimate. Many complementarians make the direct connection between the eternal Son and the male incarnation. Following their tendency to reason "from above," and by virtue of the eternal Son's nature or character, there *had* to be a male incarnation. Yet making the male incarnation an ultimate necessity imputes some form of maleness to God—contrary to all positions, which explicitly affirm that God is not male.

Sexual predication is also apparent in feminist thought. Jewett, a biblical egalitarian, alternatively uses "he" and "she" in reference to God.[55] Jewett does not claim that this solves the difficulty, and ideally he would like a new pronoun. Nevertheless, he opens himself to the criticism that, instead of removing sexual polarity, by alternating pronouns he has promoted this polarity, leaving some with a "disturbing image of God-Who-Suffers-from-Gender-Confusion."[56]

As another example, in endeavoring to counter patriarchy, Moltmann writes:

> A father who both *begets* and *gives birth* to his son is no mere male father. He is a motherly father. He can no longer be defined as single-sexed and male, but becomes bisexual or transsexual. He is the *motherly Father* of his *only-born Son*, and at the same time the *fatherly Father* of his *only begotten Son*. It was at this very point that the orthodox dogmatic tradition made its most daring affirmations. According to the Council of Toledo of 675 "we must believe that the Son was not made out of nothing, nor out of some substance or other, but from the womb of the Father (*de utero Patris*), that is that he was begotten or born (*genitus vel natus*) from the Father's own being." Whatever this declaration may be supposed to be saying about the gynaecology of the Father, these bisexual affirmations imply a radical denial of patriarchal monotheism.[57]

We have covered the difficulties of the concept of generation and causation, but here is a further problem. By speaking of "bisexual" and "gynaecology," Moltmann has further sexualized the analogies of Father and Son.

We may see a further sexualizing of the analogies *Father* and *Son* by noting a difference between Christian feminism and post-Christian feminism. Although they have several similar presuppositions and concerns, the way they speak about God is remarkably different. Christian feminists, because they seek to remain within Christianity, often change their speech about God to impersonal language. But post-Christian feminists, because they depart from Christianity, leave the analogies intact—and even intensify them, speaking about the powerful influence of such symbols. Behind this difference, both positions often sexualize the analogies.

Christian feminists adopt more depersonalized language, using language other than *Father* and *Son*, partly because they believe these names have sexual connotations. Post-Christian feminists reject Christianity because they believe the analogies have sexual connotations; but since they have left Christianity, they have no need to alter the analogies. In fact, they *overemphasize* them to strengthen their position.

Another example may be seen in the criticism leveled by post-Christian feminists against traditional theology. Hampson argues that Christianity has formulated the Trinity in terms of male sexual experience—that traditional Trinitarian theology could imply a homosexual relationship, since it has conceived of the Trinity in what sounds like homosexual terms when describing the relationships as an interpenetration of being (*perichoresis*).[58] The question arises, Did traditional theology, even while trying to speak of the mutual loving relationship between the persons of the Trinity, adopt language that is based in male sexual experience? Hampson has made such a claim, but it would be difficult to demonstrate that this lay behind the concept of perichoresis. Alternatively, is this perichoresis only problematic to post-Christian feminists because they have sexualized the analogies—hence the problem—and so they project into the past their own conceptions? Either way, or both, there is a sexualizing of the analogy. Although perichoresis (interpenetration of being) is championed as a solution to a multitude of social concerns, it raises problems in other areas—particularly where women have been violently abused by men.

Post-Christian feminists also observe the general reaction that many Christians have to changing *Father* to *Mother*, concluding that the reason is sexism. Although in some instances this is surely the case, there are other reasons why people reject such a change. Are Post-Christian feminists attributing to other positions their own conceptions? Once again, either one or both have sexualized the analogies. In several instances, all positions have slipped into sexualizing the analogies of *Son* and *Father*.

Despite arguments that *Father* and *Son* are inherently sexist, and that Christianity is irredeemably patriarchal, the Bible never attributes sexuality to God. Given that *Father*, in its context, exemplified a loving relationship, fellowship, authority, discipline, creative action, and care—and not sexual bias or tyrannical rule—many do not consider it oppressive. Although *Father* and *Son* have been and may be used for oppressive purposes, there are alternative readings of the Bible that don't give them oppressive meanings. The analogies should not be extended illegitimately and then claimed to be irredeemably oppressive.

Granted, a redefinition does not immediately solve the problems many have with these analogies. Post-Christian feminists are correct: symbols are powerful. But just as their power and influence can be used for evil, they may be transformed and used for good, though this will take time. For example, in a previous age a slave may have justified a rejection of Christianity because the symbol of God as Master was inherently oppressive. Today, however, few consider the *Master* imagery as applied to God as offensive or oppressive. Carson notes an interesting case:

> There are a little over a dozen words in the Greek New Testament that might in some contexts be rendered "slave." The only one of these that must be rendered "slave," if we follow Greek precedent, is *doulos*. In the KJV, however, the vast majority of occurrences of *doulos*, especially when referring to believers, are rendered "servant." It is difficult to resist the supposition that "slave" seemed too harsh and unattractive, not least because of the social and cultural realities of the time. Modern translations rightly render far more occurrences as "slave" than did the KJV.[59]

Thus, once the slavery issue lost its intensity, translations subsequent to the 1611 King James Version have included more instances of *slave*, for the word was no longer viewed as oppressive. Today we can hear sermons on God as Master, Jesus taking the form of a slave, or ourselves encouraged to become slaves to righteousness without hearing anything tyrannical or evil. Of course, the names *Father* and *Son* are used more in the Bible than *Master*—not because God is more male, but because God is more like a father than a master. Conceivably, *Father* and *Son*, in time, will lose the oppressive connotations that many experience. We can imagine a better future where patriarchy has declined and where the names *Father* and *Son* have lost their meaning of male rule and domination.

CONCLUSION

Each of these views or approaches to the eternal Son ends up, in different ways, with philosophical, theological, or practical problems. There is a tendency either to polarize or sexualize the analogy of *Son*, or to apply to the eternal Son only a favorite feature of Jesus' sonship—be it generation, subordination in authority, or obedience. As we have seen, the sonship of Jesus is multifaceted and diverse. To speak of Jesus as the Son can incorporate many ideas. Which of the following characteristics of Jesus is applicable to eternal Son: obedience, firstborn, humanity, suffering, subordination, maleness, incarnation, the perfecting of the Son? Is the maleness of Jesus based on an eternal maleness of the Son? Does Jesus' subordination in knowledge imply the eternal Son's subordinate knowledge?

There is even debate over how to frame the discussion about the eternal Son, and there are clearly no neat formulas. When speaking of the eternal Son, all agree that the incarnation does not teach that the eternal Son had a beginning at some point in time—an Arian "there was when he was not." Few apply the relationship between sonship and humanity to claim that the Son was eternally human. And most resist applying the maleness of Jesus to the eternal Son. In fact, all positions affirm that maleness cannot be predicated of God, although, as we will see, there are troubling inconsistencies.

This is not to imply that all conceptions of the eternal Son are problematic, but rather that a substantial number surrounding our topic have been. What gives rise to some of these formulations? Is the problem with analogy and the way we apply it to God? This is apparent in some cases, such as when some label eternal generation the univocal element in the analogy of *Son*.

Is the problem one of projection? It appears all too convenient that complementarians, who want to support their entire system that is built on subordination, find the essential distinction in the Trinity to be one of subordination. Out of a host of different features of Jesus' sonship, subordination in authority is the one that is applied for all eternity.

Is the problem the way we conceive of, make a distinction between, or equate the immanent Trinity (God as God exists freely apart from creation) and the economic Trinity (God as revealed to us)?[60] It would seem so, given that some use Jesus' maleness and subordination to conceive of the Trinity in patriarchal categories.

Is the problem that we are stuck in outdated philosophical and scientific categories that hinder our formulations? This appears to be the case when *Son* is conceived as "from above" or "from below," or when categories of substance and causation are applied to the eternal Son.

Or have we reached the limits of language? At the very least, it is clear that, once we affirm the eternal Son, we should be cautious about what we say beyond that. This caution comes from the apophatic tradition of the church, which states the impossibility of wrapping our minds around God. At some point, analogy breaks down when speaking of God.

CHAPTER 8

The Eternal Son as God, and Jesus as God Embodied

The name *Son* should not be polarized or sexualized, as doing either of these undermines our knowledge of God. We have also argued that certain features, such as generation, causation, subordination, or obedience, should not be applied to the eternal Son. But on the more positive side, what *can* we say about the eternal Son that will help further our discussion?

THE ETERNAL SON AS GOD

Over a span of several hundred years following the New Testament period, the gospel story developed to include the doctrine of the Trinity. Just as it is wrong to try to find a full-fledged account of the Trinity in the biblical texts, so it is wrong to say that we must remove the Trinity because it is a later development. In its experience of God and its reflection on its foundational texts, the church concluded that God is Trinitarian; so when we speak of God, we speak of Father, Son, and Holy Spirit.

For our purposes, we can start with this foundation: the eternal Son is God. In Trinitarian reflection, ancient through modern, orthodoxy has agreed that the eternal Son is God. In fact, the doctrine of eternal generation was intended to secure that the eternal Son is indeed God. In contrast to Arius, who claimed, regarding the Son, that "there was when he was not," the council of Nicaea, using categories of substance and causation, stated that the Son was *eternally* generated from the Father—that the Son was the *same* substance as the Father.

Likewise, we saw in our discussion of Calvin that his goal was to preserve the eternal Son as God, though he also used categories of substance and causation. We need not use these categories today; but we still want to preserve what the church, after much reflection, came to confess: that the eternal Son is God. To say that the eternal Son is God is simply stating the confession of the Christian church: that God is Trinitarian.

In other words, as believers reflected on the life of Jesus, they recognized that his life revealed a distinction in God—a distinction that is usually expressed as Father, Son, and Holy Spirit. But more than that, this revelation was not simply that Jesus pointed out a distinction; Jesus himself embodied the distinction. In Jesus, God was embodied. Here was Immanuel: God with us, the eternal Son embodied in Jesus of Nazareth. To refer to this embodiment, we will refer to Jesus as the *Son-God*, emphasizing Jesus' sonship and his embodiment of the eternal Son who is God. The eternal Son as God is the basis of the gospel story.

The eternal Son as God is foundational for Jesus' priesthood, in that Jesus as Son-God is holy, blameless, and pure (Hebrews 7:26). It is foundational for Jesus' prophetic ministry, in that as Son-God he is at the Father's side, in the unique position to fully know the Father and reveal the Father to us (John 1:18). The eternal Son as God is the basis for Jesus' messianic kingly rule. As Son-God, he is the supreme ruler over all creation (Colossians 1:15), and his throne is forever (Hebrews 1:8). As Son-God, he will come in the clouds (a sole prerogative of God in ancient culture) and usher in the kingdom. Only as Son-God can the Son's voice raise the dead (John 5:25) and can the Son sit in judgment over humanity (Matthew 25:31–46). As Son-God, Jesus is the king of all—his messianic rule grounded in this feature—adding to our point that the eternal Son is not eternally subordinate. In fact, contrary to the claim that the Son's earthly subordination needs to have a basis in an eternal subordination, the giving of authority to rule, judge, and forgive sins has its foundation in the eternal Son who is God and who has God's authority. Only God can forgive sins, judge humanity, and rule over all. So as the Son-God, Jesus is the preeminent creator (Colossians 1:16; Hebrews 1:2), sustainer (Colossians 1:17; Hebrews 1:3), and redeemer (Colossians 1:20; Hebrews 1:3).

Thus, as the Son-God, Jesus' maleness cannot be applied to the eternal Son, for the eternal Son is God—and sexuality is never ascribed to God. Whether or not everyone is consistent, *all* positions agree in principle that God is not male. God has been described with eyes, ears, heart, hands, feet, arms, womb, voice, etc., but never with genitalia. No sexuality is ever ascribed to God.[1] This is clear even in the Old Testament. Waltke notes that though the grammatical forms for God are male and the analogies are mostly male, it is agreed that in the Old Testament God was regarded as nonsexual. In Deuteronomy 4:15–16, the command is not to make an image in any form—*man or woman*. Furthermore, in the ancient Near East the custom was to sacrifice male animals to male gods and female animals to female gods; but in Israel both male and female were sacrificed to God (Leviticus 3:1; 4:23, 28).[2] We may not predicate maleness to the eternal Son, who is God.

> The short answer to Arius is:
> **No, the eternal Son is God.**
>
> The short answer to eternal subordination is:
> **No, the eternal Son is God.**
>
> The short answer to views that apply maleness to the eternal Son is:
> **No, the eternal Son is God.**

JESUS AS GOD EMBODIED

The church confesses that Jesus is God embodied. We want to draw out and develop one feature of this embodiment, one part of Jesus' sonship—namely, Jesus as the image of God—and use this to address further questions surrounding the significance of his maleness. Jesus as the Son is the exact image of God. To see the Son is to see God (John 14:9). The Son is the character of God (Hebrews 1:3) and the image of the invisible God (Colossians 1:15, cf. v. 13). Jesus shows us what God is like. Thus, the Christian understanding of God begins, progresses, and ends with Jesus.

If we are searching for analogies to describe God, we have found *the* analogy in Jesus. To refer to this feature of Jesus' embodiment, we will refer to him as the *Son-image* in order to emphasize that Jesus as Son is the image of God. As the Son-image, he reflects and reveals the glory of God to humanity. The ideas of glory and image are closely related (2 Corinthians 4:4; Hebrews 1:3). To see the Son-image is to see the glory of God (John 1:14), for the Son is the exact representation of God's being (Hebrews 1:3). As the Son-image, he fully and perfectly represents and reveals God to us, so to see the Son is to see the Father (John 1:18; 12:45; 14:9).

All positions agree that God is not male and that, given the patriarchal culture of the ancient world, there could not have been a female incarnation. There is a tendency, however, to split the discussion on Jesus' maleness into two options: Is it revelational, or only cultural? Both of these options need qualification. Because complementarians agree that God is not male, they have conceded in principle that the male incarnation is not revelational in an unqualified sense. Likewise, feminists cannot consistently maintain an only-cultural approach. They have argued, as we noted in chapter one, that in Jesus there is a "kenosis of patriarchy." This means that in the incarnation God judges male rule, for Jesus humbles himself as a male. If, in the incarnation, Jesus reveals himself as nonhierarchical, and so undermines traditional male roles, he still reveals something about God—even if it is God's accommodation to, subversion of, and judgment of that patriarchal culture.

So the debate is over the exact meaning of this male incarnation. What exactly does it tell us about God? Although all positions hold in principle that God is not male, the complementarian position, by speaking of the *ultimate* necessity of a male incarnation, opens itself to the critique that it imputes maleness to God. Complementarians make the connection between maleness and the eternal Son, so that a male incarnation is revelational of God's character. Rather than being a cultural accommodation, the male incarnation has to do with profound religious truths, including that God displays male attributes *par excellence*. In speaking about male imagery for God, they say, "His representations and incarnation are inseparable from his being."[3] Or they argue that there could not have been a female incarnation even if there was an original matriarchal society.[4]

If the maleness of Jesus, however, is part of this "glory" of God that the Son-image reveals, it makes maleness a characteristic of God. If a male incarnation is required to reveal God—no matter what time or culture—then this position applies maleness to God. It is to say that the Son-image had to be male, for it is precisely *only in being male* that he can fully reveal the glory of God to us. Again, all positions affirm that God is not male; so although Jesus is God embodied, his maleness does not reveal that God is more "male-like." In this sense, Jesus' maleness is like his nationality as a Jew, his ancient worldview, or his profession—they are all particularities of his life.

We can look at other applications of the Son-image by noting that it is this Son-image into which women and men are *both* being conformed. In the New Testament, believers are described as being renewed in the image of God. Specifically, believers are being transformed into the image of the Son (Romans 8:29; 2 Corinthians 3:18). We reflect Jesus in ever-increasing measure, until we shall be like him (1 John 3:2). We are being renewed in knowledge, righteousness, and true holiness (Colossians 3:10; Ephesians 4:24). There is a far greater future to life and redemption that transforms humanity beyond our present existence. This renewal is part of the new creation (2 Corinthians 5:17), so as we have borne the image of "the man of dust" (Adam), so shall we bear the image of "the man of heaven" (1 Corinthians 15:45–49). If Adam is the prototype, then Jesus is the "telotype"—the end pattern or type for the goal of humanity. Humanity is moving in a new direction toward the Son-image.

Regarding the extensive debate over the meaning of "image of God," I think this can be said: to be in the image of God is to be and to become like Jesus. The Son-image is the new direction and goal for all of humanity. Consequently, maleness cannot be an essential part of this image; otherwise it would mean that women are in some way transforming into a more male image. The conclusion would then be, as some in the church's history have argued, that heaven will be male or that in order for women to be saved they must become men—that is, give up all the so-called characteristics of being female: weak, seductive, easily deceived, fickle, ignorant, and even the name *woman*.

Our recreation into the image of the Son does not mean that we all become male. So when we speak of Jesus as the Son-image, as the one who images God, we must say that his maleness and Jewishness are particularities of his own life and are not part of this image into which women and men, Jew and Gentile, are being conformed. To be like the Son-image has nothing to do with being male or becoming more male-like. So women are not less able to become like Jesus because he is male, and they do not reveal the Son-image less. The direction and goal for humanity is the Son-image. This is our *full* humanity. To become more like Jesus is to become more fully human. If this Son-image into which we are being conformed has maleness attached to it, women have a permanent impediment to becoming fully human and imaging Christ.

Complementarians are careful to state that God is not male and that the use of *Son* is not sexist. Nevertheless, it appears that complementarian thinking about maleness intrudes into thinking about image. This occurs on a number of levels. For example, Hurley argues from Ephesians 5:22–23 and 1 Corinthians 11 that a woman does not image God or Christ in her relationship with her husband.[7] In agreeing with Hurley's position, Dorothy Patterson writes, "Of course, this particular imaging used by Paul to describe how the man and woman relate does not in any sense negate the woman's being in the image of God in *other ways* [italics mine]."[6] Hurley concludes, "There need be no implication whatsoever that women are not the image of God in *other senses* [italics his]."[5]

Because a woman's relationship to her husband is substantial and long-term means that in this major area of her life she does not image Jesus. Is she being recreated in the image of the Son and expressing that recreation solely outside of her marriage relationship? This position again implicitly imputes masculinity to the image of God or to the Son-image, since, at least in her relationship at home, and presumably at church, a woman, in contrast to her husband, does not image Jesus. This formulation runs contrary to her transformation into the Son-image. It clashes with the New Testament directive for all to imitate and become like Jesus and the call for women and men to become mature and attain to the whole measure of the fullness of Christ (Ephesians 4:13).

Not all complementarians would formulate the distinctions in this manner. Frame argues that women are fully in the image of God, yet in church and family women image God in his submission while men image God in his authority.[8] But is this not saying something similar—that men and women (in church and family) image God in different ways? Presumably, only outside of marriage and church do women reveal the authority aspect of the image. This leads to the question, Does a man, in his marriage, ever image God in submission? Though stating that both men and women image God, Frame writes about Adam, "As vassal lord, Adam is to extend God's *control* over the world ('subdue' in Genesis 1:28). He has the right to name the animals, an exercise of *authority* in ancient thinking (Genesis 2:19ff; cf. 2:23; 3:20, where he also names his wife!). And he is to 'fill' the earth with his *presence*."[9] Frame uses this triad of control, authority, and presence as an organizing motif for understanding God,[10] which leaves the impression that male attributes (as complementarians understand them) reveal God better.

Closely related to this discussion is the view that a *male* priest, minister, or elder better represents Jesus. But what is needed to be able to represent Jesus? Richard Norris rightly points out, "The mere *fact* that Jesus was a male settles nothing. The question . . . is that of the *significance* of this or that characteristic of Jesus."[11] How do we represent Jesus? Do we all have to become carpenters or Jews? Do we have to wear first-century clothing?

Do men need to grow beards? Do we have to adopt Jesus' ancient Jewish worldview? What is needed to image Jesus?

We have seen that the Son-image is the image into which all believers—women and men—are being conformed, renewed, and made more fully human; and thus maleness is just one particularity of Jesus' life. If maleness is essential for the Son-image to reveal God, then not only is God more male-like but maleness is also essential for us to reveal God fully. If it is necessary for elders or priests to be male in order to represent Christ fully, then it becomes a necessity for women to become more male (or else remain less like Christ). We will be left with the awkward and dubious reasoning that "God-like women are deemed unfit to be Christ-like priests."[12]

Again, this position brings maleness into the Son-image and therefore into the divine being, an outcome that all positions explicitly disallow. When some say that, other things being equal, a male represents Jesus better,[13] the problem is that not all things are equal—there are many particularities to Jesus' life that are not part of the Son-image, and maleness is one of these particularities. Looking at the Son-image, we see that a male does not better or more fully represent Jesus. Maleness has nothing to do with representing, revealing, or imaging the Son of God.

Part of the problem is that some theologize primarily with substantive categories—where God as a substance fills a male container (person), where a male substance is a more fitting container for God, or where to represent Jesus one needs to be a male substance. With a relational theology, however, we can view Jesus' union with the Son as a complete relational union in contrast to a substantive union. In this view there is no conceptual difficulty with God having a complete and full union with a female human being. With a relational theology, a relational union (incarnation) is not dependent on a male substance, and neither does one need to be a male substance to fully represent and image Christ.

CONCLUSION

The basis for revelation and salvation lies in the eternal Son who is God. As Son-God, Jesus is the image of the invisible God. As Son-God, Jesus has intimate knowledge of the Father, which is the basis for his prophetic work; and so Jesus can make the Father fully known to us. As Son-God, Jesus is holy, blameless, and pure (Hebrews 7:26), which is the basis for his priestly work, such as bringing many children to glory (Hebrews 2:10). These children who are brought to glory include men and women.

As Son-God, Jesus is fully able to save his people—both women and men—who are recreated into the Son's image. As Son-prophet and Son-priest, Jesus' revelation of God and work of salvation are inevitably linked—each established in eternal sonship. In light of this, questions like, Can Jesus' maleness be necessary for revelation but not for salvation, or vice versa? fall apart. Such contrasts or oppositions conflict with eternal sonship, which forms the basis for Jesus' prophetic *and* priestly roles. To make maleness necessary for one brings maleness into the eternal Son, which forms the foundation for all other roles.

Complementarians argue that a male savior can represent and save women. If they apply maleness to the eternal Son, however, then women are excluded. To apply maleness to the eternal Son is to apply maleness to the cornerstone of revelation and salvation. And this excludes women. If maleness is applied to the eternal Son, then this becomes the foundation for Jesus' prophetic and priestly ministry. It would mean that women reveal God less than men, and it jeopardizes women's salvation.

Nevertheless, maleness is not part of eternal sonship. So Jesus' maleness does not undermine any of his roles, including the prophetic and priestly. Thus, revelation and salvation is possible apart from a *male* redeemer.

CHAPTER 9

Jesus, Wisdom, and an "Eternal Daughter"?

Christian feminists have rightly drawn attention to the ways *Son* has been used to further oppression and patriarchy, and thus they have looked to other means to speak of Jesus' embodiment of God. One significant way is through the female figure of Wisdom, or Sophia, which is used to argue for a non-androcentric Christology. In this final chapter we will look at the significance of Wisdom to further our discussion on the maleness of Jesus. What is the connection between Jesus and Wisdom? Does this give balance or even provide a corrective to an emphasis on Son? And does this allow us to change the name of Son to *Daughter*?

We will limit our discussion to the two main sources to which Christian feminists have appealed: the figure of Wisdom in the book of Proverbs and the use of *logos* ("word") in the prologue to the Gospel of John.

WISDOM IN PROVERBS

It is sometimes argued that the female gender of the words for "wisdom"—*hokma* (Hebrew) and *sophia* (Greek)—have theological significance. That is, that we can derive conclusions about thought structure from grammatical structure. James Barr has addressed this misuse of grammatical gender.[1] The fallacy of this argument is demonstrated, for example, by comparing the gender of a word in one language with its gender in another language. Barr notes that gender in language sometimes corresponds to the actual difference between male and female, but in other cases it does not. He concludes, "The phenomenon of grammatical gender is logically haphazard in relation to the real distinctions between objects or to the distinctions thought to exist between them."[2]

Waltke concurs, "Modern linguists agree that grammatical gender serves only in part to denote sexual differences among animate beings. The primary function of various systems of gender is syntactic; gender is one of the *concord systems* that connect related words within a sentence."[3]

The essential argument regarding the figure of Wisdom, however, comes not from the female gender of the Hebrew word *hokma*, but that Wisdom is intentionally portrayed as a woman—for example, in the book of Proverbs. Johnson is concerned about the "significance of the gender of personified Wisdom,"[4] and makes the connection between (1) Christ as the Wisdom of God; (2) Wisdom portrayed as a woman; and (3) Wisdom who, in some instances, has divine attributes. The argument rests on the relationship between these three points. Johnson is aware of a number of different interpretations given to the figure of Wisdom and that not all of them fit with her thesis, although her preference is for Wisdom as a personification of God.[5]

Nevertheless, our concern particularly relates to the relevance of *female* Wisdom. The question is this, Why was such an important figure portrayed as a woman?

Waltke cites the work of Karl Brugmann, who argues that "when either [primitive people or poets] personified a lifeless concept into a living being, it was the grammatical form of the noun that, through the psychological impulse of analogy . . . decided the definite direction of the gender—whether it should be masculine or feminine."[6] The example that Waltke provides to confirm this is where Hebrew poets have personified, in certain cases, the noun *hokma*, according to gender, into Woman

Wisdom, hostess (Proverbs 9:1–6), sister (Proverbs 7:4), and mediatrix (Proverbs 1:20–33).[7] So the sages may well have pictured *hokma* as a woman based solely upon the grammatical form of the noun.

As noted, there is no definite link between gender and thought structure. Therefore *hokma*, being a female noun, does not necessarily correspond to an external reality in the Hebrew mind. The sages, however, could have portrayed *hokma* as male. The question still remains, Why, for such an exceptionally important figure, was *hokma* intentionally developed as a woman? Boström writes, "It is quite possible that one of the main reasons for presenting wisdom in personified form was as a literary and moral counterbalance to Lady Folly who is associated with seductive women and a self-destructive life-style. If this is the main reason for the personification of wisdom in these passages, then one should be extremely careful not to inject too much theological content into what may well be a purely literary phenomenon."[8]

This is another good suggestion why *hokma* was personified as a woman, and it relates to the sages' purposes in the book of Proverbs. We may see this in reference to (1) the contrast between the adulterous wife and the virtuous wife, and (2) the striking similarity between wisdom and the virtuous wife. Taking the book of Proverbs as a whole, these contrasts may be represented as follows:

The adulterous wife	The virtuous wife
She is found everywhere (7:11, 12).	She is hard to find (31:10).
She left her husband (2:17).	She is faithful to her husband (31:11).
She lies (30:20).	She speaks the truth (31:26).
Her house leads to death and is spiritually deficient (2:18; 7:27; 9:18).	Her house leads to blessing and is spiritually abundant (31:11, 28).
She is unwise and devoid of understanding (5:6; 9:13).	She is wise (31:26).
She is beautiful (6:25).	She is not necessarily beautiful (31:30).

The adulterous wife	The virtuous wife
She is manipulative (7:10).	She is trustworthy (31:11).
She is immodest and proud (7:11; 9:13).	She is modest and humble (31:25, 30).
She is a trap (23:28).	She brings freedom (31:11).
Her speech is corrupt (5:3–4; 6:24; 7:5, 21; 22:14).	Her speech is pure (31:26).
She is a curse and like decay in her husband's bones (12:4).	She is a blessing and her husband's crown (12:4).
She is quarrelsome and ill-tempered (21:9, 19; 25:24; 27:15).	She is kind and pleasant (31:10–12, 28).
She will take everything you have (5:10; 6:26).	She is worth more than money can buy (31:10–11).

Wisdom	The virtuous wife
Wisdom is a crown of splendor (1:9; 4:9).	She is her husband's crown (12:4).
Wisdom is a gift of God (2:6).	A wife is a gift from the Lord (18:22).
Wisdom is pleasant to your soul (2:10).	A wife is pleasant to the soul (31:11–12).
Wisdom will protect you from adultery (2:16; 6:24; 7:5).	Her house leads to blessing and is spiritually abundant (31:11, 28).
Wisdom brings honor (3:4, 35).	She brings honor (31:23, 31).
Wisdom is more precious than rubies (3:15; 8:11).	She is worth far more than rubies (31:10).
All her ways are pleasant (3:17).	All her ways are good and pleasant (31:12, 15, 20, 28–29).
You will have no fear of sudden disaster (3:25).	She prevents sudden disasters (31:11, 21).
Whoever finds wisdom receives favor from the Lord (8:35).	Whoever finds a wife receives favor from the Lord (18:22).
Wisdom provides truthful teaching (4:2).	She gives faithful instruction (31:26).

Wisdom and the virtuous woman are equated in Proverbs 9:1–6. Similarly, Folly and the adulteress are equated in Proverbs 9:13–18. In the book of Proverbs, the female personification of *hokma* fits the intention of the sages in contrasting the figures of Wisdom and Folly, and in presenting the numerous similarities between the excellent wife and Wisdom, who are both set in opposition to the adulterous prostitute and Folly. For instance, Wisdom and Folly both offer meals (Proverbs 9:2, 17), though one is meat and wine, the other bread and water.[9] Both make calls from the high places (Proverbs 9:3, 14), and to the simple (Proverbs 9:4, 16). One brings life, the other death (Proverbs 9: 6, 18). Both have houses, yet one is seven-pillared, the other a cemetery (Proverbs 9:1, 14, 18).

Not only is Wisdom portrayed as a woman, but so also is Folly. Folly is the exemplar of anti-Wisdom; her character is one of corrupt speech, deception, and lack of knowledge and understanding. Her house is a doorway to the grave. She is similar to another biblical character—Satan—who is the father of lies (John 8:44), deceives the world (Revelation 12:9), has the power of death (Hebrews 2:14), and whose goal is the destruction of humanity (1 Peter 5:8). Even though this personification of Folly is of secondary importance to Wisdom, no implications, however, may be drawn from the female gender of Folly (or the male gender of Satan).

Overall, these female personifications relate very well for the sages' purposes. Thus, the female figure of Wisdom (and Folly) in Proverbs may be understood more as poetic imagination rather than an actual reality—a personification of God's wisdom as a female figure.[10]

What about the claim that Jesus is directly identified with the female figures in Proverbs? At certain points, such as Proverbs 8:22–31, a *direct* identification is problematic. Most agree that Wisdom is described here as created or begotten[11] (hence, Arius' use of Proverbs 8:22). The passage describes the creation of Wisdom in the distant past, before anything else was created (see especially verses 22–26). Furthermore, a number of scholars now translate Proverbs 8:30 to read "child" rather than "master worker" or "craftsman," which fits better with the context. In this view the passage portrays a child, one who was given birth in the distant past, delighting before God. This child is one of the many personae of wisdom in the book.

A direct identification with Jesus is problematic. For example, a comparison of this passage and our discussion on sonship shows a departure in some areas. The eternal Son was not created, nor was the Son given birth. The Son was from eternity, not from the distant past. The Son, not a child, was at the Father's side (John 1:18).

We have seen that no theological significance can be derived from the gender of the word *hokma*. The personification of wisdom may be understood as a development from the gender of the noun, related to the sages' purposes in Proverbs. Moreover, there are sufficient reasons why passages like Proverbs 8:22–31 should not be applied directly to Jesus. The connection is rather *indirect*. Without doubt, Jesus is the wisdom of God (1 Corinthians 1:24); but this description is not a direct correspondence with the female personae we find in Proverbs.

Nevertheless, this is relevant, as an indirect connection, for our topic. The fact that Wisdom, in some places, has divine attributes, and that Wisdom is portrayed as a woman, adds to the argument that God is not male. The reason that Wisdom can be personified as female and with divine attributes is because God is not male. As such, the figure provides a remarkable exception to a patriarchal culture. Johnson wishes to use the figure of Wisdom to break down the "'necessary ontological connection' between the undoubted maleness of Jesus' historical person and the supposed maleness of the predominant Christian image of God closely associated with his historical appearance."[12] We agree because we have a similar concern, but have approached the discussion on Wisdom in Proverbs differently. Overall, this discussion confirms what we have already concluded: that there is no ultimate necessity in God for a male incarnation, and that God is not more male-like than female-like.

JOHN'S PROLOGUE

Many scholars have found a relationship between the Greek concepts of *sophia* ("wisdom") and *logos* ("word"). They argue that the closest parallels with the prologue to John's Gospel are found in wisdom literature.[13] Furthermore, as many refer to John's supposed use of an urprologue[14]—an early Christian hymn or poem—many Christian feminists develop this idea further and argue that John is adapting an earlier hymn to *sophia*. For them, *sophia* is clearly seen in John's prologue, lending itself to a non-androcentric Christology.

Rendel Harris raised the possibility early in the twentieth century as to whether *sophia* is an alternative title to *logos* and prior to it.[15] He argued that John's prologue developed from Proverbs 8 and Jewish wisdom literature. So in substituting sophia for logos in the prologue, Harris noted the basic similarity with Proverbs 8:22–30. In developing his argument, he found further similarities between Proverbs and the prologue, concluding that *logos* is a substitute for *sophia* from a prior source. "Thus behind the Only-Begotten Son of God to whom John introduces us, we see the Unique Daughter of God, who is His Wisdom, and we ought to understand the Only-Begotten Logos-Son as an evolution from the Only-Begotten Sophia-Daughter."[16] In other words, behind John's *logos* Christology there lies a prior *sophia* Christology.

Hartmut Gese argues in a similar manner, but with more development.[17] He also finds a direct connection between the prologue and Old Testament statements on wisdom.[18] Gese provides many parallels between *sophia* and *logos*: namely, preexistence, divinity, cause of life, creator of all, agent of revelation, one who seeks to live with people, and one who is rejected by some but through whom others may become "children of wisdom." At the end of the *logos* hymn (John 1:18), Gese finds a description of Wisdom on God's lap, the "child" known from Proverbs 8:30.[19] For Gese, wisdom theology is matured and fulfilled in John's prologue.

While biblical writers did use sources, and the possibility exists that John used an urprologue, a recreation of this urprologue is fraught with difficulties. The urprologue may well have been a hymn to *logos*. Or even if John did employ a hymn to *sophia*, he used the word *logos* rather than the word *sophia*; so we should start with the word he used, not from what he possibly adapted. An interpretation of John's prologue is not dependent on a reconstruction of a prior hymn. And as with all words, in determining the meaning of *logos* in John 1:1–18 care should be taken (1) to recognize that the context basically determines the meaning of the word;[20] (2) to take account of the semantic domain of the word;[21] and (3) not to confuse the word *logos* with a theological concept—that is, overload the word with theological meaning.[22]

Apart from these concerns, the main argument for a connection between the figure of Wisdom and John's prologue depends almost entirely on parallels.[23] Regarding John's Gospel, this approach has its difficulties because of the universal character of Johannine vocabulary. Robert Kysar has demonstrated this problem of parallels by comparing the work of Dodd and Bultmann, in which they have tried to determine the background of the prologue.[24] In their use of 320 references of primary literature outside the New Testament, only 6 percent of the passages cited are used by *both* Dodd and Bultmann. Although this critique applies specifically to non-Christian influences, the danger is present in finding biblical parallels. The parallels between the prologue and wisdom literature, as suggested by Christian feminists, are by no means *unique* to wisdom literature.

John's significant use of the Old Testament is well known and documented.[25] Despite the parallels offered for Wisdom, an argument can be made for the significant influence of the creation narrative of Genesis 1 on the prologue. The opening words of the prologue, "In the beginning" (repeated in verse 2), connect us with the "In the beginning" of Genesis 1:1. The connection of verses 1–5 with the Genesis 1 account is further observed in (1) John's use of similar words, such as *God*, *light*, and *darkness*; (2) his probable replacement of the expression "God created the heavens and the earth" (Genesis 1:1) with the phrase "All things came into being through him" in verses 3 and 10;[26] and (3) his development of parallel concepts. There is a development from the physical darkness

(Genesis 1:2) to the spiritual darkness of unbelief that has not overcome/understood (a possible dual meaning) the light of the Word (John 1:5). The theme of light develops from the creation of physical light to the light of Jesus as primarily seen in his relationships, teachings, and signs. There is also the development from the creation of physical life (Genesis 1:1–31) to the bringing of spiritual life (John 1:4).

In Genesis 1, creation is attributed to God's word by the recurring statement "And God said." It is the word of God that created the heavens and earth, that brought forth light, and that created life. In John's prologue, similarly, creation is attributed to the Logos (vv. 3, 10), who was in the beginning with God (vv. 1, 2). It is apparent that John uses *logos* in connection with the word of God from Genesis 1. John uses *logos* as a verbal echo of God speaking in Genesis 1:3–30.[27] Thus, John's *logos* is to be translated "Word." In connecting the Word with the creation account, John develops from the first Genesis to a second Genesis, from the first creation to a new creation—that is, the coming of the Logos into the world is an event as momentous as the original creation. Cullmann concludes that the connection back to the creation narrative of Genesis is so important for John that any other connection is only of secondary importance.[28]

Readers of John 1 would have recalled the Genesis account. There are, however, other Old Testament parallels, like the ministry of Moses, the tabernacle, the wilderness experience, the law, and the *shekina* (presence/dwelling) of God.[29] Also, the readers may have taken the prologue to refer to the figure of Wisdom. John may well have drawn from that concept. Alternatively, perhaps the similarities between the prologue and wisdom literature arise because both go back to creation. Numerous biblical parallels are apparent, so we grant that Wisdom is included in the parallels. But as one among several parallels, there is not a *unique* relationship.

More problematic is the claim that John essentially changed an urprologue to Wisdom, and gave it an androcentric twist. To substitute *sophia* to balance out any male inferences of *logos* is unnecessary. No theological significance can be derived from the gender of a word, including

John's use of the male noun *logos*. Finally, using the relationship between Jesus and Wisdom to speak of an eternal Daughter instead of a Son is a considerable and far-reaching step that deserves separate consideration.

AN "ETERNAL DAUGHTER"?

Given that God is beyond sexuality and that Jesus is the wisdom of God, is it legitimate to speak of an "eternal Daughter"—and in so doing emphasize that God is not male? With the tendency to opt for polar positions regarding sonship, an approach from above will say no, stating that *Son* is a name from outside our world and given by God. An approach from below may say yes, pointing out that *Son* is a name solely arising from the patriarchal culture. May we change the Trinitarian name *Son* to *Daughter* without losing any meaning—and, as it is sometimes argued—gain meaning by emphasizing that God is not male?

Redemptive-historical Ties and the Son's Continuing Ministry

We have spoken of the eternal Son as God, and Jesus as God embodied. Specifically, the eternal Son is embodied in Jesus. We have examined the sonship of Jesus, finding many features, including firstborn, heir, incarnation, prophet, priest, king, obedience, suffering, subordination, image, and resurrection. The problem with speaking of a Daughter is that our Christian vocabulary for speaking of God, and the eternal Son, arose out of this context—the context of Jesus' sonship and all its related features. Thus, speaking of Daughter has no connection to Jesus' sonship. For instance, one feature of Jesus' sonship was the male incarnation, so any use of *Daughter* disconnects from the incarnation.[30] A similar point can be made regarding Jesus as firstborn son, king, prophet, and priest.

For this reason, *Son* cannot be changed to *Daughter* without radically disengaging from redemptive history, resulting in a Son who is separated from the historical Jesus. For example, Jann Aldredge-Clanton, who separates the historical Jesus from the living Christ, writes, "Referring to Christ exclusively in the masculine gender keeps the focus on the historical Jesus. A Christ who is exclusively 'he,' 'king,' 'son,' 'master,' 'brother' cannot be the Christ who is alive in the world today."[31]

But what about today in a context where a daughter is considered equal to a son, and where we are striving to expose patriarchy as a dead end of the gospel narrative? Can we now speak of a Daughter? It is important to note that the sonship of Jesus is not limited to the past, and the church speaks of the Son's *continuing* work. Considering the relationship between sonship and priesthood, for example, Jesus' work as Son-priest *presently* continues (Hebrews 8:1–2). Today he remains our Son-priest, so we can approach God with assurance and confidence (Hebrews 10:19–22). He continues to be the Son-king who is reigning until all things are under his feet (Hebrews 2:8–9; cf. 1 Corinthians 15:25). And at the eschaton it is this Son who will be subject to the Father so that God may be all in all (1 Corinthians 15:28). There are also other analogies, relationships, typologies, and associations that fall apart with a Daughter, such as the unique relationship between the Son and Father portrayed throughout the Gospels, particularly apparent in John's Gospel (e.g., John 5:17–47; 17:1–26), or the analogy between Christ as bridegroom and the church as bride (Matthew 25:1–13; Mark 2:19–20; Luke 5:34–35; Revelation 19:7; 21:2, 9; 22:17).

In the biblical material, sonship is tied to every aspect of Christology. We have argued that sonship is a broad concept for understanding Christology. It is more comprehensive and perhaps more helpful than the common division in systematic theology between the person and work of Jesus; the division of the work of Jesus into prophet, priest, and king; or a sharp division of the person of Jesus into divinity and humanity. Sonship is so enmeshed in the story of Jesus that to change *Son* to *Daughter* makes a decisive and critical break with the gospel story and with the Son's continuing work within this story.

Given all these features of Jesus' sonship, it is clear that Christian feminists cannot achieve a thorough revision of the text. Their main concern, however, is not to modify the biblical text. Their interest is to speak of a Daughter in a new cultural situation where a daughter has all the rights, privileges, and opportunities of a son. Nevertheless, what we have seen is that even in this new cultural situation the work of the Son continues. To claim that we should only refer to Jesus as Son in his earthly ministry ignores the present ongoing situation and his future work. Given these ties, the debate over Jesus' sonship is different from the concern related to the Bible calling us sons. In this regard, when the Bible speaks of all believers as brothers or sons, a convincing argument is made that this should be translated "brothers and sisters" or "sons and daughters." This point is even conceded by some complementarians.[32] In such cases the Scriptures include both female and male. But in referring to Jesus, the title *Son* is applied to one who was male and who continues his redemptive work as Son, even to the end.

Who Is Jesus?

The use of *Daughter* moves beyond Jesus and his revelation of God into other categories that are meant to give us a deeper reality apart from the continuing gospel narrative. But we are not limited to speaking of Jesus only as Son. We have seen that there are other images for Jesus in the gospel story, such as Word or Wisdom. Instead of being a solution, the use of *Daughter* creates fogginess about who Jesus is. And alternating between *Son* and *Daughter* creates an image that has no correspondence to the life of Jesus—a puzzling image that we will find hard to relate to ourselves, our world, or the Scriptures. To use such an analogy, the Scriptures and the gospel story will have to be processed through a complex hermeneutical grid, raising the question of whether fellowship with and knowledge of Jesus is even possible.

Key reasons for the proposed change to *Daughter* are to emphasize that God is not male, to counter those who have brought masculinity into the eternity of God, and to subvert patriarchal imagination. These concerns are good, but the solution is problematic. The solution does not lie in postulating a Daughter, but rather in emphasizing that eternal sonship has no sexual connotations. The solution is to accentuate, as we have concluded, that Jesus' maleness has no part of eternal divinity, that Jesus' maleness is not foundational for his redemptive work, and that Jesus' maleness is just one particularity of his life.

In fact, the proposed solution of *Daughter* is not going to work given all the ties to sonship that we have seen. Because of these connections, a change to *Daughter* is not going to balance out, in any significant way, all the connections and the male imagery. If the eternal Son is viewed to have sexual connotations, supplemental imagery like Daughter will not counterbalance. The gospel story—which is still continuing—does not allow for Jesus to be imaged as both Son and Daughter. Even granting that the male incarnation took place in a patriarchal culture (and, hypothetically, that God could have done things differently), there are still a myriad of theological ties and related analogies within the gospel story.

The fact that eternal Son has no sexual or male connotations does not immediately solve the problem many feminists have with the use of *Father* and *Son*, for many people still use these analogies to further injustice, oppression, and male priority. However, if the gospel story exposes patriarchy as a dead end, as we have argued, then the church will continue to work toward the transformation and removal of patriarchy. And with patriarchy's decline these analogies will lose their perceived oppressive character, as did *master* and *slave* in a previous age. We can hope for a better future when these words have lost much of their power to do harm.

Epilogue

The danger facing complementarianism is to impute maleness into the divine being—and in so doing to reduce the glory of God to created things, to fall into idolatry, and to jeopardize the worth and salvation of women. The danger facing biblical egalitarianism is to attempt to work around the theological basis of patriarchy—and in so doing to miss the determinative and continuing gospel narrative, which includes new realities that are working themselves out in light of the Christ-event and the Spirit's work in the church. The danger facing feminism is to make everything only cultural—and in so doing to undermine the gospel story. By focusing on a limited set of texts, complementarians increasingly find themselves at odds with the gospel story, our culture, and our experience. By focusing on culture and experience, feminists sometimes find themselves at variance with the continuing gospel narrative.

A way forward is to assimilate the strengths and reject the weaknesses of all positions. On the one hand, this means accepting the theological basis of patriarchy and rejecting attempts to work around it. In other words, it means accepting that the Bible connects theological themes such as creation, redemption, and God's names with patriarchy, just as the Bible connects theological themes with slavery and the Sabbath. On the other hand, a way forward also involves adopting the transformation dynamic of the gospel story, which includes the enduring realities of love, freedom, the image of God, the impartiality of God, and resurrection. This transforming gospel story, together with a dialogue with the sciences, exposes and rejects patriarchy, with its "equal but subordinate" scheme, as contrary to the Trinity, the image of God, the spirit of the gospel, and the story of life.

Unlike the issue of slavery, the church is still in the midst of this debate. As we have seen, the slavery debate was not finally decided by biblical argument. Rather, through changes in culture and the conscience of society, the whole church came to view slavery as inherently contrary to Christianity. It is likely that this will happen regarding this debate as well, and we will not finally solve these issues through theological, exegetical, and hermeneutical debate.

Every position has difficulties to explain. In addition, there are entrenched presuppositions that influence the course of interpretation. Professions once limited to men are becoming available to women. The church is moving toward women in leadership, a fact recognized by complementarians. Long-held views about the limited roles, capabilities, and strength of women are being eroded. As this continues, to view women as subordinate in any manner will become unacceptable to the whole church. And, in time, the names *Son* and *Father* will lose their perceived oppressive and sexist character. They will remain in use, for the church has never thrown away its text or its story.

We conclude that, in the incarnation, God honors both sexes, a position reaching back at least to Augustine[1]—by being born male, of a woman. "When the fullness of time had come, God sent his Son, born of a woman" (Galatians 4:4).

Bibliography

Ackermann, Denise. "Being Women, Being Human." In *Women Hold Up Half the Sky: Women in the Church in Southern Africa*, edited by Denise Ackermann, Jonathan A. Draper, and Emma Mashinini, 93–105. Pietermaritzburg, South Africa: Cluster Publications, 1991.
Aldredge-Clanton, Jann. *In Search of the Christ-Sophia: An Inclusive Christology for Liberating Christians*. Mystic, CT: Twenty-Third Publications, 1995.
Allen, Leslie C. *Ezekiel 20–48*. Word Biblical Commentary 29. Waco: Word, 1990.
Allender, Dan B. *To Be Told: Know Your Story—Shape Your Future*. Colorado Springs: WaterBrook, 2005.
Anderson, Ray S. "The Incarnation of God in Feminist Christology: A Theological Critique." In *Speaking the Christian God: The Holy Trinity and the Challenge of Feminism*, edited by Alvin F. Kimel, 288–312. Grand Rapids: Eerdmans, 1992.
Andreason, M. L. *The Sabbath: Which Day and Why?* Washington, DC: Review and Herald, 1942.
Andreason, Niels-Erik A. *The Old Testament Sabbath: A Tradition-Historical Investigation*. SBL Dissertation Series 7. Missoula, MT: Society of Biblical Literature, 1972.
Avis, Paul. *Eros and the Sacred*. London: SPCK, 1989.
Ayers, David, J. "The Inevitability of Failure: The Assumptions and Implementations of Modern Feminism." In *Recovering Biblical Manhood and Womanhood: A Response to Evangelical Feminism*, edited by John Piper and Wayne Grudem, 312–31. Wheaton, IL: Crossway, 1991.
Bacchiocchi, Samuele. *Divine Rest for Human Restlessness: A Theological Study of the Good News of the Sabbath for Today*. Berrien Springs, MI: Biblical Perspectives, 1988.
———. "From Sabbath to Sunday." In *The Biblical Day of Rest*, edited by Francois Swanepoel, 36–61. Pretoria, South Africa: UNISA, 1995.
———. *From Sabbath to Sunday: A Historical Investigation of the Rise of Sunday Observance in Early Christianity*. Rome: Pontifical Gregorian University Press, 1977.
Bahnsen, Greg L. *Theonomy in Christian Ethics*. 2nd ed. Phillipsburg, NJ: Presbyterian and Reformed, 1984.
Bailey, Kenneth E. *Poet and Peasant: A Literary Cultural Approach to the Parables in Luke*. Grand Rapids: Eerdmans, 1976.
Barnes, Albert. *Ephesians, Philippians, Colossians*. In *Barnes' Notes*, edited by Robert Frew. Grand Rapids: Baker, 1996 [1884–1885].
———. *An Inquiry into the Scriptural Views of Slavery*. New York: Negro Universities Press, 1969 [1857].
Barr, James. *The Semantics of Biblical Language*. 1961. Reprint, Eugene, OR: Wipf & Stock, 2004.

Barth, Karl. *Church Dogmatics*. Vol. 4, *The Doctrine of Reconciliation, 1*. Translated by Geoffrey W. Bromiley. New York: Scribner's, 1956.

Bauckham, Richard. *God Crucified: Monotheism and Christology in the New Testament*. Grand Rapids: Eerdmans, 1999.

Beckwith, Roger T., and Wilfrid Stott. *The Christian Sunday: A Biblical and Historical Study*. Grand Rapids: Baker, 1978.

Behe, Michael J. *Darwin's Black Box: The Biochemical Challenge to Evolution*. New York: Free Press, 1996.

Bell, Albert A. *Exploring the New Testament World: An Illustrated Guide to the World of Jesus and the First Christians*. Nashville: Nelson, 1998.

Berger, Teresa. "A Female Christ Child in the Manger and a Woman on the Cross, or: The Historicity of the Jesus Event and the Inculturation of the Gospel." *Feminist Theology* 11 (1996) 32–45.

Berkhof, Hendrikus. *Christian Faith: An Introduction to the Study of the Faith*. Translated by Sierd Woudstra. Grand Rapids: Eerdmans, 1979.

Bilezikian, Gilbert. *Beyond Sex Roles: What the Bible Says about a Woman's Place in Church and Family*. Grand Rapids: Baker, 1985.

———. "A Critique of Wayne Grudem's Treatment of *Kephale* in Ancient Greek Texts." Evangelical Theological Society Papers. Portland: Micropublished by Theological Research Exchange Network, 38th Annual Conference, 1986.

Blasberg-Kuhnke, Martina. "Jesus as Women See Him." *Theology Digest* 39 (1992) 205–8.

Bloesch, Donald G. *The Battle for the Trinity: The Debate over Inclusive God-Language*. Ann Arbor, MI: Servant, 1985.

———. *Is the Bible Sexist? Beyond Feminism and Patriarchalism*. Westchester, IL: Crossway, 1982.

Bloomquist, Karen. "'Let God Be God': The Theological Necessity of Depatriarchalizing God." In *Our Naming of God*, edited by Carl E. Braaten, 45–60. Minneapolis: Fortress, 1989.

Boff, Leonardo. *Trinity and Society*. Translated by Paul Burns. Maryknoll, NY: Orbis, 1988.

Boldrey, Richard, and Joyce Boldrey. *Chauvinist or Feminist? Paul's View of Women*. Grand Rapids: Baker, 1976.

Borgen, Peder. "Logos Was the True Light: Contributions to the Interpretation of the Prologue of John." *Novum Testamentum* 14 (1972) 115–30.

Børresen, Kari E. "Women's Studies of the Christian Tradition: New Perspectives." In *Religion and Gender*, edited by Ursula King, 245–55. Oxford: Blackwell, 1995.

Boström, Lennart. *The God of the Sages: The Portrayal of God in the Book of Proverbs*. Coniectanea Biblica: Old Testament Series 29. Stockholm: Almqvist & Wiksell, 1990.

Brace, C. Loring. "Human Emergence: Natural Process or Divine Creation?" In *Scientists Confront Intelligent Design and Creationism*, edited by Andrew J. Petto and Laurie R. Godfrey, 272–306. New York: Norton, 2007.

Brock, Rita. "A Feminist Consciousness Looks at Christology." *Encounter* 41 (1980) 319–31.

Brown, Harold O. J. "The New Testament Against Itself: 1 Timothy 2:9–15 and the 'Breakthrough' of Galatians 3:28." In *Women in the Church: A Fresh Analysis of 1 Timothy 2:9–15*, edited by Andreas J. Köstenberger, Thomas R. Schreiner, and H. Scott Baldwin, 197–208. Grand Rapids: Baker, 1995.

Brownlee, William H. *Ezekiel 1–19*. Word Biblical Commentary 28. Waco: Word, 1986.

Bruce, F. F. "The Background to the Son of Man Sayings." In *Christ the Lord: Studies in Christology Presented to Donald Guthrie*, edited by Harold H. Rowdon, 50–70. Leicester, UK: Inter-Varsity, 1982.

Calvin, John. *The Library of Christian Classics, Vol. XX*, edited by John T. McNeill. Vol. 1, *Calvin: Institutes of the Christian Religion*. Translated by Ford L. Battles. Philadelphia: Westminster, 1960.

———. *Commentaries on the First Book of Moses Called Genesis*. Translated by John King. Grand Rapids: Baker, 1993.

Carmody, Denise L. *Christian Feminist Theology*. Oxford: Blackwell, 1995.

———. *Responses to 101 Questions about Feminism*. London: Chapman, 1994.

Carr, Anne. "Is a Christian Feminist Theology Possible?" *Theological Studies* 43 (1982) 279–97.
Carroll, Sean B. *Endless Forms Most Beautiful: The New Science of Evo Devo and the Making of the Animal Kingdom.* New York: Norton, 2005.
Carson, D. A. "Christological Ambiguities in the Gospel of Matthew." In *Christ the Lord: Studies in Christology Presented to Donald Guthrie*, edited by Harold H. Rowdon, 97–114. Leicester, UK: Inter-Varsity, 1982.
———. *Exegetical Fallacies.* Grand Rapids: Baker, 1984.
———. *The Inclusive Language Debate: A Plea for Realism.* Grand Rapids: Baker, 1998.
———. "Introduction." In *From Sabbath to Lord's Day: A Biblical, Historical, and Theological Investigation*, edited by D. A. Carson, 13–19. Grand Rapids: Zondervan, 1982.
———. "'Silent in the Churches': On the Role of Women in 1 Corinthians 14:33b–36." In *Recovering Biblical Manhood and Womanhood: A Response to Evangelical Feminism*, edited by John Piper and Wayne Grudem, 140–53. Wheaton, IL: Crossway, 1991.
Chopp, Rebecca S. *The Power to Speak: Feminism, Language, God.* New York: Crossroad, 1989.
Christ, Carol P. *Rebirth of the Goddess: Finding Meaning in Feminist Spirituality.* Reading, MA: Addison-Wesley, 1997.
———. "Why Women Need the Goddess: Phenomenological, Psychological, and Political Reflections." In *Womanspirit Rising: A Feminist Reader in Religion*, edited by Carol P. Christ and Judith Plaskow, 273–87. New York: Harper & Row, 1979.
Christianity Today editorial. "He Meant What He Said: 'Him, His, He.'" January 2, 1976, 22.
Clowney, Edmund P. *The Church.* Contours of Christian Theology series, edited by Gerald Bray. Downers Grove, IL: InterVarsity, 1995.
Cobb, Jimmy G. "A Study of White Protestants' Attitudes toward Negroes in Charleston, South Carolina 1790–1845." PhD diss., Baylor University, 1976.
Coetzee, Christi. "The New Testament Day of Rest/Feast Day." In *The Biblical Day of Rest*, edited by Francois Swanepoel, 73–86. Pretoria, South Africa: UNISA, 1995.
Collins, Francis S. *The Language of God: A Scientist Presents Evidence for Belief.* New York: Free Press, 2007.
Conway Morris, Simon. *Life's Solution: Inevitable Humans in a Lonely Universe.* Cambridge: Cambridge University Press, 2003.
Cooke, Bernard. "Non-Patriarchal Salvation." *Horizons* 10 (1983): 22–32.
Corrington, Gail P. *Her Image of Salvation: Female Saviors and Formative Christianity.* Louisville: Westminster John Knox, 1992.
Cranfield, C. E. B. *A Critical and Exegetical Commentary on the Epistle to the Romans*, vol. 1. International Critical Commentary. Edinburgh: T & T Clark, 1975.
Crenshaw, James L. *Old Testament Wisdom: An Introduction.* London: SCM, 1982.
Cross, F. L., and E. A. Livingstone, editors. *The Oxford Dictionary of the Christian Church.* 3rd ed. rev. Oxford: Oxford University Press, 2005.
Cullmann, Oscar. *The Christology of the New Testament.* Translated by Shirley C. Guthrie and Charles A. M. Hall. 2nd ed. London: SCM, 1963.
———. "The Reply of Professor Cullmann to Roman Catholic Critics." *Scottish Journal of Theology* 15 (1962) 36–43.
Dabney, Robert L. *Discussions of Robert Lewis Dabney.* Vol. 2 and 3. Edinburgh: Banner of Truth, 1982.
Dahms, John V. "The Subordination of the Son." *Journal of the Evangelical Theological Society* 37. (1994) 351–64.
Dalrymple, G. Brent. "The Ages of the Earth, Solar System, Galaxy, and Universe." In *Scientists Confront Intelligent Design and Creationism*, edited by Andrew J. Petto and Laurie R. Godfrey, 150–79. New York: Norton, 2007.
Daly, Mary. *Beyond God the Father.* London: Women's Press, 1986.
———. *The Church and the Second Sex.* New York: Harper & Row, 1968.
———. *Gyn/Ecology: The Metaethics of Radical Feminism.* London: Women's Press, 1991.

Darwin, Charles. *The Descent of Man, and Selection in Relation to Sex.* In *From So Simple a Beginning: The Four Great Books of Charles Darwin,* edited by Edward O. Wilson. New York: Norton, 2006 [1871].

———. *On the Origin of Species.* In *From So Simple a Beginning: The Four Great Books of Charles Darwin,* edited by Edward O. Wilson. New York: Norton, 2006 [1859].

David, Immanuel S. "What Are They Saying about Christian Feminism?" *Africa Theological Journal* 20 (1991): 210–22.

Davis, David Brion. *Inhuman Bondage: The Rise and Fall of Slavery in the New World.* Oxford: Oxford University Press, 2006.

Dawkins, Richard. *The Ancestor's Tale: A Pilgrimage to the Dawn of Evolution.* New York: Mariner, 2004.

de Lacey, D. R. "The Sabbath/Sunday Question and the Law in the Pauline Corpus." In *From Sabbath to Lord's Day: A Biblical, Historical, and Theological Investigation,* edited by D. A. Carson, 159–95. Grand Rapids: Zondervan, 1982.

Dederen, Raoul. "On Esteeming One Day as Better Than Another—Romans 14:5, 6." In *The Sabbath in Scripture and History,* edited by Kenneth A. Strand, 333–37. Washington, DC: Review and Herald, 1982.

DeJong, Peter, and Donald R. Wilson. *Husband and Wife: The Sexes in Scripture and Society.* Grand Rapids: Zondervan, 1979.

Dembski, William A. *The Design Revolution: Answering the Toughest Questions about Intelligent Design.* Downers Grove, IL: InterVarsity, 2004.

DeSalle, Rob, and Ian Tattersall. *Human Origins: What Bones and Genomes Tell Us about Ourselves.* College Station, TX: Texas A&M University Press, 2008.

Diamond, Jared. *Why Is Sex Fun? The Evolution of Human Sexuality.* New York: Basic Books, 1997.

Dinter, Paul E. "Christ's Body as Male and Female." *Cross Currents* 44 (1994) 390–99.

Douma, J. *The Ten Commandments: Manual for the Christian Life.* Translated by Nelson D. Kloosterman. Phillipsburg, NJ: Presbyterian & Reformed, 1996.

Dowell, Susan, and Linda Hurcombe. *Dispossessed Daughters of Eve: Faith and Feminism.* Rev. ed. London: SPCK, 1987.

Dressler, Harold H. P. "The Sabbath in the Old Testament." In *From Sabbath to Lord's Day: A Biblical, Historical, and Theological Investigation,* edited by D. A. Carson, 21–41. Grand Rapids: Zondervan, 1982.

Dumond, Dwight L. *Antislavery Origins of the Civil War in the United States.* Ann Arbor, MI: University of Michigan Press, 1959.

Dunn, James D. G. *Christianity in the Making.* Vol. 1, *Jesus Remembered.* Grand Rapids: Eerdmans, 2003.

———. *Christology in the Making: A New Testament Inquiry into the Origins of the Doctrine of the Incarnation.* London: SCM, 1980.

———. *Romans 1–8.* Word Biblical Commentary 38A. Waco: Word, 1988.

Edwards, F. "God from a Feminist Perspective." In *Sexism and Feminism in Theological Perspective,* edited by W. S. Vorster, 36–57. Miscellanea Congregalia 24. Pretoria, South Africa: University of South Africa, 1984.

Eller, Vernard. *The Language of Canaan and the Grammar of Feminism.* Grand Rapids: Eerdmans, 1982.

Elliot, Elisabeth. "The Essence of Femininity: A Personal Perspective." In *Recovering Biblical Manhood and Womanhood: A Response to Evangelical Feminism,* edited by John Piper and Wayne Grudem, 394–99. Wheaton, IL: Crossway, 1991.

Ellis, Carl F. *Free at Last? The Gospel in the African-American Experience.* 2nd ed. Downers Grove, IL: InterVarsity, 1996.

Engelsman, Joan C. *The Feminine Dimension of the Divine.* Philadelphia: Westminster, 1979.

Erickson, Millard J. *God in Three Persons: A Contemporary Interpretation of the Trinity.* Grand Rapids: Baker, 1995.

Ermarth, Margaret Sittler. *Adam's Fractured Rib.* Philadelphia: Fortress, 1970.

Evans, Mary J. *Woman in the Bible*. Carlisle, UK: Paternoster, 1983.
Fairbanks, Daniel J. *Relics of Eden: The Powerful Evidence of Evolution in Human DNA*. Amherst, NY: Prometheus, 2007.
Farley, Margaret A. "Feminist Consciousness and the Interpretation of Scripture." In *Feminist Interpretation of the Bible*, edited by Letty M. Russell, 41–51. Oxford: Basil Blackwell, 1985.
Fee, Gordon D. *The First Epistle to the Corinthians*. New International Commentary on the New Testament. Grand Rapids: Eerdmans, 1987.
Feynman, Richard. *The Pleasure of Finding Things Out: The Best Short Works of Richard Feynman*. Cambridge, MA: Perseus, 1999.
Foh, Susan T. *Women and the Word of God: A Response to Biblical Feminism*. Phillipsburg, NJ: Presbyterian & Reformed, 1980.
Foster, Ruth A. "The Role of Feminine Language and Imagery for God in the Development of a New Testament View of God." PhD diss., Southwestern Baptist Theological Seminary, 1989.
Frame, John M. *The Doctrine of God*. Phillipsburg, NJ: Presbyterian & Reformed, 2002.
———. *The Doctrine of the Knowledge of God*. Phillipsburg, NJ: Presbyterian & Reformed, 1987.
———. "Men and Women in the Image of God." In *Recovering Biblical Manhood and Womanhood: A Response to Evangelical Feminism*, edited by John Piper and Wayne Grudem, 225–32. Wheaton, IL: Crossway, 1991.
Freed, Edwin D. *Old Testament Quotations in the Gospel of John*. Supplements to Novum Testamentum 11. Leiden: Brill, 1965.
Frye, Roland M. "Language for God and Feminist Language: Problems and Principles." *Scottish Journal of Theology* 41 (1988): 441–69.
———. "Language for God and Feminist Language: Problems and Principles." In *Speaking the Christian God: The Holy Trinity and the Challenge of Feminism*, edited by Alvin F. Kimel, 17–43. Grand Rapids: Eerdmans, 1992.
Furnish, Victor P. "'He Gave Himself [Was Given] Up . . .': Paul's Use of a Christological Assertion." In *The Future of Christology*, edited by Abraham J. Malherbe and Wayne A. Meeks, 109–21. Minneapolis: Fortress, 1993.
Gaffin, Richard B. "Calvin and the Sabbath." MTh thesis, Westminster Theological Seminary, 1962, reprinted in 1981 with new pagination.
———. *Resurrection and Redemption: A Study in Paul's Soteriology*. Phillipsburg, NJ: Presbyterian & Reformed, 1987.
Gese, Hartmut. "Der Johannesprolog." In *Zur Biblischen Theologie: Alttestamentliche Vorträge*, 152–201. Beiträge zur evangelischen Theologie 78. Munich: Kaiser, 1977.
———. "Wisdom, Son of Man, and the Origins of Christology: The Consistent Development of Biblical Theology." *Horizons in Biblical Theology* 3 (1981) 23–57.
Gibson, Joan. "Could Christ Have Been Born a Woman? A Medieval Debate." *Journal of Feminist Studies in Religion* 8 (Spring 1992) 65–82.
Giles, Kevin. "The Biblical Argument for Slavery: Can the Bible Mislead? A Case Study in Hermeneutics." *Evangelical Quarterly* 66 (1994) 3–17.
———. *Jesus and the Father: Modern Evangelicals Reinvent the Doctrine of the Trinity*. Grand Rapids: Zondervan, 2006.
———. *The Trinity and Subordinationism: The Doctrine of God and the Contemporary Gender Debate*. Downers Grove, IL: InterVarsity, 2002.
Glancy, Jennifer A. *Slavery in Early Christianity*. Minneapolis: Fortress, 2006.
Goldberg, Steven. *Why Men Rule: A Theory of Male Dominance*. Chicago: Open Court, 1993.
Goldenberg, Naomi R. *Changing of the Gods: Feminism and the End of Traditional Religions*. Boston: Beacon, 1979.
———. *Returning Words to Flesh: Feminism, Psychoanalysis, and the Resurrection of the Body*. Boston: Beacon, 1990.
Goppelt, Leonhard. *Theology of the New Testament*. Vol. 1. Translated by John E. Alsup. Grand Rapids: Eerdmans, 1981.

Grant, Jacquelyn. *White Women's Christ and Black Women's Jesus: Feminist Christology and Womanist Reponse*. Atlanta: Scholars, 1989.

Greene, Brian. *The Elegant Universe: Superstrings, Hidden Dimensions, and the Quest for the Ultimate Theory*. New York: Vintage, 1999.

———. *The Fabric of the Cosmos: Space, Time, and the Texture of Reality*. New York: Knopf, 2004.

Grenz, Stanley J., and Denise M. Kjesbo. *Women in the Church: A Biblical Theology of Women in Ministry*. Downers Grove, IL: InterVarsity, 1995.

Groothuis, Rebecca M. *Good News for Women: A Biblical Picture of Gender Equality*. Grand Rapids: Baker, 1997.

Grudem, Wayne. *Evangelical Feminism: A New Path to Liberalism?* Wheaton, IL: Crossway, 2006.

———. "The Meaning of *Kephale* ('Head'): A Response to Recent Studies." In *Recovering Biblical Manhood and Womanhood: A Response to Evangelical Feminism*, edited by John Piper and Wayne Grudem, 425–68. Wheaton, IL: Crossway, 1991.

———. *Systematic Theology*. Grand Rapids: Zondervan, 1994.

———. "Wives Like Sarah, and the Husbands Who Honor Them: 1 Peter 3:1–7." In *Recovering Biblical Manhood and Womanhood: A Response to Evangelical Feminism*, edited by John Piper and Wayne Grudem, 194–208. Wheaton, IL: Crossway, 1991.

Gundry, Patricia. *Women Be Free!* Grand Rapids: Zondervan, 1977.

Haas, Guenther. "Patriarchy as an Evil That God Tolerated: Analysis and Implications for the Authority of Scripture." *Journal of the Evangelical Theological Society* 38 (1995) 321–36.

Halkes, Catharina. "The Rape of Mother Earth: Ecology and Patriarchy." In *Motherhood: Experience, Institution, Theology*, edited by Anne Carr and Elisabeth Schüssler Fiorenza, 91–100. Edinburgh: T. & T. Clark, 1989.

Hampson, Daphne. *After Christianity*. Valley Forge, PA: Trinity, 1996.

———. "The Challenge of Feminism [Rejoinder to P. Avis, 90: 46–50, January 1987]." *Theology* 90 (1987) 220.

———. "The Challenge of Feminism to Christianity." *Theology* 88 (1985) 341–50.

———. "On Autonomy and Heteronomy." In *Swallowing a Fishbone: Feminist Theologians Debate Christianity*, edited by Daphne Hampson, 1–16. London: SPCK, 1996.

———. *Theology and Feminism*. Oxford: Blackwell, 1990.

Hardesty, Nancy A. *Women Called to Witness: Evangelical Feminism in the 19th Century*. Nashville: Abingdon, 1984.

Harrill, J. Albert. "Slavery." In *Dictionary of New Testament Background*, edited by Craig A. Evans and Stanley E. Porter, 1124–27. Downers Grove, IL: InterVarsity, 2000.

———. *Slaves in the New Testament: Literary, Social, and Moral Dimensions*. Minneapolis: Fortress, 2006.

Harris, Murray J. *Jesus as God: The New Testament Use of* Theos *in Reference to Jesus*. Grand Rapids: Baker, 1992.

Harris, Rendel. *The Origin of the Prologue to St John's Gospel*. Cambridge: Cambridge University Press, 1917.

Hasel, Gerhard F. "The Sabbath in the Pentateuch." In *The Sabbath in Scripture and History*, edited by Kenneth A. Strand, 21–43. Washington, DC: Review and Herald, 1982.

Haught, John F. *Christianity and Science: Toward a Theology of Nature*. Maryknoll, NY: Orbis, 2007.

———. *God After Darwin: A Theology of Evolution*. 2nd ed. Boulder, CO: Westview, 2008.

Hays, Richard B. *Echoes of Scripture in the Letters of Paul*. New Haven: Yale University Press, 1989.

———. *The Moral Vision of the New Testament: A Contemporary Introduction to New Testament Ethics*. New York: HarperCollins, 1996.

Heine, Susanne. *Women and Early Christianity: Are the Feminist Scholars Right?* Translated by John Bowden. London: SCM, 1987.

Heyward, Carter. "Jesus of Nazareth/Christ of Faith: Foundations of a Reactive Christology." In *Lift Every Voice: Constructing Christian Theologies from the Underside*, edited by Susan B. Thistlethwaite and Mary P. Engel, 191–200. San Francisco: Harper & Row, 1990.

Highby, Patricia D. "Toward a Feminist Trinitarian Doctrine of God." PhD diss., Iliff School of Theology and the University of Denver, 1992.
Hinga, Teresa M. "Jesus Christ and the Liberation of Women in Africa." In *The Will to Arise*, edited by Mercy A. Oduyoye and Musimbi R. A. Kanyoro, 183–94. Maryknoll, NY: Orbis, 1992.
Hitchens, Christopher. *God Is Not Great: How Religion Poisons Everything*. New York: Twelve, 2007.
Hodge, Charles. *Systematic Theology*. Vol. 1. 1871. Reprint, Grand Rapids: Eerdmans, 1993.
Hopkins, John H. *A Scriptural, Ecclesiastical, and Historical View of Slavery, from the Days of the Patriarch Abraham, to the Nineteenth Century*. New York: Negro Universities Press, [1864] 1969.
Hopkins, Julie M. *Towards a Feminist Christology: Jesus of Nazareth, European Women and the Christological Crisis*. Kampen, Netherlands: Kok Pharos, 1994.
Humes, Edward. *Monkey Girl: Evolution, Education, Religion, and the Battle for America's Soul*. New York: Harper Perennial, 2008.
Hurley, James B. *Man and Woman in Biblical Perspective*. Leicester, UK: InterVarsity, 1981.
Jastrow, Robert. *God and the Astronomers*. New York: Norton, 1978.
Jenson, Robert W. *Systematic Theology*. Vol. 1, *The Triune God*. New York: Oxford University Press, 1997.
Jeremias, Joachim. *New Testament Theology: Part One, the Proclamation of Jesus*. Translated by John Bowden. London: SCM, 1971.
Jewett, Paul K. *God, Creation, and Revelation: A Neo-Evangelical Theology*. Grand Rapids: Eerdmans, 1991.
———. *The Lord's Day: A Theological Guide to the Christian Day of Worship*. Grand Rapids: Eerdmans, 1971.
———. *Man as Male and Female: A Study in Sexual Relationships from a Theological Point of View*. Grand Rapids: Eerdmans, 1975.
———. *The Ordination of Women: An Essay on the Office of Christian Ministry*. Grand Rapids: Eerdmans, 1980.
Johnson, Elizabeth A. "The Incomprehensibility of God and the Image of God Male and Female." *Theological Studies* 45 (1984) 441–65.
———. "Jesus the Wisdom of God: A Biblical Basis for Non-Androcentric Christology." *Ephemerides Theologicae Lovanienses* 61 (1985) 261–94.
———. "Redeeming the Name of Christ." In *Freeing Theology: The Essentials of Theology in Feminist Perspective*, edited by Catherine Mowry LaCugna, 115–37. New York: HarperCollins, 1993.
———. "Wisdom Was Made Flesh and Pitched Her Tent Among Us." In *Reconstructing the Christ Symbol: Essays in Feminist Christology*, edited by Maryanne Stevens, 95–117. Mahwah, NJ: Paulist, 1993.
Johnson, Phillip E. *Darwin on Trial*. Downers Grove, IL: InterVarsity, 1991.
Johnson, S. Lewis. "Role Distinctions in the Church: Galatians 3:28." In *Recovering Biblical Manhood and Womanhood: A Response to Evangelical Feminism*, edited by John Piper and Wayne Grudem, 154–64. Wheaton, IL: Crossway, 1991.
Käsemann, Ernst. *Commentary on Romans*. Translated by Geoffrey W. Bromiley. Grand Rapids: Eerdmans, 1980.
Kassian, Mary A. *The Feminist Gospel: The Movement to Unite Feminism with the Church*. Wheaton, IL: Crossway, 1992.
Kelly, J. N. D. *Early Christian Doctrines*. Rev. ed. San Francisco: Harper & Row, 1978.
Keylock, Leslie R. "God Our Father *and* Mother? A Bisexual Nightmare from the National Council of Churches." *Christianity Today*, November 11, 1983, 50–51.
Kline, Meredith G. *Treaty of the Great King: The Covenant Structure of Deuteronomy: Studies and Commentary*. Grand Rapids: Eerdmans, 1963.
Knight, George W., III. "Husbands and Wives as Analogues of Christ and the Church: Ephesians 5:21–33 and Colossians 3:18–19." In *Recovering Biblical Manhood and Womanhood: A Response to Evangelical Feminism*, edited by John Piper and Wayne Grudem, 165–78. Wheaton: Crossway, 1991.

———. *The New Testament Teaching on the Role Relationship of Men and Women.* Grand Rapids: Baker, 1977.

Knox, David B. *Sent by Jesus: Some Aspects of Christian Ministry Today.* Edinburgh: Banner of Truth, 1992.

König, Adrio. "Die Manlikheid Van God." *Ned. Geref. Teologiese Tydskrif* 33 (1992) 81–93.

———. *Menslike Mense.* Halfway House: Orion, 1993.

———. "Sabbath and Sanctification." In *The Biblical Day of Rest,* edited by Francois Swanepoel, 87–92. Pretoria, South Africa: UNISA, 1995.

———. *Sondag: Die Dag Van die Here.* Pretoria, South Africa: Kerk, 1964.

Krauss, Lawrence M., and Robert J. Scherrer. "The End of Cosmology?" *Scientific American,* March 2008, 47–53.

Kroeger, Catherine C., and Richard C. Kroeger. *I Suffer not a Woman: Rethinking 1 Timothy 2:11–15 in Light of Ancient Evidence.* Grand Rapids: Baker, 1992.

Kuhn, Thomas S. *The Structure of Scientific Revolutions.* 4th ed. Chicago: University of Chicago Press, 1970.

Kysar, Robert. "The Background of the Prologue of the Fourth Gospel: A Critique of Historical Methods." *Canadian Journal of Theology* 16 (1970) 250–55.

LaCugna, Catherine M. *God for Us: The Trinity and Christian Life.* New York: HarperCollins, 1991.

———. "God in Communion with Us." In *Freeing Theology: The Essentials of Theology in Feminist Perspective,* edited by Catherine Mowry LaCugna, 83–114. New York: HarperCollins, 1993.

Ladd, George E. *A Theology of the New Testament.* Grand Rapids: Eerdmans, 1974.

Lamb, Simon, and David Sington. *Earth Story: The Shaping of Our World.* Princeton: Princeton University Press, 1998.

Lane, William L. *Hebrews 1–8.* Word Biblical Commentary 47A. Dallas: Word, 1991.

LaPlante, Eve. *Salem Witch Judge: The Life and Repentance of Samuel Sewall.* New York: HarperCollins, 2007.

LaRondelle, Hans K. "Contemporary Theologies of the Sabbath." In *The Sabbath in Scripture and History,* edited by Kenneth A. Strand, 278–94. Washington, DC: Review and Herald, 1982.

Lebo, Lauri. *The Devil in Dover: An Insider's Story of Dogma v. Darwin in Small-Town America.* New York: New Press, 2008.

Letham, Robert. "The Man-Woman Debate: Theological Comment." *Westminster Theological Journal* 52 (Spring 1990) 65–78.

Lewis, C. S. "Priestesses in the Church?" In *God in the Dock: Essays on Theology,* edited by Walter Hooper, 87–94. Glasgow: Fount Paperbacks, 1979.

Lincoln, Andrew T. *Ephesians.* Word Biblical Commentary 42. Dallas: Word, 1990.

———. "From Sabbath to Lord's Day: A Biblical and Theological Perspective." In *From Sabbath to Lord's Day: A Biblical, Historical, and Theological Investigation,* edited by D. A. Carson, 343–412. Grand Rapids: Zondervan, 1982.

———. "Sabbath, Rest, and Eschatology in the New Testament." In *From Sabbath to Lord's Day: A Biblical, Historical, and Theological Investigation,* edited by D. A. Carson, 197–220. Grand Rapids: Zondervan, 1982.

Litfin, A. Duane. "Evangelical Feminism: Why Traditionalists Reject It." *Bibliotheca Sacra* 136 (1979) 258–71.

Longenecker, Bruce W. *The Triumph of Abraham's God: The Transformation of Identity in Galatians.* Nashville: Abingdon, 1998.

Longenecker, Richard N. *New Testament Social Ethics for Today.* Grand Rapids: Eerdmans, 1984.

Longman, Tremper, III. *Proverbs.* Grand Rapids: Baker, 2006.

Louw, Johannes P., and Eugene A. Nida. *Greek-English Lexicon of the New Testament Based upon Semantic Domains.* Vol. 2. New York: United Bible Societies, 1988.

Lovejoy, Arthur O. *The Great Chain of Being: A Study of the History of an Idea.* Cambridge: Harvard University Press, 1936.

Lyles, Jean C. "The God-Language Bind." *The Christian Century,* April 16, 1980.

Macquarrie, John. *Jesus Christ in Modern Thought.* London: SCM, 1990.

Maddox, John. *What Remains to Be Discovered: Mapping the Secrets of the Universe, the Origins of Life, and the Future of the Human Race*. London: Macmillan, 1998.
Manning, Chandra. *What This Cruel War Was Over: Soldiers, Slavery, and the Civil War*. New York: Knopf, 2007.
Marshall, I. Howard. *The Origins of New Testament Christology*. Leicester, UK: Inter-Varsity, 1976.
Maynard Smith, John. "The Evolution of Sex." In *The Evolution of Sex*, edited by Robert Bellig and George Stevens, 3–20. New York: Harper & Row, 1988.
McFague, Sallie. "Human Beings, Embodiment, and Our Home the Earth." In *Reconstructing Christian Theology*, edited by Rebecca S. Chopp and Mark L. Taylor, 141–69. Minneapolis: Fortress, 1994.
———. *Metaphorical Theology: Models of God in Religious Language*. London: SCM, 1982.
———. *Models of God: Theology for an Ecological, Nuclear Age*. Philadelphia: Fortress, 1987.
McKane, William. *Proverbs: A New Approach*. Old Testament Library. London: SCM, 1970.
McLaughlin, Eleanor. "Christology in Dialogue with Feminist Ideology—Bodies and Boundaries." In *Christology in Dialogue*, edited by Robert F. Berkey and Sarah A. Edwards, 308–39. Cleveland: Pilgrim, 1993.
McPherson, James M. *Battle Cry of Freedom: The Civil War Era*. New York: Oxford University Press, 1988.
———. *The Struggle for Equality: Abolitionists and the Negro in the Civil War and Reconstruction*. Princeton: Princeton University Press, 1964.
Miller, Kenneth R. *Finding Darwin's God: A Scientist's Search for Common Ground Between God and Evolution*. New York: Harper Perennial, 2007.
———. *Only a Theory: Evolution and the Battle for America's Soul*. New York: Viking, 2008.
Moll, Helmut. "Faithful to Her Lord's Example: On the Meaning of the Male Priesthood in the Catholic Church." In *The Church and Women: A Compendium*, edited by Helmut Moll, 161–76. San Francisco: Ignatius, 1988.
Mollenkott, Virginia R. *The Divine Feminine: The Biblical Imagery of God as Female*. New York: Crossroad, 1983.
———. "Unlimiting God: To Unlimit God Is to Unlimit Ourselves." *Other Side* 146 (November 1983) 11–14.
———. "Women and the Bible: A Challenge to Male Interpretation." *Sojourners* 5 (Fall 1976) 21–25.
———. *Women, Men, and the Bible*. Nashville: Abingdon, 1977.
Moltmann, Jürgen. "Is There Life after Death?" In *The End of the World and the Ends of God*, edited by John Polkinghorne and Michael Welker, 238–55. Harrisburg, PA: Trinity, 2000.
———. "The Motherly Father: Is Trinitarian Patripassianism Replacing Theological Patriarchalism?" In *God as Father?* edited by Johannes-Baptist Metz and Edward Schillebeeckx, 51–56. New York: Seabury, 1981.
———. *The Way of Jesus Christ: Christology in Messianic Dimensions*. Translated by Margaret Kohl. London: SCM, 1990.
Moltmann-Wendel, Elisabeth. *A Land Flowing with Milk and Honey: Perspectives on Feminist Theology*. Translated by John Bowden. London: SCM, 1986.
Moltmann-Wendel, Elisabeth, and Jürgen Moltmann. *God—His and Hers*. London: SCM, 1991.
Moo, Douglas. "What Does It Mean not to Teach or Have Authority over Men? 1 Timothy 2:11–15." In *Recovering Biblical Manhood and Womanhood: A Response to Evangelical Feminism*, edited by John Piper and Wayne Grudem, 179–93. Wheaton: Crossway, 1991.
Moule, C. F. D. *The Origin of Christology*. Cambridge: Cambridge University Press, 1977.
Murray, John. *Collected Writings of John Murray*. Vol. 1, *The Claims of Truth*. Edinburgh: Banner of Truth, 1976.
———. *Principles of Conduct: Aspects of Biblical Ethics*. Grand Rapids: Eerdmans, 1957.
Nolan, Brian M. *The Royal Son of God: The Christology of Matthew 1–2 in the Setting of the Gospel*. Fribourg, Switzerland: Editions Universitaires, 1979.

Noll, Mark A. *The Civil War as a Theological Crisis*. Chapel Hill: University of North Carolina Press, 2006.

Nolland, John. *Luke 1—9:20*. Word Biblical Commentary 35A. Waco: Word, 1989.

Norris, Richard A. "The Ordination of Women and the 'Maleness' of Christ." *Anglican Theological Review Supplement Series* 6 (1976) 69–80.

Ochs, Carol. *Behind the Sex of God: Toward a New Consciousness-Transcending Matriarchy and Patriarchy*. Boston: Beacon, 1977.

Oddie, William. *What Will Happen to God? Feminism and the Reconstruction of Christian Belief*. London: SPCK, 1984.

Oden, Thomas C. *Systematic Theology*. Vol. 2, *The Word of Life*. San Francisco: HarperCollins, 1989.

Oduyoye, Mercy A. *Daughters of Anowa: African Women and Patriarchy*. Maryknoll, NY: Orbis, 1995.

Ortlund, Raymond C. "Male-Female Equality and Male Headship." In *Recovering Biblical Manhood and Womanhood: A Response to Evangelical Feminism*, edited by John Piper and Wayne Grudem, 95–112. Wheaton, IL: Crossway, 1991.

Packer, James I. "Let's Stop Making Women Presbyters." *Christianity Today*, February 11, 1991, 18–21.

Pannenberg, Wolfhart. *Systematic Theology*. Vol. 1. Translated by Geoffrey W. Bromiley. Grand Rapids: Eerdmans, 1991.

Patterson, Dorothy. "Aspects of a Biblical Theology of Womanhood." DTh diss., University of South Africa, 1997.

Patterson, Paige. "The Meaning of Authority in the Local Church." In *Recovering Biblical Manhood and Womanhood: A Response to Evangelical Feminism*, edited by John Piper and Wayne Grudem, 248–59. Wheaton, IL: Crossway, 1991.

Peacocke, Arthur. *Theology for a Scientific Age: Being and Becoming—Natural, Divine, and Human*. Minneapolis: Fortress, 1993.

Pennock, Robert T. *Tower of Babel: The Evidence Against the New Creationism*. Cambridge, MA: MIT Press, 2000.

Petto, Andrew J., and Laurie R. Godfrey, eds. *Scientists Confront Intelligent Design and Creationism*. New York: Norton, 2007.

Piper, John. "A Vision of Biblical Complementarity: Manhood and Womanhood Defined According to the Bible." In *Recovering Biblical Manhood and Womanhood: A Response to Evangelical Feminism*, edited by John Piper and Wayne Grudem, 31–59. Wheaton, IL: Crossway, 1991.

Piper, John, and Wayne Grudem. "Charity, Clarity, and Hope: The Controversy and the Cause of Christ." In *Recovering Biblical Manhood and Womanhood: A Response to Evangelical Feminism*, edited by John Piper and Wayne Grudem, 403–22. Wheaton, IL: Crossway, 1991.

———. "An Overview of Central Concerns: Questions and Answers." In *Recovering Biblical Manhood and Womanhood: A Response to Evangelical Feminism*, edited by John Piper and Wayne Grudem, 60–92. Wheaton, IL: Crossway, 1991.

———, editors. *Recovering Biblical Manhood and Womanhood: A Response to Evangelical Feminism*. Wheaton: Crossway, 1991.

Plantinga, Cornelius, Jr. "Social Trinity and Tritheism." In *Trinity, Incarnation, and Atonement: Philosophical and Theological Essays*, edited by Ronald J. Feenstra and Cornelius Plantinga Jr., 21–47. Notre Dame, IN: University of Notre Dame Press, 1989.

Plaskow, Judith. *Sex, Sin and Grace: Women's Experience and the Theologies of Reinhold Niebuhr and Paul Tillich*. Lanham, MD: University Press of America, 1980.

Polkinghorne, John. *Belief in God in an Age of Science*. New Haven: Yale University Press, 1998.

———. *Science and Theology: An Introduction*. Minneapolis: Fortress, 1998.

Poythress, Vern S. "The Church as Family: Why Male Leadership in the Family Requires Male Leadership in the Church." In *Recovering Biblical Manhood and Womanhood: A Response to Evangelical Feminism*, edited by John Piper and Wayne Grudem, 233–47. Wheaton, IL: Crossway, 1991.

———. *Symphonic Theology: The Validity of Multiple Perspectives in Theology.* Grand Rapids: Zondervan, 1987.

———. "Two Hermeneutical Tensions in Evangelical Feminism." Paper presented at the Eastern Regional ETS Conference. Philadelphia, April 5, 1991.

Prothero, Donald R. *Evolution: What the Fossils Say and Why It Matters.* New York: Columbia University Press, 2007.

Reid, Brian H. "American Civil War." In *The Oxford Companion to Military History*, edited by Richard Holmes, 35–40. Oxford: Oxford University Press, 2001.

Repcheck, Jack. *The Man Who Found Time: James Hutton and the Discovery of the Earth's Antiquity.* Cambridge, MA: Perseus, 2003.

Ridderbos, Herman. *The Coming of the Kingdom.* Translated by H. de Jongste. Philadelphia: Presbyterian & Reformed, 1962.

Ridley, Mark. *Evolution.* Oxford: Blackwell, 2004.

Ridley, Matt. *The Red Queen: Sex and the Evolution of Human Nature.* New York: Harper Perennial, 2003.

Roughgarden, Joan. *Evolution's Rainbow: Diversity, Gender, and Sexuality in Nature and People.* Berkeley: University of California Press, 2004.

Ruether, Rosemary R. "Can Christology Be Liberated from Patriarchy?" In *Reconstructing the Christ Symbol: Essays in Feminist Christology*, edited by Maryanne Stevens, 7–29. Mahwah, NJ: Paulist, 1993.

———. "Feminism and Patriarchal Religion: Principles of Ideological Critique of the Bible." *Journal for the Study of the Old Testament* 22 (1982) 54–66.

———. "Feminist Theology and Spirituality." In *Christian Feminism: Visions of a New Humanity*, edited by Judith L. Weidman, 9–32. New York: Harper & Row, 1984.

———. "Is Feminism the End of Christianity? A Critique of Daphne Hampson's *Theology and Feminism*." *Scottish Journal of Theology* 43 (1990) 390–400.

———. *Mary—the Feminine Face of the Church.* Philadelphia: Westminster, 1977.

———. *New Woman New Earth: Sexist Ideologies and Human Liberation.* New York: Seabury, 1975.

———. *Sexism and God-Talk: Towards a Feminist Theology.* London: SCM, 1983.

———. *To Change the World: Christology and Cultural Criticism.* London: SCM, 1981.

Russell, Letty M. *Household of Freedom: Authority in Feminist Theology.* Philadelphia: Westminster, 1987.

Sacred Congregation for the Doctrine of the Faith, *Declaration on the Question of the Admission of Women to the Ministerial Priesthood (Inter Insigniores),* (October 15, 1976).

Sanders, E. P. *Paul and Palestinian Judaism: A Comparison of Patterns of Religion.* Minneapolis: Fortress, 1977.

Scanzoni, Letha D., and Nancy A. Hardesty. *All We're Meant to Be: Biblical Feminism for Today.* Rev. ed. Grand Rapids: Eerdmans, 1992.

Schnackenburg, Rudolf. *The Gospel according to St John.* Vol. 1, *Introduction and Commentary on Chapters 1–4.* Translated by Kevin Smyth. New York: Crossroad, 1990.

Schreiner, Thomas R. "Head Coverings, Prophecies and the Trinity: 1 Corinthians 11:2–16." In *Recovering Biblical Manhood and Womanhood: A Response to Evangelical Feminism*, edited by John Piper and Wayne Grudem, 124–39. Wheaton, IL: Crossway, 1991.

———. "An Interpretation of 1 Timothy 2:9–15: A Dialogue with Scholarship." In *Women in the Church: A Fresh Analysis of 1 Timothy 2:9–15*, edited by Andreas J. Köstenberger, Thomas R. Schreiner and H. Scott Baldwin, 105–54. Grand Rapids: Baker, 1995.

Schüssler Fiorenza, Elisabeth. *Discipleship of Equals: A Critical Feminist ekklesia-Logy of Liberation.* New York: Crossroad, 1993.

———. "Emerging Issues in Feminist Biblical Interpretation." In *Christian Feminism: Visions of a New Humanity*, edited by Judith L. Weidman, 33–54. New York: Harper & Row, 1984.

———. *In Memory of Her: A Feminist Theological Reconstruction of Christian Origins.* New York: Crossroad, 1983.

―――. *Jesus, Miriam's Child, Sophia's Prophet: Critical Issues in Feminist Christology*. London: SCM, 1995.

―――. "The Will to Choose or to Reject: Continuing Our Critical Work." In *Feminist Interpretation of the Bible*, edited by Letty M. Russell, 125–36. Oxford: Basil Blackwell, 1985.

Scott, Eugenie C. "Creation Science Lite: 'Intelligent Design' as the New Anti-Evolutionism." In *Scientists Confront Intelligent Design and Creationism*, edited by Andrew J. Petto and Laurie R. Godfrey, 59–109. New York: Norton, 2007.

Scott, Martin. *Sophia and the Johannine Jesus*. Journal for the Study of the New Testament Supplement Series 71. Sheffield: JSOT Press, 1992.

Selman, M. J. "First-Born." In *New Bible Dictionary*. 2nd ed. Edited by J. D. Douglas, 377–78. Leicester, UK: Inter-Varsity, 1982.

Seneca. *Seneca Ad Lucilium Epistulae Morales: With an English Translation by Richard M. Gummere*. Cambridge: Harvard University Press, 1917.

Shermer, Michael. "An Unauthorized Autobiography of Science." *Scientific American*, December 2007, 48–49.

―――. *Why Darwin Matters: The Case against Intelligent Design*. New York: Owl, 2006.

Shields, David L. "Christ: A Male Feminist View." *Encounter* 45 (1984) 221–32.

Shubin, Neil. *Your Inner Fish: A Journey into the 3.5 Billion-Year History of the Human Body*. New York: Pantheon, 2008.

Shults, F. LeRon. *Christology and Science*. Grand Rapids: Eerdmans, 2008.

―――. *Reforming the Doctrine of God*. Grand Rapids: Eerdmans, 2005.

―――. *Reforming Theological Anthropology: After the Philosophical Turn to Relationality*. Grand Rapids: Eerdmans, 2003.

Silva, Moises. *Biblical Words and Their Meaning: An Introduction to Lexical Semantics*. Grand Rapids: Zondervan, 1983.

Smith, H. S. *In His Image, but . . . : Racism in Southern Religion, 1780–1910*. Durham, NC: Duke University Press, 1972.

Sölle, Dorothee. *The Strength of the Weak: Toward a Christian Feminist Identity*. Translated by Robert Kimber and Rita Kimber. Philadelphia: Westminster, 1984.

―――. *Thinking about God: An Introduction to Theology*. Translated by John Bowden. London: SCM, 1990.

Spanner, Douglas. "Men, Women and God." *Churchman* 108, no. 2 (1994) 101–18.

Specht, Walter F. "The Sabbath in the New Testament." In *The Sabbath in Scripture and History*, edited by Kenneth A. Strand, 92–113. Washington, DC: Review and Herald, 1982.

―――. "Sunday in the New Testament." In *The Sabbath in Scripture and History*, edited by Kenneth A. Strand, 114–29. Washington, DC: Review and Herald, 1982.

Stark, Rodney. *For the Glory of God: How Monotheism Led to Reformations, Science, Witch-Hunts, and the End of Slavery*. Princeton: Princeton University Press, 2003.

Steinhardt, Paul J., and Neil Turok. *Endless Universe: Beyond the Big Bang*. New York: Doubleday, 2007.

Stevens, Maryanne. "Introduction." In *Reconstructing the Christ Symbol: Essays in Feminist Christology*, edited by Maryanne Stevens, 1–5. Mahwah, NJ: Paulist, 1993.

Stewart, James B. *Holy Warriors: The Abolitionists and American Slavery*. New York: Hill & Wang, 1976.

Storkey, Elaine. *What's Right with Feminism*. London: SPCK, 1985.

Suchocki, Marjorie. "The Challenge of Mary Daly." *Encounter* 41 (1980) 307–17.

―――. "God, Sexism, and Transformation." In *Reconstructing Christian Theology*, edited by Rebecca S. Chopp and Mark L. Taylor, 25–48. Minneapolis: Fortress, 1994.

―――. "The Unmale God: Reconsidering the Trinity." *Quarterly Review* 3 (1983): 34–49.

Swartley, Willard M. *Slavery, Sabbath, War, and Women: Case Issues in Biblical Interpretation*. Scottdale, PA: Herald, 1983.

Templeton, Charles. *Farewell to God: My Reasons for Rejecting the Christian Faith*. Toronto: McClelland & Stewart, 1999.

Thistlethwaite, Susan. *Sex, Race, and God: Christian Feminism in Black and White.* New York: Crossroad, 1991.
Thompson, John. *Modern Trinitarian Perspectives.* Oxford: Oxford University Press, 1994.
Thornwell, James H. *The Collected Writings of James Henley Thornwell, vol. IV—Ecclesiastical.* Edinburgh: Banner of Truth, 1974 [1873].
Toon, Peter. *Our Triune God: A Biblical Portrayal of the Trinity.* Wheaton, IL: Victor, 1996.
Torrance, Thomas F. "The Christian Apprehension of God the Father." In *Speaking the Christian God: The Holy Trinity and the Challenge of Feminism,* edited by Alvin F. Kimel, 120–43. Grand Rapids: Eerdmans, 1992.
———. *The Christian Doctrine of God: One Being Three Persons.* New York: T. & T. Clark, 2001.
Trible, Phyllis. "Depatriarchalizing in Biblical Interpretation." *Journal of the American Academy of Religion* 41 (1973) 30–48.
———. "Five Loaves and Two Fishes: Feminist Hermeneutics and Biblical Theology." *Theological Studies* 50 (1989) 279–95.
———. *God and the Rhetoric of Sexuality.* Overtures to Biblical Theology. Philadelphia: Fortress, 1978.
———. "If the Bible's So Patriarchal, How Come I Love It?" *Bible Review* 8 (1992) 44–47, 55.
———. "Postscript: Jottings on the Journey." In *Feminist Interpretation of the Bible,* edited by Letty M. Russell, 147–49. Oxford: Blackwell, 1985.
———. *Texts of Terror: Literary-Feminist Readings of Biblical Narratives.* Philadelphia: Fortress, 1984.
Tucker, Ruth A. *Women in the Maze: Questions and Answers on Biblical Equality.* Downers Grove, IL: InterVarsity, 1992.
Tyson, Neil deGrasse. *Death by Black Hole: And Other Cosmic Quandaries.* New York: Norton, 2007.
van der Walt, B. J. *The Bible as Eye-Opener on the Position of Women.* Potchefstroom, South Africa: Potchefstroom University for Christian Higher Education, 1988.
van Huyssteen, J. Wentzel. *Alone in the World? Human Uniqueness in Science and Theology.* Grand Rapids: Eerdmans, 2006.
———. *Duet or Duel? Theology and Science in a Postmodern World.* London: SCM, 1998.
Van Leeuwen, Mary S. *Gender and Grace: Love, Work and Parenting in a Changing World.* Downers Grove, IL: InterVarsity, 1990.
Volf, Miroslav. *Exclusion and Embrace: A Theological Exploration of Identity, Otherness, and Reconciliation.* Nashville: Abingdon, 1996.
Vos, Geerhardus. *The Self-Disclosure of Jesus: The Modern Debate about the Messianic Consciousness.* New York: Doran, 1926.
Wade, Nicholas. *Before the Dawn: Recovering the Lost History of Our Ancestors.* New York: Penguin, 2007.
Walker, Alan. *Franz Liszt: Volume One, the Virtuoso Years 1811–1847.* Rev. ed. Ithaca, NY: Cornell University Press, 1988.
Waltke, Bruce K. *The Book of Proverbs: Chapters 1–15.* New International Commentary on the Old Testament. Grand Rapids: Eerdmans, 2004.
———. *Creation and Chaos: An Exegetical and Theological Study of Biblical Cosmogony.* Portland, OR: Western Conservative Baptist Seminary, 1974.
———. "The Role of Women in the Bible." *Crux* 31, no. 3 (1995) 29–40.
———. "Shared Leadership or Male Headship." *Christianity Today,* October 3, 1986, 13-I.
Waltke, Bruce K., and M. O'Connor. *An Introduction to Biblical Hebrew Syntax.* Winona Lake, IN: Eisenbrauns, 1990.
Warfield, Benjamin B. *Calvin and Calvinism.* Grand Rapids: Baker, 1991.
Webb, William J. *Slaves, Women, and Homosexuals: Exploring the Hermeneutics of Cultural Analysis.* Downers Grove, IL: InterVarsity, 2001.
Weinrich, William C. "Feminism in the Church: The Issue of Our Day." *Concordia Theological Quarterly* 50, no. 2 (April 1986) 139–44.
Westerholm, Stephen. *Israel's Law and the Church's Faith: Paul and His Recent Interpreters.* Grand Rapids: Eerdmans, 1988.

Williams, D. T. "God as Father: The Maleness of God." *Koers* 55, no. 2 (1990) 259–75.
Williams, Neil H. "The Maleness of Christ: Revelational or Cultural?" DTh diss., University of South Africa, 1999.
Williams, Rowan. "Women and the Ministry: A Case for Theological Seriousness." In *Feminine in the Church*, edited by Monica Furlong, 11–27. London: SPCK, 1984.
Wilson-Kastner, Patricia. *Faith, Feminism, and the Christ*. Philadelphia: Fortress, 1983.
Wise, Kurt P. "Geology." In *In Six Days: Why Fifty Scientists Choose to Believe in Creation*, edited by John F. Ashton, 351–55. Green Forest, AR: Master Books, 2001.
Witherington, Ben, III. *Paul's Narrative Thought World: The Tapestry of Tragedy and Triumph*. Louisville: Westminster John Knox, 1994.
Woit, Peter. *Not Even Wrong: The Failure of String Theory and the Search for Unity in Physical Law*. New York: Basic Books, 2006.
Wood, Kenneth H. "The 'Sabbath Days' of Colossians 2:16, 17." In *The Sabbath in Scripture and History*, edited by Kenneth A. Strand, 338–42. Washington, DC: Review and Herald, 1982.
Wren, Brian. *What Language Shall I Borrow? God-Talk in Worship: A Male Response to Feminist Theology*. New York: Crossroad, 1989.
Wright, N. T. *Evil and the Justice of God*. Downers Grove, IL: InterVarsity, 2006.
———. *Jesus and the Victory of God*. Christian Origins and the Question of God. Minneapolis: Fortress, 1996.
———. *The Last Word: Beyond the Bible Wars to a New Understanding of the Authority of Scripture*. New York: HarperSanFrancisco, 2005.
———. *The Letter to the Romans*. In *The New Interpreter's Bible*. Vol. 10, *Acts–First Corinthians*. Nashville: Abingdon, 2002.
———. *The New Testament and the People of God*. Christian Origins and the Question of God. Minneapolis: Fortress, 1992.
———. *Paul: A Fresh Perspective*. Minneapolis: Fortress, 2005.
———. *The Resurrection of the Son of God*. Christian Origins and the Question of God. Minneapolis: Fortress, 2003.
———. *Surprised by Hope: Rethinking Heaven, the Resurrection, and the Mission of the Church*. New York: HarperOne, 2008.
Yarbrough, Robert W. "The Hermeneutics of 1 Timothy 2:9–15." In *Women in the Church: A Fresh Analysis of 1 Timothy 2:9–15*, edited by Andreas J. Köstenberger, Thomas R. Schreiner, and H. Scott Baldwin, 155–96. Grand Rapids: Baker, 1995.
Zappone, Katherine E. "Woman's Special Nature: A Different Horizon for Theological Anthropology." In *The Special Nature of Women?* edited by Anne Carr and Elisabeth Schüssler Fiorenza. London: SCM, 1991.
Zikmund, Barbara B. "Feminist Consciousness in Historical Perspective." In *Feminist Interpretation of the Bible*, edited by Letty M. Russell, 21–29. Oxford: Blackwell, 1985.
Zimmerli, Walther. *Old Testament Theology in Outline*. Translated by David E. Green. Edinburgh: T. & T. Clark, 1993.
Zizioulas, John D. *Being as Communion: Studies in Personhood and the Church*. Crestwood, NY: St. Vladimir's Seminary Press, 1985.

Endnotes

Introduction

1. Patricia Wilson-Kastner, *Faith, Feminism, and the Christ* (Philadelphia: Fortress, 1983), 90.
2. Joan Gibson documents this medieval debate in Joan Gibson, "Could Christ Have Been Born a Woman? A Medieval Debate," *Journal of Feminist Studies in Religion* 8 (Spring 1992): 65–82.
3. Ibid., 69.
4. Thomas Aquinas, *Summa Theologica* I, 92.
5. Michael Shermer, "An Unauthorized Autobiography of Science," *Scientific American*, December 2007, 48–49.
6. Neil H. Williams, "The Maleness of Christ: Revelational or Cultural?" (DTh diss., University of South Africa, 1999).

Chapter 1: A Summary of Various Views

1. For example, Daphne Hampson argues that Sallie McFague is not really a theist. See Daphne Hampson, *Theology and Feminism* (Oxford: Basil Blackwell, 1990), 158–60.
2. J. I. Packer, "Let's Stop Making Women Presbyters," *Christianity Today* (February 11, 1991): 20.
3. For summary argumentation, see Helmut Moll, "Faithful to Her Lord's Example: On the Meaning of the Male Priesthood in the Catholic Church," in *The Church and Women: A Compendium*, ed. Helmut Moll (San Francisco: Ignatius, 1988); and Sacred Congregation for the Doctrine of the Faith, *Declaration on the Question of the Admission of Women to the Ministerial Priesthood (Inter Insigniores)* (October 15, 1976).
4. For example, George W. Knight III, *The New Testament Teaching on the Role Relationship of Men and Women* (Grand Rapids: Baker, 1977); James B. Hurley, *Man and Woman in Biblical Perspective* (Leicester: InterVarsity, 1981); or the extensive coverage of the complementarian position in *Recovering Biblical Manhood and Womanhood: A Response to Evangelical Feminism*, eds. John Piper and Wayne Grudem (Wheaton: Crossway, 1991) have no section on Jesus' maleness.
5. Susan T. Foh, *Women and the Word of God: A Response to Biblical Feminism* (Phillipsburg,

NJ: Presbyterian and Reformed, 1980); Mary A. Kassian, *The Feminist Gospel: The Movement to Unite Feminism with the Church* (Wheaton: Crossway, 1992); William Oddie, *What Will Happen to God? Feminism and the Reconstruction of Christian Belief* (London: SPCK, 1984); Donald G. Bloesch, *Is the Bible Sexist? Beyond Feminism and Patriarchalism* (Westchester, IL: Crossway, 1982); Donald G. Bloesch, *The Battle for the Trinity: The Debate Over Inclusive God-Language* (Ann Arbor, MI: Servant Publications, 1985).

6. Oddie, *What Will Happen to God?* xiv.
7. Foh, *Women and the Word of God*, 158.
8. Kassian, *Feminist Gospel*, 146.
9. Douglas Moo, quoted by Leslie R. Keylock in "God Our Father and Mother? A Bisexual Nightmare from the National Council of Churches," *Christianity Today* (November 11, 1983): 51.
10. Editorial, *Christianity Today*, "He Meant What He Said: 'Him, His, He,'" (January 2, 1976): 22.
11. Vernard Eller, *The Language of Canaan and the Grammar of Feminism* (Grand Rapids: Eerdmans, 1982), 39.
12. Bruce Waltke, "Shared Leadership or Male Headship," *Christianity Today* (October 3, 1986): 13-I; Roland M. Frye, "Language for God and Feminist Language: Problems and Principles," *Scottish Journal of Theology* 41 (1988): 451–53.
13. Foh, *Women and the Word of God*, 153, 163.
14. Ruth A. Foster, "The Role of Feminine Language and Imagery for God in the Development of a New Testament View of God" (PhD diss., Southwestern Baptist Theological Seminary, 1989), 305.
15. A. Duane Litfin, "Evangelical Feminism: Why Traditionalists Reject It," *Bibliotheca Sacra* 136 (July–September 1979): 270.
16. Eller, *Language of Canaan*.
17. Bloesch, *Is the Bible Sexist?* 75–76.
18. Eller, *Language of Canaan*, 43.
19. C. S. Lewis, "Priestesses in the Church?" in C. S. Lewis, *God in the Dock: Essays on Theology*, ed. Walter Hooper (Glasgow: Fount Paperbacks, 1979), 90–91.
20. Oddie, *What Will Happen to God?* 123. (The nineteenth-century philosopher Ludwig Feuerbach argued that religion was a projection of the ideals and aspirations of men.)
21. Bloesch, *Battle for the Trinity*, 36; see also Kassian, *Feminist Gospel*, 145.
22. Kassian, *Feminist Gospel*, 146.
23. Roland M. Frye, "Language for God and Feminist Language: Problems and Principles," in *Speaking the Christian God: The Holy Trinity and the Challenge of Feminism*, ed. Alvin F. Kimel (Grand Rapids: Eerdmans, 1992), 42.
24. Bloesch, *Battle for the Trinity*, 35.
25. Kassian, *Feminist Gospel*, 145.
26. Bloesch, *Is the Bible Sexist?* 76, 79.
27. Bloesch, *Battle for the Trinity*, 32.
28. Foh, *Women and the Word of God*, 149.
29. Bloesch, *Is the Bible Sexist?* 85–86; Waltke, "Shared Leadership or Male Headship," 13-I; William C. Weinrich, "Feminism in the Church: The Issue of Our Day," *Concordia Theological Quarterly* 50, no. 2 (April 1986): 142; Vern S. Poythress, "The Church as Family: Why Male Leadership in the Family Requires Male Leadership in the Church," in Piper and Grudem, *Recovering Biblical Manhood and Womanhood*, 239; Raymond C. Ortlund, "Male-Female Equality and Male Headship," in Piper and Grudem, *Recovering Biblical Manhood and Womanhood*, 99–105; Wayne Grudem, *Systematic Theology* (Grand Rapids: Zondervan, 1994), 461–66.
30. Weinrich writes, "The disparagement of the sexual differentiation of humankind into

male and female as having no theological significance lies at the base of much defense of homosexual behavior." Weinrich, "Feminism in the Church," 143, no. 1. Similarly, Piper and Grudem write, "We believe that the feminist minimization of sexual role differentiation contributes to the confusion of sexual identity that, especially in second and third generations, gives rise to more homosexuality in society." John Piper and Wayne Grudem, "An Overview of Central Concerns: Questions and Answers," in Piper and Grudem, *Recovering Biblical Manhood and Womanhood*, 82.

31. D. T. Williams, "God as Father: The Maleness of God," *Koers* 55, no. 2 (1990): 267; Piper and Grudem, "Overview of Central Concerns," 86–87.
32. Weinrich, "Feminism in the Church," 142.
33. Foh, *Women and the Word of God*, 144.
34. Ibid., 158–60.
35. Margaret Sittler Ermarth, *Adam's Fractured Rib* (Philadelphia: Fortress, 1970), 127.
36. Williams, "God as Father," 268.
37. For example, Thomas R. Schreiner, "Head Coverings, Prophecies and the Trinity: 1 Corinthians 11:2–16," in Piper and Grudem, *Recovering Biblical Manhood and Womanhood*, 127, 133; Wayne Grudem, "The Meaning of Kephale ('Head'): A Response to Recent Studies," in Piper and Grudem, *Recovering Biblical Manhood and Womanhood*, 426; Wayne Grudem, "Wives Like Sarah, and the Husbands Who Honor Them: 1 Peter 3:1–7," in Piper and Grudem, *Recovering Biblical Manhood and Womanhood*, 199; George W. Knight III, "Husbands and Wives as Analogues of Christ and the Church: Ephesians 5:21–33 and Colossians 3:18–19," in Piper and Grudem, *Recovering Biblical Manhood and Womanhood*, 168, 176; Poythress, "The Church as Family," 240.
38. Douglas Moo, "What Does It Mean Not to Teach or Have Authority Over Men? 1 Timothy 2:11–15," in Piper and Grudem, *Recovering Biblical Manhood and Womanhood*, 193.
39. Ibid., 190.
40. D. A. Carson, "'Silent in the Churches': On the Role of Women in 1 Corinthians 14:33b–36," in Piper and Grudem, *Recovering Biblical Manhood and Womanhood*, 151–52.
41. Robert Letham, "The Man-Woman Debate: Theological Comment," *Westminster Theological Journal* 52 (Spring 1990): 74. See also Waltke, "Shared Leadership or Male Headship," 13-I.
42. Some complementarians, however, argue that the role differentiation extends beyond church and family. See John Piper, "A Vision of Biblical Complementarity: Manhood and Womanhood Defined According to the Bible," in Piper and Grudem, *Recovering Biblical Manhood and Womanhood*, 31–59.
43. John M. Frame, "Men and Women in the Image of God," in Piper and Grudem, *Recovering Biblical Manhood and Womanhood*, 229.
44. Litfin, "Evangelical Feminism," 264.
45. Bloesch, *Is the Bible Sexist?* 79–80, 90.
46. Letham, "Man-Woman Debate," 65–78.
47. For example, Ruth A. Tucker corrects Susan Foh for stating that biblical feminists do not believe that the Bible is inerrant. For Tucker, it is not a question of inerrancy but of hermeneutics. Ruth A. Tucker, *Women in the Maze: Questions and Answers on Biblical Equality* (Downers Grove, IL: InterVarsity, 1992), 203.
48. Paul K. Jewett, *Man as Male and Female: A Study in Sexual Relationships from a Theological Point of View* (Grand Rapids: Eerdmans, 1975), 168.
49. Paul K. Jewett, *God, Creation, and Revelation: A Neo-Evangelical Theology* (Grand Rapids: Eerdmans, 1991), 324.
50. Paul K. Jewett, *The Ordination of Women: An Essay on the Office of Christian Ministry* (Grand Rapids: Eerdmans, 1980), 55.
51. Virginia R. Mollenkott, *Women, Men, and the Bible* (Nashville: Abingdon, 1977), 68.
52. Rebecca M. Groothuis, *Good News for Women: A Biblical Picture of Gender Equality* (Grand Rapids: Baker, 1997), 109.

53. Letha D. Scanzoni and Nancy A. Hardesty, *All We're Meant to Be: Biblical Feminism for Today*, rev. ed. (Grand Rapids: Eerdmans, 1992), 74.
54. Ibid., 73–74.
55. Stanley J. Grenz and Denise M. Kjesbo, *Women in the Church: A Biblical Theology of Women in Ministry* (Downers Grove, IL: InterVarsity, 1995), 209.
56. Tucker, *Women in the Maze*, 26.
57. Groothuis, *Good News for Women*, 111; Scanzoni and Hardesty, *All We're Meant to Be*, 19.
58. Gilbert Bilezikian, *Beyond Sex Roles: What the Bible Says about a Woman's Place in Church and Family* (Grand Rapids: Baker, 1985), 25; B. J. van der Walt, *The Bible as Eye-Opener on the Position of Women* (Potchefstroom, South Africa: Potchefstroom University for Christian Higher Education, 1988), 10.
59. Tucker, *Women in the Maze*, 33–34.
60. Mollenkott, *Women, Men, and the Bible*, 55–56.
61. Grenz and Kjesbo, *Women in the Church*, 164–65; Groothuis, *Good News for Women*, 134–35.
62. van der Walt, *The Bible as Eye-Opener*, 8–9; Mary S. Van Leeuwen, *Gender and Grace: Love, Work and Parenting in a Changing World* (Downers Grove, IL: InterVarsity, 1990), 41; Groothuis, *Good News for Women*, 127–28.
63. Grenz and Kjesbo, *Women in the Church*, 165.
64. Mollenkott, *Women, Men, and the Bible*, 132; Grenz and Kjesbo, *Women in the Church*, 165–69; Groothuis, *Good News for Women*, 139–40.
65. Bilezikian, *Beyond Sex Roles*, 124.
66. van der Walt, *The Bible as Eye-Opener*, 3.
67. Ibid., 38.
68. Bilezikian, *Beyond Sex Roles*, 129–32.
69. van der Walt, *The Bible as Eye-Opener*, 33.
70. Mollenkott, *Women, Men, and the Bible*, 111–12; Gilbert Bilezikian, "A Critique of Wayne Grudem's Treatment of Kephale in Ancient Greek Texts," Evangelical Theological Society Papers (Portland: Micropublished by Theological Research Exchange Network, 38th Annual Conference, 1986); Groothuis, *Good News for Women*, 159.
71. Groothuis, *Good News for Women*, 127.
72. van der Walt, *The Bible as Eye-Opener*, 31.
73. Jewett, *Man as Male and Female*, 142.
74. Grenz and Kjesbo, *Women in the Church*, 101.
75. Ibid., 106–7.
76. Bilezikian, *Beyond Sex Roles*, 126–28.
77. Grenz and Kjesbo, *Women in the Church*, 106.
78. Virginia R. Mollenkott, "Women and the Bible: A Challenge to Male Interpretation," *Sojourners* 5 (Fall 1976): 25; Mollenkott, *Women, Men, and the Bible*, 63, 122–24; Grenz and Kjesbo, *Women in the Church*, 152.
79. Jewett, *The Ordination of Women*, 35.
80. Groothuis, *Good News for Women*, 111–12.
81. Ibid., 98, 112.
82. Adrio König, "Die Manlikheid Van God," *Ned. Geref. Teologiese Tydskrif* 33 (1992): 91.
83. Jewett, *God, Creation, and Revelation*, 323–24.
84. Jewett, *The Ordination of Women*, 36, 43.
85. Virginia R. Mollenkott, *The Divine Feminine: The Biblical Imagery of God as Female* (New York: Crossroad, 1983), 4.
86. See Virginia R. Mollenkott, "Unlimiting God: To Unlimit God Is to Unlimit Ourselves," *Other Side*, no. 146 (November 1983): 11–14.
87. Mollenkott, *Women, Men, and the Bible*, 58.

88. Ibid., 60.
89. Jewett, *Man as Male and Female*, 167.
90. Jewett, *The Ordination of Women*, 41.
91. Ibid., 45.
92. Groothuis, *Good News for Women*, 97–98.
93. Mollenkott, *Divine Feminine*, 110.
94. Grenz and Kjesbo, *Women in the Church*, 146.
95. Ibid., 148.
96. Mary J. Evans, *Woman in the Bible* (Carlisle, UK: Paternoster, 1983), 22.
97. Ibid., 23–24.
98. Jewett, *Man as Male and Female*, 94–103.
99. Groothuis, *Good News for Women*, 110.
100. Elaine Storkey, *What's Right with Feminism* (London: SPCK, 1985), 156.
101. For some of these examples see Jewett, *Man as Male and Female*, 170; Grenz and Kjesbo, *Women in the Church*, 63–97.
102. Jewett, *Man as Male and Female*, 130–31.
103. van der Walt, *The Bible as Eye-Opener*, 19–20; Scanzoni and Hardesty, *All We're Meant to Be*, 83–87; Grenz and Kjesbo, *Women in the Church*, 94; Groothuis, *Good News for Women*, 190–98.
104. Bilezikian, *Beyond Sex Roles*, 195–206.
105. Grenz and Kjesbo, *Women in the Church*, 220.
106. Leeuwen, *Gender and Grace*, 241–42.
107. Elisabeth Moltmann-Wendel and Jürgen Moltmann, *God—His and Hers* (London: SCM, 1991), 78; see also Rosemary R. Ruether, *Sexism and God-Talk: Towards a Feminist Theology* (London: SCM, 1983), 12–13.
108. Teresa M. Hinga, "Jesus Christ and the Liberation of Women in Africa," in *The Will to Arise*, ed. Mercy A. Oduyoye and Musimbi R. A. Kanyoro (Maryknoll, NY: Orbis, 1992), 192.
109. Christian feminists see complementarianism as a "romantic term which bears the suspicion of another rationalization for subordination." Anne Carr, "Is a Christian Feminist Theology Possible?" *Theological Studies* 43 (1982): 288.
110. Margaret A. Farley, "Feminist Consciousness and the Interpretation of Scripture," in *Feminist Interpretation of the Bible*, ed. Letty M. Russell (Oxford: Basil Blackwell, 1985), 46.
111. Somewhat tongue in cheek, Susan Dowell and Linda Hurcombe note the entry in the New Hutchinson's Twentieth Century Encyclopedia: "Eve," see "Adam." Dowell and Hurcombe, *Dispossessed Daughters of Eve: Faith and Feminism*, rev. ed. (London: SPCK, 1987), 1.
112. Wilson-Kastner, *Faith, Feminism, and the Christ*, 104.
113. Ibid., 115.
114. Marjorie Suchocki, "The Challenge of Mary Daly," *Encounter* 41 (1980): 312.
115. Jacquelyn Grant, *White Women's Christ and Black Women's Jesus: Feminist Christology and Womanist Response* (Atlanta: Scholars, 1989), 58.
116. Ruether, *Sexism and God-Talk*, 18.
117. Suchocki, "The Challenge of Mary Daly," 307.
118. Rosemary R. Ruether, "Is Feminism the End of Christianity? A Critique of Daphne Hampson's *Theology and Feminism*," *Scottish Journal of Theology* 43, no. 3 (1990): 393–94.
119. Rosemary R. Ruether, "Feminism and Patriarchal Religion: Principles of Ideological Critique of the Bible," *Journal for the Study of the Old Testament* 22 (1982): 63.
120. Ruether, *Sexism and God-Talk*, 135.
121. Ibid., 137.
122. Bernard Cooke, "Non-Patriarchal Salvation," *Horizons* 10 (1983): 28.
123. Rowan Williams, "Women and the Ministry: A Case for Theological Seriousness," in *Feminine in the Church*, ed. Monica Furlong (London: SPCK, 1984), 22.

124. Elisabeth Schüssler Fiorenza, *Jesus, Miriam's Child, Sophia's Prophet: Critical Issues in Feminist Christology* (London: SCM, 1995), 47.
125. Ibid., 188. Fiorenza coined the word "kyriarchal" from the Greek words for "master/lord" and "to rule/dominate" to reference intersecting and shifting social structures of domination and oppression.
126. Eleanor McLaughlin, "Christology in Dialogue with Feminist Ideology—Bodies and Boundaries," in *Christology in Dialogue*, eds. Robert F. Berkey and Sarah A. Edwards (Cleveland: Pilgrim, 1993), 329–34.
127. Maryanne Stevens, "Introduction," in *Reconstructing the Christ Symbol: Essays in Feminist Christology*, ed. Maryanne Stevens (Mahwah, NJ: Paulist, 1993), 1.
128. Denise L. Carmody, *Responses to 101 Questions about Feminism* (London: Geoffrey Chapman, 1994), 32.
129. Wilson-Kastner, *Faith, Feminism, and the Christ*, 92.
130. Karen Bloomquist, "'Let God Be God': The Theological Necessity of Depatriarchalizing God," in *Our Naming of God*, ed. Carl E. Braaten (Minneapolis: Fortress, 1989), 59.
131. David Shields mentions three examples where Jesus overturns the patriarchal culture: (1) Jesus' interaction with the unclean hemorrhaging woman; (2) the outcast Syrophoenician woman whom Jesus engages in a verbal exchange; (3) Mary, who takes a traditional male place of learning at Jesus' feet and is commended for listening like any other male disciple. David L. Shields, "Christ: A Male Feminist View," *Encounter* 45 (1984): 227. See also Wilson-Kastner, *Faith, Feminism, and the Christ*, 72.
132. Bloomquist, "Let God Be God," 57.
133. Martina Blasberg-Kuhnke writes, "Jesus' experience of Abba is connected with human-male domination: 'And call no one your father on earth, for you have one Father—the one in heaven' (Mt 23:9)." Martina Blasberg-Kuhnke, "Jesus as Women See Him," *Theology Digest* 39 (1992): 207.
134. Wilson-Kastner, *Faith, Feminism, and the Christ*, 90.
135. Elizabeth A. Johnson, "Redeeming the Name of Christ," in *Freeing Theology: The Essentials of Theology in Feminist Perspective*, ed. Catherine Mowry LaCugna (New York: HarperCollins, 1993), 118–19.
136. Ibid., 120; McLaughlin, "Christology in Dialogue with Feminist Ideology," 311; Kari E. Børresen, "Women's Studies of the Christian Tradition: New Perspectives," in *Religion and Gender*, ed. Ursula King (Oxford: Blackwell, 1995), 248.
137. Richard A. Norris, "The Ordination of Women and the 'Maleness' of Christ," *Anglican Theological Review Supplement Series*, no. 6 (1976): 73; Wilson-Kastner, *Faith, Feminism, and the Christ*, 90; Elizabeth A. Johnson, "Jesus the Wisdom of God: A Biblical Basis for Non-Androcentric Christology," *Ephemerides Theologicae Lovanienses* 61 (1985): 294; Paul Avis, *Eros and the Sacred* (London: SPCK, 1989), 44; Immanuel S. David, "What Are They Saying about Christian Feminism?" *Africa Theological Journal* 20, no. 3 (1991): 214–15.
138. Rosemary R. Ruether, "Feminist Theology and Spirituality," in *Christian Feminism: Visions of a New Humanity*, ed. Judith L. Weidman (New York: Harper & Row, 1984), 21; Rosemary R. Ruether, "Can Christology Be Liberated from Patriarchy?" in Stevens, *Reconstructing the Christ Symbol*, 12; Denise L. Carmody, *Christian Feminist Theology* (Oxford: Blackwell, 1995), 186–87.
139. Julie M. Hopkins, *Towards a Feminist Christology: Jesus of Nazareth, European Women and the Christological Crisis* (Kampen, Netherlands: Kok Pharos, 1994), 90–91.
140. Avis, *Eros and the Sacred*, 42.
141. Teresa Berger, "A Female Christ Child in the Manger and a Woman on the Cross, or: The Historicity of the Jesus Event and the Inculturation of the Gospel," *Feminist Theology* 11 (1996): 43.
142. Rosemary R. Ruether, *New Woman New Earth: Sexist Ideologies and Human Liberation* (New

York: Seabury, 1975), xiii; Marjorie Suchocki, "The Unmale God: Reconsidering the Trinity," *Quarterly Review* 3 (1983): 35; Bloomquist, "Let God Be God," 48, 51; Denise Ackermann, "Being Women, Being Human," in *Women Hold up Half the Sky: Women in the Church in Southern Africa*, eds. Denise Ackermann, Jonathan A. Draper, and Emma Mashinini (Pietermaritzburg, South Africa: Cluster Publications, 1991), 98; Susan Thistlethwaite, *Sex, Race, and God: Christian Feminism in Black and White* (New York: Crossroad, 1991), 112.
143. Sallie McFague, *Metaphorical Theology: Models of God in Religious Language* (London: SCM, 1982), 145.
144. Ruether, "Feminism and Patriarchal Religion," 58–59; Catharina Halkes, "The Rape of Mother Earth: Ecology and Patriarchy," in *Motherhood: Experience, Institution, Theology*, eds. Anne Carr and Elisabeth Schüssler Fiorenza (Edinburgh: T & T Clark, 1989), 97; Mercy A. Oduyoye, *Daughters of Anowa: African Women and Patriarchy* (Maryknoll, NY: Orbis Books, 1995), 178.
145. Catherine M. LaCugna, *God for Us: The Trinity and Christian Life* (New York: HarperCollins, 1991), 311.
146. Carr, "Is a Christian Feminist Theology Possible?" 285.
147. Elizabeth A. Johnson, "The Incomprehensibility of God and the Image of God Male and Female," *Theological Studies* 45 (1984): 443.
148. LaCugna, *God for Us*, 311.
149. F. Edwards, "God from a Feminist Perspective," in *Sexism and Feminism*, ed. W. S. Voster (Pretoria, South Africa: University of South Africa, 1984), 54; Dorothee Sölle, *The Strength of the Weak: Toward a Christian Feminist Identity*, trans. Robert Kimber and Rita Kimber (Philadelphia: Westminster, 1984), 113; Carmody, *Responses to 101 Questions*, 29; Carmody, *Christian Feminist Theology*, 198.
150. Phyllis Trible, "Postscript: Jottings on the Journey," in Russell, *Feminist Interpretation of the Bible*, 148.
151. Sallie McFague, *Models of God: Theology for an Ecological, Nuclear Age* (Philadelphia: Fortress, 1987), 98.
152. Carmody, *Responses to 101 Questions*, 28.
153. Carmody, "Feminist Theology and Spirituality," 16.
154. Rosemary R. Ruether, *Mary—the Feminine Face of the Church* (Philadelphia: Westminster, 1977), 45–46; Ruether, *To Change the World*, 49–50; Ruether, *Sexism and God-Talk*, 128–29; Wilson-Kastner, *Faith, Feminism, and the Christ*, 96, 101–4; Børresen, "Women's Studies," 251–52.
155. Dorothee Sölle, *Thinking about God: An Introduction to Theology*, trans. John Bowden (London: SCM, 1990), 182; Catherine M. LaCugna, "God in Communion with Us," in *Freeing Theology: The Essentials of Theology in Feminist Perspective*, ed. Catherine Mowry LaCugna (New York: HarperCollins, 1993), 84–85.
156. Marjorie Suchocki, "God, Sexism, and Transformation," in *Reconstructing Christian Theology*, eds. Rebecca S. Chopp and Mark L. Taylor (Minneapolis: Fortress, 1994), 38.
157. Patricia D. Highby, "Toward a Feminist Trinitarian Doctrine of God" (PhD diss., Iliff School of Theology and University of Denver, 1992), 241.
158. Norris, "The Ordination of Women," 75–76; Johnson, "The Incomprehensibility of God," 462; LaCugna, *God for Us*, 280; Carmody, *Christian Feminist Theology*, 196.
159. Elisabeth Schüssler Fiorenza, "The Will to Choose or to Reject: Continuing Our Critical Work," in Russell, *Feminist Interpretation of the Bible*, 129.
160. Rebecca S. Chopp, *The Power to Speak: Feminism, Language, God* (New York: Crossroad, 1989), 71; Sölle, *Thinking about God*, 74.
161. Phyllis Trible, *Texts of Terror: Literary-Feminist Readings of Biblical Narratives* (Philadelphia: Fortress, 1984).
162. McFague, *Metaphorical Theology*, 164.
163. Ruether, *Sexism and God-Talk*, 53; Barbara B. Zikmund, "Feminist Consciousness in

Historical Perspective," in Russell, *Feminist Interpretation of the Bible*, 22–23; Dowell and Hurcombe, *Dispossessed Daughters of Eve*, 34; Sölle, *Thinking about God*, 75; Gail P. Corrington, *Her Image of Salvation: Female Saviors and Formative Christianity* (Louisville: Westminster/John Knox, 1992), 30–31.

164. Ruether, *Sexism and God-Talk*, 141; Susanne Heine, *Women and Early Christianity: Are the Feminist Scholars Right?* trans. John Bowden (London: SCM, 1987), 134–41; Elisabeth Schüssler Fiorenza, *Discipleship of Equals: A Critical Feminist ekklesia-Logy of Liberation* (New York: Crossroad, 1993), 170–71.
165. Phyllis Trible, "Depatriarchalizing in Biblical Interpretation," *Journal of the American Academy of Religion* 41 (1973): 30.
166. Elisabeth Schüssler Fiorenza, *In Memory of Her: A Feminist Theological Reconstruction of Christian Origins* (New York: Crossroad, 1983), 236.
167. McFague, *Metaphorical Theology*, 166.
168. Trible, "Depatriarchalizing in Biblical Interpretation," 35–38; Phyllis Trible, "Five Loaves and Two Fishes: Feminist Hermeneutics and Biblical Theology," *Theological Studies* 50 (1989): 291; Phyllis Trible, "If the Bible's So Patriarchal, How Come I Love It?" *Bible Review* 8 (1992): 47, 55.
169. Schüssler Fiorenza, *Discipleship of Equals*, 70; Paul E. Dinter, "Christ's Body as Male and Female," *Cross Currents* 44 (1994): 398–99.
170. Phyllis Trible, *God and the Rhetoric of Sexuality* (Philadelphia: Fortress, 1978), 201; Trible, "Five Loaves and Two Fishes," 290.
171. Trible, "Depatriarchalizing in Biblical Interpretation," 45; Ruether, *Mary—the Feminine Face of the Church*, 22–23, 46–47; Trible, *God and the Rhetoric of Sexuality*, 161; Ruether, *Sexism and God-Talk*, 140.
172. For example, Joan C. Engelsman, *The Feminine Dimension of the Divine* (Philadelphia: Westminster, 1979), 119; Ruether, *Sexism and God-Talk*, 117; Letty M. Russell, *Household of Freedom: Authority in Feminist Theology* (Philadelphia: Westminster, 1987), 54–56; Schüssler Fiorenza, *Jesus, Miriam's Child, Sophia's Prophet*, 131–62. Schüssler Fiorenza argues in *In Memory of Her* that the first Christian theology is Sophialogy.
173. Elizabeth A. Johnson, "Wisdom Was Made Flesh and Pitched Her Tent Among Us," in Stevens, *Reconstructing the Christ Symbol*, 107–8; Carmody, *Christian Feminist Theology*, 182–87.
174. Johnson, "Jesus the Wisdom of God," 263–67.
175. Ibid., 288.
176. Ibid., 293.
177. Ibid.
178. Johnson, "Redeeming the Name of Christ," 127–28.
179. Johnson, "Jesus the Wisdom of God," 288–89; Johnson, "Wisdom Was Made Flesh," 108.
180. Ruether, *Sexism and God-Talk*, 165.
181. Elisabeth Moltmann-Wendel, *A Land Flowing with Milk and Honey: Perspectives on Feminist Theology*, trans. John Bowden (London: SCM, 1986), 39.
182. Wilson-Kastner, *Faith, Feminism, and the Christ*, 90.
183. Sallie McFague, "Human Beings, Embodiment, and Our Home the Earth," in *Reconstructing Christian Theology*, eds. Rebecca S. Chopp and Mark L. Taylor (Minneapolis: Fortress, 1994), 141.
184. Ruether, *Sexism and God-Talk*, 167.
185. Bloomquist, "Let God Be God," 47; Suchocki, "God, Sexism, and Transformation," 45.
186. Edwards, "God from a Feminist Perspective," 48–49; Schüssler Fiorenza, *Discipleship of Equals*, 97.
187. Carol Ochs, *Behind the Sex of God: Toward a New Consciousness-Transcending Matriarchy and Patriarchy* (Boston: Beacon, 1977), 133–34.

188. Commenting on destructive dualisms and New Testament teaching, Ruether writes, "The Gospels do not operate with a dualism of masculine and feminine. The widow, the prostitute, and the Samaritan woman are not representatives of the 'feminine,' but rather they represent those who have no honor in the present system of religious righteousness." Ruether, *Sexism and God-Talk*, 137.
189. Naomi R. Goldenberg, *Changing of the Gods: Feminism and the End of Traditional Religions* (Boston: Beacon, 1979), 10, 25.
190. Hampson, *Theology and Feminism*, 21.
191. Ibid., 102; See also Mary Daly, *Beyond God the Father* (London: Women's Press, 1986), 99–100.
192. Daphne Hampson, *After Christianity* (Valley Forge, PA: Trinity Press International, 1996), 67.
193. Daly, *Beyond God the Father*, 95.
194. Daphne Hampson, "The Challenge of Feminism to Christianity," *Theology* 88 (1985): 341.
195. Hampson, *Theology and Feminism*, 98–99.
196. Daly, *Beyond God the Father*, 162.
197. Hampson, *After Christianity*, 66.
198. Hampson, *Theology and Feminism*, 104.
199. Ibid.
200. Ibid., 15.
201. Hampson, *After Christianity*, 69.
202. Hampson, *Theology and Feminism*, 87.
203. Daly, *Beyond God the Father*, 73.
204. Hampson, "Challenge of Feminism to Christianity," 342; Daphne Hampson, "On Autonomy and Heteronomy," in *Swallowing a Fishbone: Feminist Theologians Debate Christianity*, ed. Daphne Hampson (London: SPCK, 1996), 7.
205. Daly, *Beyond God the Father*, xxiii–xxiv.
206. Hampson, *Theology and Feminism*, 84.
207. Goldenberg, *Changing of the Gods*, 21.
208. Hampson, *Theology and Feminism*, 162.
209. Ibid., 29.
210. Ibid., 34.
211. Ibid., 158.
212. Ibid., 159.
213. Ibid., 108.
214. This saturation is such that the word *God* becomes problematic. Daly, for example, because she believes it is impossible to remove male imagery from *God*, no longer uses the word.
215. Goldenberg, *Changing of the Gods*, 93.
216. Mary Daly, *Gyn/Ecology: The Metaethics of Radical Feminism* (London: Women's Press, 1991), 89. See also Carol P. Christ, *Rebirth of the Goddess: Finding Meaning in Feminist Spirituality* (Reading, MA: Addison-Wesley, 1997), 2.
217. Carol P. Christ, "Why Women Need the Goddess: Phenomenological, Psychological, and Political Reflections," in *Womanspirit Rising: A Feminist Reader in Religion*, eds. Carol P. Christ and Judith Plaskow (New York: Harper & Row, 1979), 275.
218. Naomi R. Goldenberg, *Returning Words to Flesh: Feminism, Psychoanalysis, and the Resurrection of the Body* (Boston: Beacon, 1990), 197.
219. Christ, "Why Women Need the Goddess," 276–86; Christ, *Rebirth of the Goddess*, 22.
220. Hampson, *Theology and Feminism*, 161.
221. Christ, *Rebirth of the Goddess*, 23.
222. Hampson, *Theology and Feminism*, 75.
223. Ibid., 94.

224. Ibid., 95.
225. Hampson, *After Christianity*, 180–81.
226. Hampson, "Challenge of Feminism to Christianity," 344.
227. Hampson, *After Christianity*, 6.
228. Hampson, *Theology and Feminism*, 75.
229. Daly, *Beyond God the Father*, 77.
230. Ibid., 80.
231. Ibid., 96.
232. Ibid., 69–97.
233. Goldenberg, *Changing of the Gods*, 22.
234. Hampson, "Challenge of Feminism to Christianity," 344–45.
235. Daly, *Beyond God the Father*, 78–79.
236. Hampson, *Theology and Feminism*, 71.
237. Hampson, *After Christianity*, 72.
238. Hampson, *Theology and Feminism*, 62–66.
239. Judith Plaskow, *Sex, Sin and Grace: Women's Experience and the Theologies of Reinhold Niebuhr and Paul Tillich* (Lanham, MD: University Press of America, 1980); Daphne Hampson, "The Challenge of Feminism [Rejoinder to P. Avis, 90: 46–50, January 1987]," *Theology* 90 (1987): 220.
240. Christ, *Rebirth of the Goddess*, 31–49.
241. Hampson, *After Christianity*, 284.
242. Daly, *Beyond God the Father*, 114–22.
243. Hampson, *Theology and Feminism*, 24.
244. Hampson, *After Christianity*, 121, 125.
245. Ibid., 150.
246. Ibid., 12.
247. Daly, *Beyond God the Father*, 74.
248. Ibid., 8.
249. Ibid., 19.
250. There are even more numerous Old Testament examples, such as not wearing clothes woven of different material (Lev. 19:19). For our purposes, even in the New Testament we have culture-specific commands that are no longer binding.
251. Foh comes close to arguing that women should still wear head coverings. Foh, *Women and the Word of God*, 36.
252. Piper and Grudem, "Overview of Central Concerns," 75; Schreiner, "Head Coverings, Prophecies and the Trinity," 132.
253. Mary Daly, *The Church and the Second Sex* (New York: Harper & Row, 1968), 38; Groothuis, *Good News for Women*, 161.

Chapter 2: The Slavery Debate—Implications for Our Topic

1. Patricia Gundry, *Women Be Free!* (Grand Rapids: Zondervan, 1977), 53.
2. John H. Hopkins, *A Scriptural, Ecclesiastical, and Historical View of Slavery, from the Days of the Patriarch Abraham, to the Nineteenth Century* (New York: Negro Universities Press, 1969 [1864]), 6.
3. Steven Goldberg, *Why Men Rule: A Theory of Male Dominance* (Chicago, IL: Open Court, 1993).
4. Bruce K. Waltke, "The Role of Women in the Bible," *Crux* 31, no. 3 (1995): 36. David Ayers, also referring to Goldberg, writes, "The arguments over the universality of sex differences are crucial and represent more than mere academic quibbling. Only through such discussion can biological differences be established as having social relevance. If across the dazzling variety of cultures such similarities consistently emerge, it is a distortion of logic to

assume that each society has found an essentially similar way through socialization alone." David J. Ayers, "The Inevitability of Failure: The Assumptions and Implementations of Modern Feminism," in Piper and Grudem, *Recovering Biblical Manhood and Womanhood*, 316.
5. Goldberg, *Why Men Rule*, 49.
6. Hopkins, *A Scriptural, Ecclesiastical, and Historical View of Slavery*, 47.
7. Waltke, "Role of Women in the Bible," 32.
8. S. Lewis Johnson, "Role Distinctions in the Church: Galatians 3:28," in Piper and Grudem, *Recovering Biblical Manhood and Womanhood*, 164.
9. Harold O. J. Brown, "The New Testament Against Itself: 1 Timothy 2:9–15 and the 'Breakthrough' of Galatians 3:28," in *Women in the Church: A Fresh Analysis of 1 Timothy 2:9–15*, eds. Andreas J. Köstenberger, Thomas R. Schreiner, and H. Scott Baldwin (Grand Rapids: Baker, 1995), 199.
10. James H. Thornwell, *The Collected Writings of James Henley Thornwell, vol. IV—Ecclesiastical* (Edinburgh: Banner of Truth, 1974 [1873]), 414.
11. Carl F. Ellis, *Free at Last? The Gospel in the African-American Experience*, 2nd ed. (Downers Grove, IL: InterVarsity, 1996), 45–46.
12. Hopkins, *A Scriptural, Ecclesiastical, and Historical View of Slavery*, 7; H. S. Smith, *In His Image, but . . . : Racism in Southern Religion, 1780–1910* (Durham, NC: Duke University Press, 1972), 11.
13. Chandra Manning, *What This Cruel War Was Over: Soldiers, Slavery, and the Civil War* (New York: Alfred A. Knopf, 2007), 142.
14. Hopkins, *A Scriptural, Ecclesiastical, and Historical View of Slavery*, 97.
15. James M. McPherson, *Battle Cry of Freedom: The Civil War Era* (New York: Oxford University Press, 1988), 244.
16. James McPherson writes, "One of the most formidable obstacles to the abolition of slavery and the extension of equal rights to free Negroes was the widespread popular and scientific belief, North as well as South, in the innate inferiority of the Negro race." James M. McPherson, *The Struggle for Equality: Abolitionists and the Negro in the Civil War and Reconstruction* (Princeton, NJ: Princeton University Press, 1964), 134.
17. Hopkins, *A Scriptural, Ecclesiastical, and Historical View of Slavery*, 6, 15.
18. Waltke, "Role of Women in the Bible," 30.
19. Dorothy Patterson, "Aspects of a Biblical Theology of Womanhood," (DTh diss., University of South Africa, 1997), 107. See also Waltke, "Role of Women in the Bible," 36–37.
20. Guenther Haas, "Patriarchy as an Evil That God Tolerated: Analysis and Implications for the Authority of Scripture," *Journal of the Evangelical Theological Society* 38, no. 3 (1995): 321–36.
21. Smith, *In His Image*, 206.
22. Hopkins, *A Scriptural, Ecclesiastical, and Historical View of Slavery*, 97.
23. John Piper and Wayne Grudem, "An Overview of Central Concerns: Questions and Answers," in *Recovering Biblical Manhood and Womanhood: A Response to Evangelical Feminism*, eds. John Piper and Wayne Grudem (Wheaton: Crossway, 1991), 36.
24. Ibid., 43.
25. Thornwell, *vol. IV—Ecclesiastical*, 389.
26. Robert L. Dabney, *Discussions of Robert Lewis Dabney*, vol. 2 (Edinburgh: Banner of Truth, 1982 [1891]), 199–217.
27. Smith, *In His Image*, vii.
28. Frame writes, "Women and men equally image God, even in their sexual differences, even in their differences with regard to authority and submission. The reason is that the image of God embraces everything that is human. Both men and women, therefore, resemble God and are called to represent Him throughout the creation, exercising control, authority, and

presence in His name. This doctrine is not at all inconsistent with the subordination of women to men in the home and in the church. All human beings are under authority, both divine and human. Their submission to authority, as well as their authority itself, images God." John M. Frame, "Men and Women in the Image of God," in Piper and Grudem, *Recovering Biblical Manhood and Womanhood*, 231–32.
29. Smith, *In His Image*, 134–35.
30. Hopkins, *A Scriptural, Ecclesiastical, and Historical View of Slavery*, 13–14; Smith, *In His Image*, 135.
31. Thornwell, *vol. IV—Ecclesiastical*, 429.
32. Jimmy G. Cobb, "A Study of White Protestants' Attitudes Toward Negroes in Charleston, South Carolina 1790–1845," (PhD diss., Baylor University, 1976), 101.
33. Vern S. Poythress, "The Church as Family: Why Male Leadership in the Family Requires Male Leadership in the Church," in Piper and Grudem, *Recovering Biblical Manhood and Womanhood*, 240.
34. Thornwell, *vol. IV—Ecclesiastical*, 407.
35. Vern S. Poythress, "Two Hermeneutical Tensions in Evangelical Feminism," paper presented at the Eastern Regional ETS Conference, Philadelphia, April 5, 1991.
36. Ibid., 1–2.
37. Poythress writes, "When we take into account the complementarian practices in first century cultures and in first century church, feminist readings of the key texts cannot plausibly be sustained. Evangelical feminists are thus forced into the position articulated in 1979 by DeJong and Wilson in *Husband and Wife*. According to this view, NT texts aim at transforming but not at immediately overthrowing patriarchal practice. One cannot directly appeal to any NT proof text in order to justify modern feminist sentiments. Only in the long run do the implications of the transforming forces in the NT become evident." Poythress, "Two Hermeneutical Tensions," 9.
38. Thornwell, *vol. IV—Ecclesiastical*, 428–29.
39. Hopkins, *A Scriptural, Ecclesiastical, and Historical View of Slavery*, 41.
40. Thornwell, *vol. IV—Ecclesiastical*, 393.
41. Ibid., 384.
42. Piper and Grudem, "Overview of Central Concerns," 66.
43. Smith, *In His Image*, 200.
44. McPherson writes, "Within two years proslavery writers had answered *Uncle Tom's Cabin* with at least fifteen novels whose thesis [was] that slaves were better off than free workers in the North." McPherson, *Battle Cry of Freedom*, 90; see also 56, 208.
45. Hopkins, *A Scriptural, Ecclesiastical, and Historical View of Slavery*, 284–300.
46. Ibid., 301.
47. Ibid., 33.
48. *Recovering Biblical Manhood and Womanhood: A Response to Evangelical Feminism*, eds. John Piper and Wayne Grudem (Wheaton: Crossway, 1991).
49. Kassian, *Feminist Gospel*, 61–65.
50. Robert L. Dabney, *Discussions of Robert Lewis Dabney*, vol. 3 (Edinburgh: Banner of Truth, 1982), 40–41.
51. Hopkins, *A Scriptural, Ecclesiastical, and Historical View of Slavery*, 333, 350.
52. Ibid., 48.
53. Dabney, *Discussions*, vol. 3, 41.
54. Thornwell, *vol. IV—Ecclesiastical*, 393.
55. Ibid., 390.
56. Kassian, *Feminist Gospel*, 225.
57. Ibid., 227–33.
58. Dabney, *Discussions*, vol. 2, 100.

59. Smith, *In His Image*, 239–40.
60. Paige Patterson, "The Meaning of Authority in the Local Church," in Piper and Grudem, *Recovering Biblical Manhood and Womanhood*, 259.
61. Hopkins, *A Scriptural, Ecclesiastical, and Historical View of Slavery*, 349.
62. Thornwell, *vol. IV—Ecclesiastical*, 419–20.
63. Schreiner writes, "Those who erase the distinction in roles between men and women in the present age are probably guilty of falling prey to a form of overrealized eschatology, for the creational order established with reference to men and women will be terminated in the coming age (cf. Matt. 22:30)." Thomas R. Schreiner, "An Interpretation of 1 Timothy 2:9–15: A Dialogue with Scholarship," in *Women in the Church: A Fresh Analysis of 1 Timothy 2:9–15*, eds. Andreas J. Köstenberger, Thomas R. Schreiner, and H. Scott Baldwin (Grand Rapids: Baker, 1995), 138.
64. Waltke writes, "It will not do to obscure the New Testament teaching about husband-headship by appealing to Galatians 3:28. . . . While in the eschaton, of which we are already members, that is true, until the redemption of our bodies we still participate in the first creation with its distinction between the sexes." Waltke, "Role of Women in the Bible," 37.
65. Carr writes, "To envision God as future, as ahead, rather than above and over against the human and natural world, is a reorientation that helps women to see the feminist dilemmas in the church as a temporary one." Anne Carr, *Transforming Grace* (New York: HarperCollins, 1990), 153; quoted in F. LeRon Shults, *Reforming the Doctrine of God* (Grand Rapids: Eerdmans, 2005), 196.
66. Foh, *Women and the Word of God*, 32. Oddie also writes, "Even the extreme case of the institution of slavery itself . . . can, in its concrete expression, actually cease to be demonic if master and slave now see their relationship in the light of Christ: the actual granting of freedom operating on the socio-political plane may then become almost irrelevant. St. Paul, in sending back to his master Philemon the runaway slave Onesimus, now a Christian, sends him back 'for good, no longer as a slave, but as more than a slave—as a dear brother, very dear indeed to me and how much more to you, both as a man and as a Christian' (Phil. 15–16). But their earthly relationship of master and slave (surprisingly for our modern expectations) is, so far as we can see, to remain, not abolished but in a vital way made part of the divine order: slaves, says Paul elsewhere, should be obedient to their masters." Oddie, *What Will Happen to God?* 53–54.
67. Albert Barnes, *An Inquiry Into the Scriptural Views of Slavery* (New York: Negro Universities Press, 1969 [1857]), 289.
68. For example, why did Paul command submission? It is because this submission fitted well with the culture of the day where women were commanded by Jewish and Roman law to obey their husbands and women were not highly regarded. Paul's commands regarding submission are to keep the peace in a culture where women were more ignorant and generally prohibited from speaking in public. See Richard Boldrey and Joyce Boldrey, *Chauvinist or Feminist? Paul's View of Women* (Grand Rapids: Baker, 1976), 70; Groothuis, *Good News for Women*, 169–70; van der Walt, *The Bible as Eye-Opener*, 21–22.
69. Daly, before moving to a post-Christian feminine position, wrote, "The New Testament gave advice to women (and to slaves) which would help them to bear the subhuman (by today's standards) conditions imposed upon them. It would be foolish to erect, on this basis, a picture of 'immutable' feminine qualities and virtues. Thus, although obedience was required of women and slaves, there is nothing about obedience which makes it intrinsically more appropriate for women than for men." Daly, *The Church and the Second Sex*, 33.
70. Eve LaPlante, *Salem Witch Judge: The Life and Repentance of Samuel Sewall* (New York: HarperCollins, 2007), 301.
71. Hopkins, *Inquiry Into the Scriptural Views of Slavery*, 118–22.
72. Albert Barnes, *Ephesians, Philippians, Colossians*, in *Barnes' Notes*, ed. Robert Frew (Grand

Rapids: Baker, 1996 [1884–1885]), 122.
73. Hopkins, *A Scriptural, Ecclesiastical, and Historical View of Slavery*, 229.
74. Ibid., 231.
75. Barnes, *Inquiry Into the Scriptural Views of Slavery*, 162–65.
76. Adrio König, *Menslike Mense* (Halfway House: Orion, 1993), 148.
77. James B. Stewart, *Holy Warriors: The Abolitionists and American Slavery* (New York: Hill and Wang, 1976), 4, 62.
78. Hopkins, *Inquiry Into the Scriptural Views of Slavery*, 341–46.
79. Ibid., 345.
80. Smith, *In His Image*, 134.
81. Hopkins, *Inquiry Into the Scriptural Views of Slavery*, 220.
82. Dwight L. Dumond, *Antislavery Origins of the Civil War in the United States* (Ann Arbor, MI: The University of Michigan Press, 1959), 48–49.
83. Barnes, *Inquiry Into the Scriptural Views of Slavery*, 102–3.
84. Ibid., 288.
85. Ibid., 294.
86. Ibid., 340.
87. Kevin Giles writes, "In regard to slavery and the subordination of women the truth of the matter is that while the Bible supports both at one level, at another level there is a critique of both these oppressive structures. There are within Scripture great principles laid down clearly, for those with eyes to see, which point beyond the advice given to particular people at particular times on these matters." Kevin Giles, "The Biblical Argument for Slavery: Can the Bible Mislead? A Case Study in Hermeneutics," *Evangelical Quarterly* 66 (1994): 16. See also Boldrey and Boldrey, *Chauvinist or Feminist?* 48; Mollenkott, "Women and the Bible," 20.
88. Ruether, "Is Feminism the End of Christianity?" 396.
89. Willard Swartley writes, "Abolitionist writers gave priority to theological principles and basic moral imperatives, which in turn put slavery under moral judgment. The point we should learn from this is that theological principles and basic moral imperatives should be primary biblical resources for addressing social issues today." Willard M. Swartley, *Slavery, Sabbath, War, and Women: Case Issues in Biblical Interpretation* (Scottdale, PA: Herald, 1983), 61.
90. Hopkins, *Inquiry Into the Scriptural Views of Slavery*, 357.
91. Hampson, "On Autonomy and Heteronomy," 3.
92. Piper and Grudem, "Overview of Central Concerns," 66.
93. For example, Wayne Grudem, *Evangelical Feminism: A New Path to Liberalism?* (Wheaton: Crossway, 2006), 78–79.
94. Dumond, *Antislavery Origins of the Civil War in the United States*, 40.
95. David Brion Davis, *Inhuman Bondage: The Rise and Fall of Slavery in the New World* (Oxford: Oxford University Press, 2006), 37.
96. Albert A. Bell, *Exploring the New Testament World: An Illustrated Guide to the World of Jesus and the First Christians* (Nashville: Thomas Nelson, 1998), 193.
97. Jennifer A. Glancy, *Slavery in Early Christianity* (Minneapolis: Fortress, 2006), 14, 27, 70.
98. A central theme of Glancy's book is on the sexual availability and abuse of slaves. Glancy, *Slavery in Early Christianity*. Bell writes, "The frequent references in the laws to children born of slave women and free men suggest that such liaisons were common." Bell, *Exploring the New Testament*, 238.
99. Glancy, *Slavery in Early Christianity*, 21.
100. Ibid., 51.
101. Bell, *Exploring the New Testament*, 238.
102. J. Albert Harrill, "Slavery," in *Dictionary of New Testament Background*, eds. Craig A. Evans and Stanley E. Porter (Downers Grove, IL: InterVarsity, 2000), 1125.
103. Rodney Stark, *For the Glory of God: How Monotheism Led to Reformations, Science, Witch-*

Hunts, and the End of Slavery (Princeton, NJ: Princeton University Press, 2003), 296; Davis, *Inhuman Bondage*, 44.
104. Bell, *Exploring the New Testament*, 100.
105. J. Albert Harrill, *Slaves in the New Testament: Literary, Social, and Moral Dimensions* (Minneapolis: Fortress, 2006), 158.
106. Harrill, *Slaves in the New Testament*, 158–59.
107. Davis, *Inhuman Bondage*, 45.
108. Ibid.
109. Glancy, *Slavery in Early Christianity*, 51; Davis, *Inhuman Bondage*, 42.
110. Stark, *For the Glory of God*, 297.
111. Ibid., 299.
112. Seneca, Moral Epistles, 47 "On Master and Slave," in *Seneca Ad Lucilium Epistulae Morales: With an English Translation by Richard M. Gummere* (Cambridge, MA: Harvard University Press, 1917), 307, see also 303.
113. Harrill, "Slavery," 1127.
114. Ibid., 1125.
115. Davis, *Inhuman Bondage*, 43.
116. Stark, *For the Glory of God*, 291; see also 299–301.
117. "Slavery," in *The Oxford Dictionary of the Christian Church*, eds. F. L. Cross and E. A. Livingstone, 3rd ed. rev. (Oxford: Oxford University Press, 2005), 1519.
118. Stark, *For the Glory of God*, 329–34.
119. Piper and Grudem, "Overview of Central Concerns," 65.
120. Edmund P. Clowney, *The Church*, Contours of Christian Theology series, ed. Gerald Bray, (Downers Grove, IL: InterVarsity, 1995), 228.
121. Patterson, "Aspects of a Biblical Theology of Womanhood," 60.
122. Knight, "Husbands and Wives," 177.
123. Hopkins, *A Scriptural, Ecclesiastical, and Historical View of Slavery*, 8; Smith, *In His Image*, 196.
124. Mark A. Noll, *The Civil War as a Theological Crisis* (Chapel Hill, NC: The University of North Carolina Press, 2006), 50.
125. McPherson, *The Struggle for Equality*, 136. Similarly, Swartley writes, "In the slavery debate, both sides used the whole Bible remarkably well, and the whole Bible was perceived to support opposing positions!" Swartley, *Slavery, Sabbath, War, and Women*, 60.
126. Eve LaPlante, a direct descendant of Sewall, recently wrote an intriguing and moving account of his life in her book *Salem Witch Judge*. The details on Sewell that follow are taken from her material.
127. LaPlante, *Salem Witch Judge*, 300–4.
128. Ibid., 304–311. The full title was "Talitha Cumi: or an invitation to women to look after their inheritance in the heavenly mansions." *Talitha Cumi* refers to the Aramaic in Mark 5:21: "Little girl, stand up." Sewell probably wrote this at the deathbed of his daughter.
129. See Harrill, *Slaves in the New Testament*, 193–96, for a fine analysis of this Baptist resolution.
130. Copies of the SBC and PCA resolutions can be viewed at http://www.sbc.net/resolutions/amResolution.asp?ID=899 and http://www.pcahistory.org/pca/race.html.
131. For example, McPherson, *Battle Cry of Freedom*, 65, 196, 241; Manning, *What This Cruel War Was Over*, 32, 37, 205, 210, 217.
132. Brian Reid writes that the war "resulted from a fundamental disagreement between two sections, North and South, about the place of chattel slavery in the Union. Without the slavery question there would have been no war. The southern emphasis on 'states rights' was essentially a coded phrase for the defense of slavery." Brian H. Reid, "American Civil War," in *The Oxford Companion to Military History*, ed. Richard Holmes (Oxford: Oxford University Press, 2001), 35. Davis notes President Lincoln's perspective on the Thirteenth Amendment,

which abolished slavery, as a document that "rooted out 'the original disturbing cause' of the great rebellion and civil war." Davis, *Inhuman Bondage*, 322. See also pp. 297–322 for how the issue of slavery as the cause of the war was repressed. Stark writes, "The Civil War was primarily about slavery, not about the economic interests of the industrial North versus those of the agricultural South." Stark, *For the Glory of God*, 346.
133. McPherson, *Battle Cry of Freedom*, 241.
134. Ibid., 78–79.
135. Ibid., 51, 106, 129, 168.
136. Ibid., 241.
137. Ibid., 71.
138. Ibid., 40.
139. Manning, *What This Cruel War Was Over*, 21.
140. Ibid., 11–12, 169.
141. "The most powerful motivator remained Confederate troops' certainty that they must fight to prevent the abolition of slavery, the worst of all possible disasters that could befall southern white men and their families." Manning, *What This Cruel War Was Over*, 138. See also pp. 32, 210.
142. McPherson, *Battle Cry of Freedom*, 84.
143. Ibid., 152, 203.
144. Richard B. Hays, *Echoes of Scripture in the Letters of Paul* (New Haven, CT, and London: Yale University Press, 1989), 160.
145. Ibid., 156.
146. Robert W. Jenson, *Systematic Theology*, vol. 1, *The Triune God* (New York: Oxford University Press, 1997), 5.
147. Contrary to post-Christian feminist claims, we have noted that the Bible embeds slavery in its message. There is significant slavery imagery applied to God, Jesus, our relationship to God, and our relationship to other people. Consistency asks that post-Christian feminists also take account of the power and influence of these images. Nevertheless, we grant that post-Christian feminist concerns are more foundational and that patriarchal imagery is more extensive and embedded than slavery.

Chapter 3: The Sabbath Debate—Further Implications for Our Topic

1. The Sabbath is usually neglected in discussions on gender. Willard Swartley is one exception, and I have used his outline of the different Sabbath positions as a basis for my own. See Willard M. Swartley, *Slavery, Sabbath, War, and Women: Case Issues in Biblical Interpretation* (Scottdale, PA: Herald, 1983), 65–90.
2. Samuele Bacchiocchi, *Divine Rest for Human Restlessness: A Theological Study of the Good News of the Sabbath for Today* (Berrien Springs, MI: Biblical Perspectives, 1988), 34.
3. M. L. Andreason, *The Sabbath: Which Day and Why?* (Washington, DC: Review and Herald, 1942), 236.
4. Ibid., 53.
5. Ibid., 56–57.
6. Bacchiocchi, *Divine Rest for Human Restlessness*, 42.
7. Niels-Erik A. Andreason, *The Old Testament Sabbath: A Tradition-Historical Investigation* (Missoula, MT: The Society of Biblical Literature, 1972), 174, 199.
8. Andreason, *The Sabbath*, 148.
9. Walter F. Specht, "The Sabbath in the New Testament," in *The Sabbath in Scripture and History*, ed. Kenneth A. Strand (Washington, DC: Review and Herald, 1982), 94.
10. Samuele Bacchiocchi, *From Sabbath to Sunday: A Historical Investigation of the Rise of Sunday Observance in Early Christianity* (Rome: Pontifical Gregorian University Press, 1977).
11. Gerhard F. Hasel, "The Sabbath in the Pentateuch," in Strand, *Sabbath in Scripture and*

History, 36.
12. Ibid., 37.
13. Hans K. LaRondelle, "Contemporary Theologies of the Sabbath," in Strand, *Sabbath in Scripture and History*, 285.
14. Ibid., 293.
15. Walter F. Specht, "Sunday in the New Testament," in Strand, *Sabbath in Scripture and History*, 123–24.
16. Andreason, *The Sabbath: Which Day and Why?* 169–70.
17. Ibid., 171.
18. Raoul Dederen, "On Esteeming One Day as Better Than Another—Romans 14:5, 6," in Strand, *Sabbath in Scripture and History*, 335–36.
19. Kenneth H. Wood, "The 'Sabbath Days' of Colossians 2:16, 17," in Strand, *Sabbath in Scripture and History*, 338–41.
20. Andreason, *The Sabbath*, 173–74.
21. Specht, "Sunday in the New Testament," 124–25.
22. LaRondelle, "Contemporary Theologies of the Sabbath," 288–89; Specht, "Sabbath in the New Testament," 126.
23. Specht, "Sabbath in the New Testament," 111.
24. Bacchiocchi, "From Sabbath to Sunday," in *The Biblical Day of Rest*, ed. Francois Swanepoel (Pretoria, South Africa: UNISA, 1995), 60.
25. John Murray, *Collected Writings of John Murray*, vol. 1, *The Claims of Truth* (Edinburgh: Banner of Truth, 1976), 206–8; John Murray, *Principles of Conduct: Aspects of Biblical Ethics* (Grand Rapids: Eerdmans, 1957), 30–35.
26. Murray writes, "In a word, sin does not abrogate creation ordinances and redemption does not make superfluous their obligation and fulfillment." Murray, *Claims of Truth*, 206.
27. Murray, *Claims of Truth*, 216.
28. Ibid., 221.
29. Greg L. Bahnsen, *Theonomy in Christian Ethics*, 2nd ed. (Phillipsburg, NJ: Presbyterian and Reformed, 1984), 228–30.
30. Ibid., 230.
31. Roger T. Beckwith and Wilfrid Stott, *The Christian Sunday: A Biblical and Historical Study* (Grand Rapids: Baker, 1978), 13–14, 44–45.
32. Ibid., 12.
33. Ibid., 44.
34. J. Douma, *The Ten Commandments: Manual for the Christian Life*, trans. Nelson D. Kloosterman (Phillipsburg, NJ: Presbyterian and Reformed, 1996), 138.
35. Christi Coetzee, "The New Testament Day of Rest/Feast Day," in Swanepoel, *Biblical Day of Rest*, 74.
36. Paul K. Jewett, *The Lord's Day: A Theological Guide to the Christian Day of Worship* (Grand Rapids: Eerdmans, 1971), 100–5.
37. Ibid., 105.
38. Ibid., 107.
39. Ibid., 117.
40. Ibid., 83–84.
41. Ibid., 152, 164.
42. Ibid., 92.
43. Adrio König, "Sabbath and Sanctification," in Swanepoel, *Biblical Day of Rest*, 88–89.
44. D. R. de Lacey, "The Sabbath/Sunday Question and the Law in the Pauline Corpus," in *From Sabbath to Lord's Day: A Biblical, Historical, and Theological Investigation*, ed. D. A. Carson (Grand Rapids: Zondervan, 1982), 173, 180–84.
45. König, "Sabbath and Sanctification," 89. See also Adrio König, *Sondag: Die Dag Van die Here*

(Pretoria, South Africa: N. G. Kerk, 1964), 29–36.
46. D. A. Carson, "Introduction," in Carson, *From Sabbath to Lord's Day*, 16.
47. H. P. Dressler, "The Sabbath in the Old Testament," in Carson, *From Sabbath to Lord's Day*, 34.
48. A. T. Lincoln, "From Sabbath to Lord's Day: A Biblical and Theological Perspective," in Carson, *From Sabbath to Lord's Day*, 368.
49. de Lacey, "Sabbath/Sunday Question," 195, n. 166.
50. Ibid., 181.
51. Ibid., 182–83.
52. Ibid., 185.
53. König, "Sabbath and Sanctification," 90; A. T. Lincoln, "Sabbath, Rest, and Eschatology in the New Testament," in Carson, *From Sabbath to Lord's Day*, 215.
54. Lincoln, "Sabbath, Rest, and Eschatology in the New Testament," 214.
55. Ibid.
56. Ibid., 216.
57. Jewett, *The Lord's Day*, 100–6.
58. Calvin, *The Library of Christian Classics, Vol. XX*, ed. John T. McNeill, vol. 1, *Calvin: Institutes of the Christian Religion*, trans. Ford L. Battles (Philadelphia: Westminster, 1960), 395.
59. Ibid., 399.
60. Ibid.
61. Ibid.
62. Douma corrects a misconception that claims that Calvin allowed for meetings at intervals longer than a week. Douma, *Ten Commandments*, 124.
63. John Calvin, *Commentaries on the First Book of Moses Called Genesis*, trans. John King (Grand Rapids: Baker, 1993), 106.
64. Richard B. Gaffin, "Calvin and the Sabbath" (MTh thesis, Westminster Theological Seminary, 1962), reprinted in 1981 with new pagination, 54.
65. Beckwith and Stott, *Christian Sunday*, 6.
66. Bahnsen, for example, does not explain how, according to his theonomic position, this change to the Decalogue is permissible. According to Bahnsen, apart from ceremonial law that was rescinded by Jesus' work, a Christian is obligated to obey the entire Old Testament law. His Sunday-Sabbath view contradicts his thesis that the Old Testament law (Decalogue inclusive) is binding in exhaustive detail and not abrogated by Christ (p. 264). Bahnsen's stress on the Mosaic law at the expense of the situation in which the law was given does not allow him to hold consistently to his thesis—that is, account for a change to the Sabbath commandment. His emphasis on the Mosaic law does not take sufficient account of the cultural situation in which the law was given. Hence Bahnsen's criticism of Meredeth Kline's work that derives interpretative implications from ancient Near East treaties (pp. 571–84). See Bahnsen, *Theonomy in Christian Ethics*, 213, 310, 312–13.
67. Coetzee writes, "Therefore it must be clear: a command or decision that the Sabbath as day of rest within the New Covenant, thus for Christians, must be moved from the seventh day (Saturday) to the first day (Sunday) does not exist, not from Jesus Christ, or from his apostles, or anywhere in the New Testament." Coetzee, "New Testament Day of Rest/Feast Day," 78.
68. N. T. Wright, *Surprised by Hope: Rethinking Heaven, the Resurrection, and the Mission of the Church* (New York: HarperOne, 2008), 62.
69. See, for example, in Westerholm, "It is clear that, for Paul, Torah was a unit." Stephen Westerholm, *Israel's Law and the Church's Faith: Paul and His Recent Interpreters* (Grand Rapids: Eerdmans, 1988), 208. Or in Longenecker, "In most forms of Judaism, the law was perceived to be an indivisible whole." Bruce W. Longenecker, *The Triumph of Abraham's God: The Transformation of Identity in Galatians* (Nashville: Abingdon, 1998), 32. Although this

would take us far from our topic, we could also include a discussion on the temporality of the Torah.
70. E. P. Sanders, *Paul and Palestinian Judaism: A Comparison of Patterns of Religion* (Minneapolis: Fortress, 1977).
71. For example, N. T. Wright, *The New Testament and the People of God* (Minneapolis: Fortress, 1992), 151–52.
72. Beckwith and Stott, *Christian Sunday*, 7; Bruce K. Waltke, "The Role of Women in the Bible," *Crux* 31, no. 3 (1995): 30; Douma, *Ten Commandments*, 181.
73. As we have seen with Calvin's position on the Sabbath, it is possible to hold to a creation ordinance and yet maintain a different principle. Similarly, most egalitarians find the principle in the marriage ordinance as one of "source" rather than "headship," and thus see no need for a structural change.
74. Douma, *Ten Commandments*, 138.
75. It is sometimes argued that wife submission comes under the fifth commandment of honoring father and mother and its general application of submission to all authority. For such argumentation see Douma, *Ten Commandments*, 181. But this argument begs the question. To demonstrate that it came under the Decalogue, one would have to assume the point under discussion.
76. Waltke, "Role of Women in the Bible," 34, 36–37.
77. Wright, *Surprised by Hope*, 55.
78. Ibid. See also N. T. Wright, *The Resurrection of the Son of God* (Minneapolis: Fortress, 2003), 607–8.
79. Vern S. Poythress, "Two Hermeneutical Tensions in Evangelical Feminism," paper presented at the Eastern Regional ETS Conference, Philadelphia, April 5, 1991, 2; Wayne Grudem, *Systematic Theology* (Grand Rapids: Zondervan, 1994), 938–39.

Chapter 4: Origins, Sex, and Evolution

1. Rob DeSalle and Ian Tattersall, *Human Origins: What Bones and Genomes Tell Us about Ourselves* (College Station, TX: Texas A&M University Press, 2008), 69.
2. Charles Darwin, *On the Origin of Species*, in *From So Simple a Beginning: The Four Great Books of Charles Darwin*, ed. Edward O. Wilson (New York: Norton, 2006 [1859]), 489–90.
3. Ibid., 502.
4. Charles Darwin, *The Descent of Man, and Selection in Relation to Sex*, in *From So Simple a Beginning: The Four Great Books of Charles Darwin*, ed. Edward O. Wilson (New York: Norton, 2006 [1871]). Darwin provides numerous examples for his theory of sexual selection, spending four chapters on birds alone (pp. 1043–1155).
5. The middle of the twentieth century saw the rise of the subdiscipline of paleoanthropology: the study of human origins that includes areas of archaeology, diet, anatomy, geology, and fossils. DeSalle and Tattersall, *Human Origins*, 22.
6. Donald R. Prothero, *Evolution: What the Fossils Say and Why It Matters* (New York: Columbia University Press, 2007).
7. There is debate over whether to use *hominin* or *hominid*. I am following the approach that uses hominid to refer to humans and their related extinct forms.
8. Prothero, *Evolution*, 318–22.
9. Ibid., 113.
10. Francis S. Collins, *The Language of God: A Scientist Presents Evidence for Belief* (New York: Free Press, 2007), 133–34.
11. DeSalle and Tattersall, *Human Origins*, 70. It appears that there is not one agreed on figure, depending on how the comparison is made. Whatever the exact percentage, we are very closely related to chimps. In fact, in terms of DNA similarity, we are closer to chimps than chimps are to gorillas.

12. Collins, *Language of God*, 127–30.
13. Daniel J. Fairbanks, *Relics of Eden: The Powerful Evidence of Evolution in Human DNA* (Amherst, NY: Prometheus Books, 2007), 12–13.
14. For example, Michael Shermer, *Why Darwin Matters: The Case Against Intelligent Design* (New York: Owl Books, 2006), 12–13.
15. Fairbanks, *Relics of Eden*, 124.
16. Prothero, *Evolution*, 257–60.
17. Ibid., 99.
18. DeSalle and Tattersall write, "There are, in fact, five major ways genomes in populations can change with time—natural selection, migration, genetic drift, altered mating patterns such as inbreeding, and mutation." DeSalle and Tattersall, *Human Origins*, 77. See also Nicholas Wade, *Before the Dawn: Recovering the Lost History of Our Ancestors* (New York: Penguin, 2007), 80.
19. Sean B. Carroll, *Endless Forms Most Beautiful: The New Science of Evo Devo and the Making of the Animal Kingdom* (New York: Norton, 2005), 9.
20. Carroll, *Endless Forms Most Beautiful*, 9.
21. Ibid., 139, 145.
22. Ibid., 11, 131.
23. Ibid., 135.
24. Ibid., 180.
25. Ibid., 180, 289.
26. Ibid., 65–69.
27. Ibid., 10.
28. Neil Shubin, *Your Inner Fish: A Journey Into the 3.5 Billion-Year History of the Human Body* (New York: Pantheon Books, 2008).
29. Ibid., 39.
30. Ibid., 185–86.
31. Ibid., 85.
32. Ibid., 90–93.
33. Ibid., 190–92.
34. Ibid., 192.
35. Ibid., 193–96.
36. Ibid., 196.
37. See Prothero, *Evolution*, 108–11. Added to this point of visible embryological similarities is now the work of evo-devo that shows that organisms have the same genetic tool kit, thus the visible similarities correspond to underlying genetic similarities. Miller, in comparing the vertebrate embryos of fish, frog, chick, and mouse, writes, "For years biologists have noted that embryos from different vertebrate classes show certain striking similarities as they develop. Critics of evolution have instead preferred to emphasize the distinct differences between such embryos. A deeper comparison can now be made with the tools of molecular genetics. A genetic map of the nervous system compartments in which master control genes are active shows that the very same sets of genes are expressed in corresponding compartments of each type of embryo." Kenneth R. Miller, *Only a Theory: Evolution and the Battle for America's Soul* (New York: Viking, 2008), 132.
38. Prothero, *Evolution*, 344–45.
39. Lawrence M. Krauss and Robert J. Scherrer, "The End of Cosmology?" *Scientific American* (March 2008): 47.
40. This idea was originally proposed in the 1920s by the scientist-priest Georges Lemaître.
41. Paul J. Steinhardt and Neil Turok, *Endless Universe: Beyond the Big Bang* (New York: Doubleday, 2007).
42. The concept of "brane" as defined by Steinhardt and Turok is "derived from 'membrane,' a basic object in string theory consisting of a one-, two-, or higher-dimensional surface that

can move through space, stretch, curve, wiggle, and collide with other similar constituents. In this terminology, a string is a 1-brane, a membrane is a 2-brane, and the three-dimensional space we live in is a 3-brane." Steinhardt and Turok, *Endless Universe*, 260. To illustrate the theory they refer to double-glazed glass (p. 139): a window that has two pieces of glass with air in between. Our universe is on a brane—one of the pieces of glass—separated by a small gap (a separate spatial dimension) from another hidden world lying on the other piece of glass. About every trillion years or so these branes collide, causing the start of another Big Bang. The theory provides intriguing answers to some of the difficulties with the standard model, including the infinite temperature and density at the beginning, the inconceivably vast and split-second expansion required, and the place of dark energy.

43. Neil deGrasse Tyson, *Death by Black Hole: And Other Cosmic Quandaries* (New York: Norton, 2007), 192.
44. Jack Repcheck, *The Man Who Found Time: James Hutton and the Discovery of the Earth's Antiquity* (Cambridge, MA: Perseus Publishing, 2003).
45. Simon Lamb and David Sington, *Earth Story: The Shaping of Our World* (Princeton, NJ: Princeton University Press, 1998), 12–16.
46. Repcheck, *The Man Who Found Time*, 152–53.
47. Quoted in Repcheck, *The Man Who Found Time*, 1.
48. Shubin, *Your Inner Fish*, 11.
49. G. Brent Dalrymple, "The Ages of the Earth, Solar System, Galaxy, and Universe," in *Scientists Confront Intelligent Design and Creationism*, eds. Andrew J. Petto and Laurie R. Godfrey (New York: Norton, 2007), 150.
50. Prothero, *Evolution*, 145.
51. Ibid., 58.
52. The classic treatment of revolutions in science is Kuhn. He notes that science every so often undergoes a paradigm change, like a hermit crab getting rid of its shell. Thomas S. Kuhn, *The Structure of Scientific Revolutions*, 2nd ed. (Chicago: The University of Chicago Press, 1970).
53. A number of scientists, including Carl Sagan, have noted that evolution is both a fact and a theory. Kenneth Miller writes, "Evolution is both a fact and a theory. It is a fact that evolutionary change took place. And evolution is also a theory that seeks to explain the detailed mechanism behind that change." Kenneth R. Miller, *Finding Darwin's God: A Scientist's Search for Common Ground Between God and Evolution* (New York: Harper Perennial, 2007), 54.
54. John Polkinghorne, *Science and Theology: An Introduction* (Minneapolis: Fortress, 1998), 119.
55. DeSalle and Tattersall, *Human Origins*, 41.
56. String theory hopes to resolve the incompatibilities between the theories of relativity and quantum mechanics and provide a new unified theory. It holds that the smallest parts of matter are not atoms, electrons, or quarks, but one-dimensional loops of vibrating strings. The different vibrations of these strings give rise to all other particles. The theory also postulates that space has other hidden dimensions, six other dimensions (or seven with M-theory) hiding or curled up in our common three (plus time). I have the aesthetic hope that string theory is correct, which would mean that at the smallest level of existence there is *music*, the vibration of strings. For a readable overview, see Brian Greene, *The Elegant Universe: Superstrings, Hidden Dimensions, and the Quest for the Ultimate Theory* (New York: Vintage Books, 1999), and Brian Greene, *The Fabric of the Cosmos: Space, Time, and the Texture of Reality* (New York: Alfred A. Knopf, 2004), 327–412. For an argument against string theory, see Peter Woit, *Not Even Wrong: The Failure of String Theory and the Search for Unity in Physical Law* (New York: Basic Books, 2006).
57. Many trace the beginnings of the ID movement to Phillip E. Johnson, *Darwin on Trial* (Downers Grove, IL: InterVarsity, 1991).
58. Michael J. Behe, *Darwin's Black Box: The Biochemical Challenge to Evolution* (New York: The Free Press, 1996), 39.

59. William A. Dembski, *The Design Revolution: Answering the Toughest Questions about Intelligent Design* (Downers Grove, IL: InterVarsity, 2004), 33–37, 75–77.
60. DeSalle and Tattersall, *Human Origins*, 20.
61. Richard Feynman, *The Pleasure of Finding Things Out: The Best Short Works of Richard Feynman* (Cambridge, MA: Perseus Books, 1999), 12.
62. Miller, *Finding Darwin's God*, 240.
63. Ibid., 140–61.
64. Ibid., 157.
65. Ibid., 160.
66. Shermer, *Why Darwin Matters*, 69.
67. One of Kenneth Miller's concerns with Phillip Johnson's book, *Darwin on Trial*, is that Johnson attacks evolutionary theory but fails to provide any alternative or better explanation. Miller, *Finding Darwin's God*, 123.
68. Miller, *Only a Theory*, 177.
69. For a fine discussion of the trial see Edward Humes, *Monkey Girl: Evolution, Education, Religion, and the Battle for America's Soul* (New York: Harper Perennial, 2008). And for a more personal account see Lauri Lebo, *The Devil in Dover: An Insider's Story of Dogma v. Darwin in Small-Town America* (New York: The New Press, 2008).
70. Judge Jones concluded that ID was not science for three reasons: "(1) ID violates the centuries-old ground rules of science by invoking and permitting supernatural causation; (2) the argument of irreducible complexity, central to ID, employs the same flawed and illogical contrived dualism that doomed creation science in the 1980s; and (3) ID's negative attacks on evolution have been refuted by the scientific community. . . . It is additionally important to note that ID has failed to gain acceptance in the scientific community, it has not generated peer-reviewed publications, nor has it been the subject of testing and research." Quoted in Eugenie C. Scott, "Creation Science Lite: 'Intelligent Design' as the New Anti-Evolutionism," in Petto and Godfrey, *Scientists Confront Intelligent Design and Creationism*, 100–1.
71. Even Behe concedes that the earth is ancient and that life descended from a common ancestor. Behe, *Darwin's Black Box*, 5.
72. John F. Haught, *Christianity and Science: Toward a Theology of Nature* (Maryknoll, NY: Orbis, 2007), 141. Polkinghorne speaks of the "many-layered character" of reality. John Polkinghorne, *Belief in God in an Age of Science* (New Haven, CT: Yale University Press, 1998), 19.
73. Alan Walker, *Franz Liszt: Volume One, the Virtuoso Years 1811–1847*, rev. ed. (Ithaca, NY: Cornell University Press, 1988), 154.
74. For example, Charles Templeton, a former mass evangelist, gives the evidence from science as one reason for his rejection of Christianity. See Charles Templeton, *Farewell to God: My Reasons for Rejecting the Christian Faith* (Toronto: McClelland & Stewart, 1999), 6–7, 48–50.
75. Darwin, *Descent of Man*, 1248.
76. Fairbanks, *Relics of Eden*, 109–10.
77. For a current summary of human evolution, see DeSalle and Tattersall, *Human Origins*, 113–37.
78. Prothero, *Evolution*, 339; DeSalle and Tattersall, *Human Origins*, 113–14.
79. Current indications are that Neanderthals were a different species. Although they buried their dead, they did not possess our symbolic capacities. DeSalle and Tattersall, *Human Origins*, 178, 191–94.
80. Mark Ridley, *Evolution* (Oxford: Blackwell, 2004), 546, 550.
81. C. Loring Brace, "Human Emergence: Natural Process or Divine Creation?" in Petto and Godfrey, *Scientists Confront Intelligent Design and Creationism*, 274.
82. Collins, *Language of God*, 126.

83. Wade, *Before the Dawn*, 58.
84. Fairbanks, *Relics of Eden*, 14.
85. John Maddox, *What Remains to Be Discovered: Mapping the Secrets of the Universe, the Origins of Life, and the Future of the Human Race* (London: Macmillan, 1998), 252.
86. Richard Dawkins, *The Ancestor's Tale: A Pilgrimage to the Dawn of Evolution* (New York: Mariner Books, 2004), 424.
87. Speaking of genes, the Y chromosome, which only males carry, is deteriorating, decaying—disappearing. It once was home to thousands of genes, and now only has twenty-seven. Based on its decay scientists estimate that it will disappear in 125,000 years. This leaves two options: what determines maleness will jump to another chromosome, or there will only be females. Given the advantages of the sexes, male determination will probably jump to another chromosome. Or perhaps nature herself will solve the problem of patriarchy. See DeSalle and Tattersall, *Human Origins*, 139–40.
88. Joan Roughgarden, *Evolution's Rainbow: Diversity, Gender, and Sexuality in Nature and People* (Berkeley: University of California Press, 2004), 17.
89. Dawkins, *Ancestor's Tale*, 431.
90. Ridley, *Evolution*, 315.
91. Quoted in Matt Ridley, *The Red Queen: Sex and the Evolution of Human Nature* (New York: Harper Perennial, 2003), 29.
92. Ridley, *Evolution*, 320.
93. See Ridley for the following illustration, originally provided by John Maynard Smith. Ridley, *Evolution*, 320.
94. Ridley, *Evolution*, 323.
95. John Maynard Smith, "The Evolution of Sex," in *The Evolution of Sex*, eds. Robert Bellig and George Stevens (New York: Harper & Row, 1988), 16; Ridley, *Red Queen*, 63–64.
96. Ridley, *Evolution*, 323–27.
97. Roughgarden, *Evolution's Rainbow*, 17.
98. Ibid., 18.
99. Roughgarden, *Evolution's Rainbow*, 171.
100. John Haught writes, "Some version of hierarchy, theology rightly insists, remains essential to any intelligible conception of cosmic meaning. To deny hierarchy altogether would be to plunge our lives and minds into a swamp of unqualified relativism, wherein religious and ethical claims would have no basis and nothing could plausibly be said to have any enduring importance." John F. Haught, *God After Darwin: A Theology of Evolution*, 2nd ed. (Boulder, CO: Westview Press, 2008), 78.
101. For example, David B. Knox, *Sent by Jesus: Some Aspects of Christian Ministry Today* (Edinburgh: Banner of Truth, 1992), 45–47.
102. See Arthur O. Lovejoy, *The Great Chain of Being: A Study of the History of an Idea* (Cambridge, MA: Harvard University Press, 1936).
103. Dawkins, *Ancestor's Tale*, 248; DeSalle and Tattersall, *Human Origins*, 203.
104. Ridley, *Evolution*, 327–37.
105. Shermer, *Why Darwin Matters*, 134–35.
106. Ridley, *Evolution*, 329.
107. Dawkins, *Ancestor's Tale*, 207–11.
108. Ibid., 205.
109. Ibid.
110. Ibid., 207–11.
111. Ridley, *Evolution*, 329; Roughgarden, *Evolution's Rainbow*, 47–48.
112. Jared Diamond, *Why Is Sex Fun? The Evolution of Human Sexuality* (New York: Basic Books, 1997), 26.
113. Roughgarden, *Evolution's Rainbow*, 46–47.

114. Douglas Spanner, "Men, Women and God," *Churchman* 108, no. 2 (1994): 107–8.
115. Knox, *Sent by Jesus*, 45–46.
116. J. Wentzel van Huyssteen, *Duet or Duel? Theology and Science in a Postmodern World* (London: SCM Press, 1998).
117. F. LeRon Shults, *Christology and Science* (Grand Rapids: Eerdmans, 2008), 2–4.
118. For example, van Huyssteen critiques the faulty argument that the Big Bang was the moment of creation by God. van Huyssteen, *Duet or Duel?* 44–45.
119. As described by Robert Jastrow, *God and the Astronomers* (New York: W. W. Norton & Company, 1978), 28, 112–13.
120. Darwin, *On the Origin of Species*, 755.
121. The question may arise: When did we become the image of God? The question will probably never have a clear and direct answer, because with evolutionary theory the boundaries are blurred. Presumably, at some stage in our development, we developed the capacity to relate to God—just as we developed the capacity for symbolic thought and language. And at some stage God called us to be caring rulers over creation.
122. For an example from biblical studies see Ben Witherington III, *Paul's Narrative Thought World: The Tapestry of Tragedy and Triumph* (Louisville: Westminster/John Knox, 1994). For an example from practical theology see Dan B. Allender, *To Be Told: Know Your Story—Shape Your Future* (Colorado Springs: WaterBrook Press, 2005).
123. N. T. Wright, *The New Testament and the People of God* (Minneapolis: Fortress, 1992).
124. N. T. Wright, *Jesus and the Victory of God* (Minneapolis: Fortress, 1996).
125. N. T. Wright, *The Last Word: Beyond the Bible Wars to a New Understanding of the Authority of Scripture* (New York: HarperSanFrancisco, 2005).
126. N. T. Wright, *Evil and the Justice of God* (Downers Grove, IL: InterVarsity, 2006).
127. Wright, *The New Testament and the People of God*, 38.
128. Ibid., 40.
129. Wright, *Evil and the Justice of God*, 45.
130. Wright, *Jesus and the Victory of God*, 219.
131. Ibid., 197.
132. Ibid., 651.
133. N. T. Wright, *Paul: A Fresh Perspective* (Minneapolis: Fortress, 2005), 11.
134. Ibid., 7–13.
135. N. T. Wright, "The Letter to the Romans," in *The New Interpreter's Bible*, vol. 10, *Acts–First Corinthians* (Nashville: Abingdon, 2002), 586–87.
136. Wright, *New Testament and the People of God*, 141–42.
137. Wright, *The Last Word*, 121–27.
138. Haught, *Christianity and Science*, xi.
139. This emphasis on "surprising developments" in the gospel story, particularly seen in the life of Jesus, I owe to Steve Taylor.
140. See http://heasarc.gsfc.nasa.gov/docs/cosmic/nearest_star_info.html.
141. Arthur Peacocke, *Theology for a Scientific Age: Being and Becoming—Natural, Divine, and Human* (Minneapolis: Fortress, 1993), 170–73.
142. Darwin, *On the Origin of Species*, 760.
143. Wright, *Paul: A Fresh Perspective*, 11–12.
144. J. Wentzel van Huyssteen, *Alone in the World? Human Uniqueness in Science and Theology* (Grand Rapids: Eerdmans, 2006).
145. Simon Conway Morris, *Life's Solution: Inevitable Humans in a Lonely Universe* (Cambridge: Cambridge University Press, 2003).
146. Ibid., 111–12.
147. Ibid., 119.
148. Ibid., 119, 282–84, 298–99, 329, for example.

149. Shults, *Christology and Science*.
150. Jürgen Moltmann, "Is There Life After Death?" in *The End of the World and the Ends of God*, eds. John Polkinghorne and Michael Welker (Harrisburg, PA: Trinity Press International, 2000), 239.
151. Perhaps a requirement for the title of professor emeritus should be a book of "retractions."
152. http://neo.jpl.nasa.gov/apophis/
153. Tyson, *Death by Black Hole*, 264–65.
154. Ibid., 266–67.
155. Haught notes that the scientific method cannot speak of the truly new and that there are "levels of depth in nature that science simply cannot reach." Haught, *Christianity and Science*, 35.
156. This is one of the weakest arguments from the new atheists. For example, Christopher Hitchens writes that religion "comes from the bawling and fearful infancy of our species, and is a babyish attempt to meet our inescapable demand for knowledge (as well as for comfort, reassurance, and other infantile needs)." Christopher Hitchens, *God Is Not Great: How Religion Poisons Everything* (New York: Twelve, 2007), 64.

Chapter 5: Jesus' Maleness and Creation

1. The slogan of Mars Hill Graduate School in Seattle.
2. See the work of John Frame. Considering these perspectives, he notes that the three interrelate in our interpretation. One informs and corrects the other in a hermeneutical spiral. Frame writes, "We come to know Scripture through our senses and minds (self) and through Scripture's relations with the rest of the world. But then what we read in Scripture must be allowed to correct the ideas we have formed about these other areas. Then as we understand the other areas better, we understand Scripture better." John M. Frame, *The Doctrine of the Knowledge of God* (Phillipsburg, NJ: Presbyterian and Reformed, 1987), 89.
3. Ruether writes, "Human experience is the starting point and the ending point of the hermeneutical circle. . . . Systems of authority try to . . . make received symbols dictate what can be experienced as well as the interpretation of that which is experienced. In reality, the relation is the opposite. If a symbol does not speak authentically to experience, it becomes dead or must be altered to provide new meaning." Rosemary R. Ruether, *Sexism and God-Talk: Towards a Feminist Theology* (London: SCM, 1983), 12–13. Likewise, Schüssler Fiorenza argues, "A feminist critical interpretation of the Bible, I would therefore argue, cannot take as its point of departure the normative authority of the biblical archetype, but must begin with women's experience in their struggle for liberation." Elisabeth Schüssler Fiorenza, "Emerging Issues in Feminist Biblical Interpretation," in *Christian Feminism: Visions of a New Humanity*, ed. Judith L. Weidman (New York: Harper & Row, 1984), 45. See also Elisabeth Schüssler Fiorenza, "The Will to Choose or to Reject: Continuing Our Critical Work," in *Feminist Interpretation of the Bible*, ed. Letty M. Russell (Oxford: Basil Blackwell, 1985), 128.
4. Bruce K. Waltke, "The Role of Women in the Bible," *Crux* 31, no. 3 (1995): 36. See also Schreiner, "An Interpretation of 1 Timothy 2:9–15," in *Women in the Church: A Fresh Analysis of 1 Timothy 2:9–15*, eds. Andreas J. Köstenberger, Thomas R. Schreiner, and H. Scott Baldwin (Grand Rapids: Baker, 1995), 106–7.
5. Schreiner, "An Interpretation of 1 Timothy 2:9–15," 106.
6. John H. Hopkins, *A Scriptural, Ecclesiastical, and Historical View of Slavery, from the Days of the Patriarch Abraham, to the Nineteenth Century* (New York: Negro Universities Press, 1969 [1864]), 6.
7. When she held egalitarian views.
8. Concerning passages that appear to teach subordination, Jewett writes that Paul's insight had "historical limitations." Paul K. Jewett, *Man as Male and Female: A Study in Sexual*

Relationships from a Theological Point of View (Grand Rapids: Eerdmans, 1975), 138–39. Jewett argues that Paul does prohibit women from the teaching office, but this prohibition is counter to the plain teaching of the rest of the New Testament. For Jewett, there is no way to harmonize Paul's thinking on this subject (pp. 112–113). See also Paul K. Jewett, *The Ordination of Women: An Essay on the Office of Christian Ministry* (Grand Rapids: Eerdmans, 1980), 65, 67–68. Mollenkott adopted a similar view, saying, "Paul's arguments reflect his personal struggles over female subordination and show vestiges both of Greek philosophy (particularly Stoicism) and of the rabbinical training he had received from his own socialization and especially from Rabbi Gamaliel." Virginia R. Mollenkott, *Women, Men, and the Bible* (Nashville: Abingdon, 1977), 95. See also Virginia R. Mollenkott, "Women and the Bible: A Challenge to Male Interpretation," *Sojourners* 5 (Fall 1976): 22. Mollenkott maintains that there is an inherent contradiction between parts of Paul's teaching, between his subordinationist teaching and his good relationships with other women leaders in the church. She does not believe, however, that this denigrates the authority of Scripture.

9. Richard N. Longenecker, *New Testament Social Ethics for Today* (Grand Rapids: Eerdmans, 1984), 92.
10. Gordon D. Fee, *The First Epistle to the Corinthians*, The New International Commentary on the New Testament, eds. N. B. Stonehouse, F. F. Bruce, G. D. Fee (Grand Rapids: Eerdmans, 1987), 699–708. Even if we grant Fee's exegesis and arguments on 1 Corinthians 14:34–35, stepping back a bit, as yet no one has removed 1 Corinthians 14:34–35 from a translation. In other words, this text is still in our Bible and still informs the church's understanding.
11. For example, the Kroegers concentrate on the cultural background of Ephesus, including Gnosticism, mystery religions, and Greek myths, to argue for a different reading of 1 Timothy 2:11–15. Catherine C. Kroeger and Richard C. Kroeger, *I Suffer Not a Woman: Rethinking 1 Timothy 2:11–15 in Light of Ancient Evidence* (Grand Rapids: Baker, 1992).
12. Some egalitarian interpretations of 1 Timothy 2:11–15 include: (1) Commenting on 1 Timothy 2:12, Grenz writes, "On the basis of his [Paul's] choice of the present active indicative (*epitrepo*) rather than the imperative, egalitarians conclude that Paul is not voicing a timeless command, but a temporary directive applicable to a specific situation: 'I am not presently allowing.'" Stanley J. Grenz and Denise M. Kjesbo, *Women in the Church: A Biblical Theology of Women in Ministry* (Downers Grove, IL: InterVarsity, 1995), 130. (2) Richard and Joyce Boldrey argue that Paul's command is given because most women were unlearned and were considered inferior and incapable of acting without supervision. Richard Boldrey and Joyce Boldrey, *Chauvinist or Feminist? Paul's View of Women* (Grand Rapids: Baker, 1976), 23–24, 64. (3) Peter DeJong and Donald R. Wilson say that Paul is "addressing the threats to unity that are inherent in any dominant-subordinate relationship, whether political, economic, or familial." Peter DeJong and Donald R. Wilson, *Husband and Wife: The Sexes in Scripture and Society* (Grand Rapids: Zondervan, 1979), 147, see also 144–47, 160. (4) Patricia Gundry favors two possible positions: women are not allowed to teach at this time (until they are better learned), or not allowed to teach because it was not in accord with the culture. Patricia Gundry, *Women Be Free!* (Grand Rapids: Zondervan, 1977), 75–77. (5) van der Walt interprets Paul's teaching in 1 Timothy 2:12 as that he does not permit a woman to *dominate* her husband. B. J. van der Walt, *The Bible as Eye-Opener on the Position of Women* (Potchefstroom, South Africa: Potchefstroom University for Christian Higher Education, 1988), 37. (6) Catherine and Richard Kroeger translate *authentein* so that 1 Timothy 2:12–13 reads, "I do not permit woman to teach nor to represent herself as originator of man but she is to be in conformity [with the Scriptures] [or that she keeps a secret.] For Adam was created first, then Eve." In this view, what women are not allowed to teach is explained by the phrase "represent herself as originator of man." Kroeger and Kroeger, *I Suffer Not a Woman*, 103.
13. Daphne Hampson, *Theology and Feminism* (Oxford: Basil Blackwell, 1990), 151–52.

14. Rita Brock, "A Feminist Consciousness Looks at Christology," *Encounter* 41 (1980): 322; Carter Heyward, "Jesus of Nazareth/Christ of Faith: Foundations of a Reactive Christology," in *Lift Every Voice: Constructing Christian Theologies from the Underside*, eds. Susan B. Thistlethwaite and Mary P. Engel (San Francisco: Harper & Row, 1990), 196.
15. Again, much of the gospel story is about God breaking into this world; and this arrival of newness is not a violation of the laws of nature. See John F. Haught, *God After Darwin: A Theology of Evolution*, 2nd ed. (Boulder, CO: Westview Press, 2008), 17.
16. For example, Hampson, *Theology and Feminism*, 84–85.
17. Robert W. Yarbrough, "The Hermeneutics of 1 Timothy 2:9–15," in *Women in the Church: A Fresh Analysis of 1 Timothy 2:9–15*, eds. Andreas J. Köstenberger, Thomas R. Schreiner, and H. Scott Baldwin (Grand Rapids: Baker, 1995), 192.
18. Some readers may wonder how this emphasis on the gospel transformation dynamic relates to William Webb's thesis of a movement in redemptive history. I view Webb's "redemptive movement" as one part of the gospel transformation dynamic—an illustration *within* Scripture itself to the transforming work of the gospel story. See William J. Webb, *Slaves, Women, and Homosexuals: Exploring the Hermeneutics of Cultural Analysis* (Downers Grove, IL: InterVarsity, 2001).
19. J. I. Packer, "Let's Stop Making Women Presbyters," *Christianity Today* (February 11, 1991): 20.
20. Elisabeth Elliot, "The Essence of Femininity: A Personal Perspective," in *Recovering Biblical Manhood and Womanhood: A Response to Evangelical Feminism*, eds. John Piper and Wayne Grudem (Wheaton: Crossway, 1991), 398.
21. Piper and Grudem, "Overview of Central Concerns," 46–49.
22. George W. Knight III, *The New Testament Teaching on the Role Relationship of Men and Women* (Grand Rapids: Baker, 1977), 9–10.
23. Ibid., 55–56.
24. Waltke, "Role of Women in the Bible," 36.
25. Dorothy Patterson, "Aspects of a Biblical Theology of Womanhood," (DTh diss., University of South Africa, 1997), 124.
26. Ibid., 150–51.
27. Ibid., 140.
28. David B. Knox, *Sent by Jesus: Some Aspects of Christian Ministry Today* (Edinburgh: Banner of Truth, 1992), 45–46.
29. Ibid., 47.
30. Harold O. J. Brown, "The New Testament Against Itself: 1 Timothy 2:9–15 and the 'Breakthrough' of Galatians 3:28," in *Women in the Church: A Fresh Analysis of 1 Timothy 2:9–15*, eds. Andreas J. Köstenberger, Thomas R. Schreiner, and H. Scott Baldwin (Grand Rapids: Baker, 1995), 201, 206, 208.
31. Ibid., 200.
32. Thomas R. Schreiner, "Head Coverings, Prophecies and the Trinity: 1 Corinthians 11:2–16," in Piper and Grudem, *Recovering Biblical Manhood and Womanhood*, 128.
33. Schreiner, "An Interpretation of 1 Timothy 2:9–15," 145.
34. Schreiner, "Head Coverings, Prophecies and the Trinity," 139, cf. 138.
35. Steven Goldberg, *Why Men Rule: A Theory of Male Dominance* (Chicago, IL: Open Court, 1993), 115.
36. Katherine Zappone writes, "Attention to both biology and socio-cultural factors ought to be part of a feminist theological redefinition of human nature. This would mean that differences between men and women, and differences between women, shape the starting point of our theory building. What this requires of us, first and foremost, is the ability to move beyond the fear of 'difference' as an analytic category." Katherine E. Zappone, "Woman's Special Nature: A Different Horizon for Theological Anthropology," in *The Special Nature of Women?*

eds. Anne Carr and Elisabeth Schüssler Fiorenza (Netherlands: Stichting Concilium, 1991), 92.
37. Raymond C. Ortlund, "Male-Female Equality and Male Headship," in Piper and Grudem, *Recovering Biblical Manhood and Womanhood*, 99.
38. Ibid., 97–98.
39. Patterson, "Aspects of a Biblical Theology of Womanhood," 155–58.
40. Ibid., 149, 159.
41. Rebecca M. Groothuis, *Good News for Women: A Biblical Picture of Gender Equality* (Grand Rapids: Baker, 1997), 75.
42. T. F. Torrance, *The Christian Doctrine of God: One Being Three Persons* (New York: T & T Clark, 2001), 102, 124.
43. John D. Zizioulas, *Being as Communion: Studies in Personhood and the Church* (Crestwood, NY: St. Vladimir's Seminary Press, 1985), 18.
44. F. LeRon Shults, *Reforming Theological Anthropology: After the Philosophical Turn to Relationality* (Grand Rapids: Eerdmans, 2003), 31; F. LeRon Shults, *Reforming the Doctrine of God* (Grand Rapids: Eerdmans, 2005), 58–59, see also 5–6.
45. Robert Letham, "The Man-Woman Debate: Theological Comment," *Westminster Theological Journal* 52 (Spring 1990): 74.
46. Ortlund, "Male-Female Equality," 111–12.
47. Paige Patterson, "The Meaning of Authority in the Local Church," in Piper and Grudem, *Recovering Biblical Manhood and Womanhood*, 257.
48. John M. Frame, "Men and Women in the Image of God," in Piper and Grudem, *Recovering Biblical Manhood and Womanhood*, 228.
49. A. Duane Litfin, "Evangelical Feminism: Why Traditionalists Reject It," *Bibliotheca Sacra* 136 (July–September 1979): 265.
50. Patterson, "Aspects of a Biblical Theology of Womanhood," 124, 206; George W. Knight III, "Husbands and Wives as Analogues of Christ and the Church: Ephesians 5:21–33 and Colossians 3:18–19," in Piper and Grudem, *Recovering Biblical Manhood and Womanhood*, 177.
51. H. S. Smith, *In His Image, but . . . : Racism in Southern Religion, 1780–1910* (Durham, NC: Duke University Press, 1972), viii.
52. Edmund P. Clowney, *The Church*, Contours of Christian Theology series, ed. Gerald Bray, (Downers Grove, IL: InterVarsity, 1995), 228.
53. Knight, "Husbands and Wives," 171–72.
54. Patterson, "Aspects of a Biblical Theology of Womanhood," 201.
55. Knight, "Husbands and Wives," 172.
56. Patterson, "Aspects of a Biblical Theology of Womanhood," 210.
57. Ibid., 220.
58. Ibid., 219.
59. For example, Dorothy Patterson writes, "In marriage, the wife voluntarily becomes a helper to her husband just as in redemption Jesus Christ chose to humble Himself to die on the cross during His incarnation." Patterson, "Aspects of a Biblical Theology of Womanhood," 206.
60. John Piper and Wayne Grudem, "Charity, Clarity, and Hope: The Controversy and the Cause of Christ," in Piper and Grudem, *Recovering Biblical Manhood*, 414.
61. Susan T. Foh, *Women and the Word of God: A Response to Biblical Feminism* (Phillipsburg, NJ: Presbyterian and Reformed, 1980), 197.
62. A. T. Lincoln, *Ephesians*, Word Biblical Commentary, eds. D. A. Hubbard and G. W. Barker, vol. 42 (Dallas: Word, 1990), 367–80.
63. Ibid., 393.
64. Richard B. Hays, *The Moral Vision of the New Testament: A Contemporary Introduction to New*

Testament Ethics (New York: HarperCollins, 1996), 364.
65. I am indebted to Steve Taylor for his help with the following two paragraphs.
66. As is well known, Calvin started his *Institutes* connecting the knowledge of God and the knowledge of self.
67. Take, for example, the story of Kurt Wise, who over several months took a pair of scissors to a Bible and cut out every verse that conflicted with evolution. The result was a Bible that disintegrated. Kurt P. Wise, "Geology," in *In Six Days: Why Fifty Scientists Choose to Believe in Creation*, ed. John F. Ashton (Green Forest, AR: Master Books, 2001), 353–54.
68. For another example of strong ties between Christianity and social movements, note the thesis of Nancy Hardesty's book: "Nineteenth-century American feminism was deeply rooted in evangelical revivalism. Its theology and practice motivated and equipped women and men to adopt a feminist ideology, to reject stereotyped sex roles, and to work for positive changes in marriage, church, society, and politics. Most woman's rights leaders—whether in the church, education, reform organizations, or the media—were products of evangelical backgrounds or were deeply influenced by evangelical culture, whether or not they acknowledged that debt or maintained any allegiance to it in later life." Nancy A. Hardesty, *Women Called to Witness: Evangelical Feminism in the 19th Century* (Nashville: Abingdon, 1984), 9.

Chapter 6: Jesus' Maleness and His Sonship

1. Ruether's well-known question. Rosemary R. Ruether, *To Change the World: Christology and Cultural Criticism* (London: SCM, 1981), 45; Rosemary R. Ruether, *Sexism and God-Talk: Towards a Feminist Theology* (London: SCM, 1983), 116.
2. M. J. Selman, "First-Born," in *New Bible Dictionary*, 2nd ed., ed. J. D. Douglas (Leicester: InterVarsity, 1982), 378.
3. Technically, Ishmael, not Isaac, was Abraham's firstborn.
4. William L. Lane, *Hebrews 1–8*, Word Biblical Commentary, vol. 47a, eds. David A. Hubbard and Glenn W. Barker, (Dallas: Word, 1991), 26.
5. Leonhard Goppelt, *Theology of the New Testament*, vol. 1, trans. John E. Alsup (Grand Rapids: Eerdmans, 1981), 202.
6. John Nolland, *Luke 1– 9:20*, Word Biblical Commentary, vol. 35a, eds. David A. Hubbard and Glenn W. Barker (Waco: Word, 1989), 173–74.
7. Herman Ridderbos, *The Coming of the Kingdom*, trans. H. de Jongste (Philadelphia: Presbyterian and Reformed, 1962), 31.
8. James D. G. Dunn, *Christianity in the Making*, vol. 1, *Jesus Remembered* (Grand Rapids: Eerdmans, 2003), 724–62.
9. William H. Brownlee, *Ezekiel 1–19*, Word Biblical Commentary, vol. 28, eds. David A. Hubbard and Glenn W. Barker (Waco: Word, 1986), xli. Moule allows for this interpretation, while preferring the dominant background to be Daniel 7. C. F. D. Moule, *The Origin of Christology* (Cambridge: Cambridge University Press, 1977), 12. John Macquarrie overreacts by rejecting apocalyptic imagery and concentrating only on Jesus in his humanity. John Macquarrie, *Jesus Christ in Modern Thought* (London: SCM, 1990), 41–42. Many, however, argue that the term used by Ezekiel is not to be identified with "Son of Man" in the New Testament. See Geerhardus Vos, *The Self-Disclosure of Jesus: The Modern Debate about the Messianic Consciousness* (New York: George H. Doran Company, 1926), 250; Joachim Jeremias, *New Testament Theology: Part One, the Proclamation of Jesus*, trans. John Bowden (London: SCM, 1971), 268; George E. Ladd, *A Theology of the New Testament* (Grand Rapids: Eerdmans, 1974), 147; I. Howard Marshall, *The Origins of New Testament Christology* (Leicester: InterVarsity, 1976), 66; James D. G. Dunn, *Christology in the Making: A New Testament Inquiry into the Origins of the Doctrine of the Incarnation* (London: SCM, 1980), 65–97; F. F. Bruce, "The Background to the Son of Man Sayings," in *Christ the*

Lord: Studies in Christology Presented to Donald Guthrie, ed. Harold H. Rowdon (Leicester: InterVarsity, 1982), 50–70. The primary reason for this rejection is that Ezekiel's use cannot account for the apocalyptic use of Son of Man in the Gospels.

10. Leslie C. Allen, *Ezekiel 20–48*, Word Biblical Commentary, vol. 29, eds. David A. Hubbard and Glenn W. Barker (Waco: Word, 1990), 9.
11. William Brownlee writes, "When Ezekiel is addressed as 'son of man,' this means that he is spoken to as a member of the human race, not as a male." Brownlee, *Ezekiel 1–19*, 25.
12. Oscar Cullmann, *The Christology of the New Testament*, 2nd ed., trans. Shirley C. Guthrie and Charles A. M. Hall (London: SCM, 1963), 153.
13. N. T. Wright, *The New Testament and the People of God* (Minneapolis: Fortress, 1992), 291–97.
14. Carson says, "It is likely that Jesus chose 'the Son of man' as his favorite self-designation precisely because it was ambiguous." Carson allows for the background of Daniel 7 as well as the frail human side to the term that better fits the suffering motif of the Son of Man. D. A. Carson, "Christological Ambiguities in the Gospel of Matthew," in *Christ the Lord: Studies in Christology Presented to Donald Guthrie*, ed. Harold H. Rowdon (Leicester: InterVarsity, 1982), 113.
15. Jürgen Moltmann, *The Way of Jesus Christ: Christology in Messianic Dimensions*, trans. Margaret Kohl (London: SCM, 1990), 14.
16. Brian M. Nolan, *The Royal Son of God: The Christology of Matthew 1–2 in the Setting of the Gospel* (Fribourg, Switzerland: Editions Universitaires, 1979), 218; Cullmann, *Christology*, 299–305; Hendrikus Berkhof, *Christian Faith: An Introduction to the Study of the Faith*, trans. Sierd Woudstra (Grand Rapids: Eerdmans, 1979), 282–83.
17. Concerning the wilderness trial, Ridderbos writes, "It is a test to which Jesus has to submit in order to prove his perfect obedience to the Father and his commitment to the Father's mandate. The tempter's intention, accordingly, is not to deprive Jesus of his messianic certainty." Ridderbos, *The Coming of the Kingdom*, 157.
18. See, for example, Gordon D. Fee, *The First Epistle to the Corinthians*, The New International Commentary on the New Testament, eds. N. B. Stonehouse, F. F. Bruce, G. D. Fee (Grand Rapids: Eerdmans, 1987), 760.
19. Cullmann, *Christology*, 293, italics original. Cullmann clarified (modified?) his position by stating that the functional does not exclude the ontological. See Oscar Cullmann, "The Reply of Professor Cullmann to Roman Catholic Critics," *Scottish Journal of Theology* 15 (1962): 36–43.
20. Ernst Käsemann, *Commentary on Romans*, trans. Geoffrey W. Bromiley (Grand Rapids: Eerdmans, 1980), 11.
21. Richard B. Gaffin, *Resurrection and Redemption: A Study in Paul's Soteriology* (Phillipsburg, NJ: Presbyterian and Reformed, 1987), 100.
22. James D. G. Dunn, *Romans 1–8*, Word Biblical Commentary, vol. 38a, eds. David A. Hubbard and Glenn W. Barker (Waco: Word, 1988), 14.
23. C. E. B. Cranfield, *A Critical and Exegetical Commentary on the Epistle to the Romans*, vol. 1, The International Critical Commentary on the Holy Scriptures of the Old and New Testaments, ed. J. A. Emerton, C. E. B. Cranfield, and G. N. Stanton (Edinburgh: T & T Clark, 1975), 61.
24. Käsemann, *Commentary on Romans*, 11.
25. Lane, *Hebrews 1–8*, 118.
26. Wright, *New Testament and the People of God*, 395.
27. For example, Richard Bauckham argues that the highest Christology is present in all New Testament writings, for in the New Testament we find the full identity of Jesus with God—Jesus identified with divine sovereignty, creation, and the divine name. Richard Bauckham, *God Crucified: Monotheism and Christology in the New Testament* (Grand Rapids: Eerdmans, 1999), 26–27.

28. For example, from John we could have also looked at John 5:17–18; 10:30, 33, 36; 19:7. Or from Paul, Colossians 1:13–20.
29. N. T. Wright, "The Letter to the Romans," in *The New Interpreter's Bible*, vol. 10, *Acts–First Corinthians* (Nashville: Abingdon, 2002), 580.
30. Cullmann, *Christology*, 301; Dunn, *Romans 1–8*, 501; Victor P. Furnish, "'He Gave Himself [Was Given] Up': Paul's Use of a Christological Assertion," in *The Future of Christology*, eds. Abraham J. Malherbe and Wayne A. Meeks (Minneapolis: Fortress, 1993), 118; Wright, *Letter to the Romans*, 612.
31. This passage shows the impossibility of separating being and function.
32. Jenson writes, "The phrase 'Father, Son, and Holy Spirit' is simultaneously a very compressed telling of the total narrative by which Scripture identifies God and a personal name for the God so specified; in it, name and narrative description not only appear together . . . but are identical." Robert W. Jenson, *Systematic Theology*, vol. 1, *The Triune God* (New York: Oxford University Press, 1997), 46.

Chapter 7: What Have We Done with the Eternal Son?

1. Origen, *De Principiis* 1.2.1–13.
2. J. N. D. Kelly, *Early Christian Doctrines*, rev. ed. (San Francisco: Harper & Row, 1978), 233, see also 232–37. Charles Hodge notes four possible options, and concludes that the members of the council didn't explain exactly what they had in mind—that eternal generation could mean sameness of substance, or likeness (the Son as image), or derivation of essence, or something else incomprehensible to us. Charles Hodge, *Systematic Theology*, vol. 1 (1871; repr., Grand Rapids: Eerdmans, 1993), 468.
3. Jewett writes, "Analogical language, to be meaningful, must of course rest upon some univocal element between the human reality from which it is taken and the divine reality to which it refers. In our exposition of the doctrine of the Trinity, so far as God's name—Father, Son, and Spirit—is concerned, we have identified the univocal element in the concept of origins. The second and third persons in the Godhead originate, as persons, with the first person, who is therefore called 'Father.' The Father 'begets' the Son and 'breathes' ('spirates') the Spirit. But obviously in using such terms as 'begetting' and 'breathing' to describe how the second and third persons of the Godhead have their origin in the first place, we speak analogically, not univocally. And since this is so, feminine figures could as well be used without altering the substance of our thought about God." Paul K. Jewett, *God, Creation, and Revelation: A Neo-Evangelical Theology* (Grand Rapids: Eerdmans, 1991), 323–24.
4. Wayne Grudem, "The Meaning of Kephale ('Head'): A Response to Recent Studies," in *Recovering Biblical Manhood and Womanhood: A Response to Evangelical Feminism*, eds. John Piper and Wayne Grudem (Wheaton: Crossway, 1991), 456–57, 539–40; Wayne Grudem, *Systematic Theology* (Grand Rapids: Zondervan, 1994), 251.
5. Thomas R. Schreiner, "Head Coverings, Prophecies and the Trinity: 1 Corinthians 11:2–16," in Piper and Grudem, *Recovering Biblical Manhood and Womanhood*, 129–30.
6. Karl Barth, *Church Dogmatics*, vol. 4, *The Doctrine of Reconciliation, I*, trans. Geoffrey W. Bromiley (New York: Charles Scribner's Sons, 1956), 201–2.
7. Ibid., 209.
8. Ibid., 202.
9. For example, Peter Toon connects eternal generation, a male incarnation, and male priority in order to justify non-inclusive language. In *Our Triune God: A Biblical Portrayal of the Trinity* (Wheaton: Victor, 1996), 240, he writes:

> There is holy order in the creation where the male man is first in order and the female man is second in order; but, at the same time there is a perfect equality in terms of essential being of the male and female man. In the New Testament Jesus Christ, the male Man who is the Word made flesh, is proclaimed as the true image of God.

To maintain holy order we need also to maintain the long-established custom of speaking of God's creatures made in his image as man or as mankind. We do not have to be saying 'man and woman' and 'he and she' all the time. The use of the word man in the traditional sense conveys the notion of order for he being first in order contains in himself she who is second in order. It is wholly appropriate that the word man can mean both the human race and the male species; and that the word woman can only mean female man and never the human race. This, in a trinitarian perspective, mirrors the truth that the Father is first and the Son is included in the Father, for he is begotten of the Father before all ages.

10. Although our discussion is confined to the eternal generation of the Son, even scantier scriptural evidence is offered for the procession of the Spirit, such as John 14:16, 26; 1 Corinthians 2:10.
11. Benjamin B. Warfield, *Calvin and Calvinism* (Grand Rapids: Baker, 1991), 277.
12. Wolfhart Pannenberg, *Systematic Theology*, vol. 1, trans. Geoffrey W. Bromiley (Grand Rapids: Eerdmans, 1991), 306.
13. Ibid., 306.
14. D. A. Carson, *Exegetical Fallacies* (Grand Rapids: Baker, 1984), 29–30.
15. Vern S. Poythress, *Symphonic Theology: The Validity of Multiple Perspectives in Theology* (Grand Rapids: Zondervan, 1987), 74–79.
16. Murray J. Harris, *Jesus as God: The New Testament Use of Theos in Reference to Jesus* (Grand Rapids: Baker, 1992), 86–87.
17. Calvin, *The Library of Christian Classics, Vol. XX*, ed. John T. McNeill, vol. 1, *Calvin: Institutes of the Christian Religion*, trans. Ford L. Battles (Philadelphia: Westminster, 1960), 159.
18. Warfield, *Calvin and Calvinism*, 247.
19. Kelly, *Early Christian Doctrines*, 240, cf. 105–6.
20. Leonardo Boff, *Trinity and Society*, trans. Paul Burns (Maryknoll, NY: Orbis, 1988), 137–47; Pannenberg, *Systematic Theology*, vol. 1, 300–327. Millard Erickson writes, "I would propose that there are no references to the Father begetting the Son or the Father (and the Son) sending the Spirit that cannot be understood in terms of the temporal role assumed by the second and third persons of the Trinity, respectively. They do not indicate any intrinsic relationship among the three. Further, to speak of one of the persons as unoriginate and the others as either eternally begotten or proceeding from the Father is to introduce an element of causation or origination that must ultimately involve some type of subordination among them." Millard J. Erickson, *God in Three Persons: A Contemporary Interpretation of the Trinity* (Grand Rapids: Baker, 1995), 309.
21. Calvin, *Institutes of the Christian Religion*, 149–54.
22. Ibid., 154.
23. Miroslav Volf, *Exclusion and Embrace: A Theological Exploration of Identity, Otherness, and Reconciliation* (Nashville: Abingdon, 1996), 180.
24. Ibid.
25. Ibid., 187.
26. Pannenberg, *Systematic Theology*, vol. 1, 325.
27. Ibid., 298, cf. 334.
28. J. Wentzel van Huyssteen, *Alone in the World? Human Uniqueness in Science and Theology* (Grand Rapids: Eerdmans, 2006), 113.
29. Cornelius Plantinga Jr., "Social Trinity and Tritheism," in *Trinity, Incarnation, and Atonement: Philosophical and Theological Essays*, eds. Ronald J. Feenstra and Cornelius Plantinga Jr. (Notre Dame, IN: University of Notre Dame Press, 1989), 28.
30. For example, John Thompson writes, "There is and must be total equality; this was guaranteed in the patristic era by the success of the *homoousion*, which means that each person is fully divine. At the same time, since Son and Spirit have their source in and come

from the Father, owing their being to him, there inevitably arises a form of subordination." This "total equality" of the Son is qualified. Calvin, not influenced by modern discussions on equality, saw that such a position did not preserve the full equality of the Son and denied the Son as *autotheos*. John Thompson, *Modern Trinitarian Perspectives* (Oxford: Oxford University Press, 1994), 146.

31. Grudem, *Systematic Theology*, 251.
32. Robert Letham, "The Man-Woman Debate: Theological Comment," *Westminster Theological Journal* 52 (Spring 1990): 68.
33. Grudem, *Systematic Theology*, 249.
34. Ibid., 257.
35. John Dahms approaches such a position when he uses John 14:28 to justify the eternal ontological subordination of the Son. Dahms claims that any interpretations that deny this essential and eternal subordination "implicitly deny the unity of the incarnate Son" and are of the same error as Nestorianism (p. 352). To justify eternal subordination he also uses Matthew 24:36 and Mark 13:32, which speak of the limitation of knowledge of the Son. Dahms is led to suggest that this limitation is part of eternal sonship (p. 356). Thus, he consistently applies subordination but arrives at a Christology from which the church has always distanced itself. John V. Dahms, "The Subordination of the Son," *Journal of the Evangelical Theological Society* 37, no. 3 (1994): 351–64.
36. For a historical overview of the church's opposition to subordinationism, see the work of Kevin Giles. Kevin Giles, *Jesus and the Father: Modern Evangelicals Reinvent the Doctrine of the Trinity* (Grand Rapids: Zondervan, 2006), 129–71; and Kevin Giles, *The Trinity and Subordinationism: The Doctrine of God and the Contemporary Gender Debate* (Downers Grove, IL: InterVarsity, 2002), 32–59.
37. Grudem, Letham, Schreiner, and others.
38. Barth, *Doctrine of Reconciliation, I*, 200–10.
39. Thompson, *Modern Trinitarian Perspectives*, 48.
40. Ibid., 154.
41. Mary A. Kassian, *The Feminist Gospel: The Movement to Unite Feminism with the Church* (Wheaton: Crossway, 1992), 145.
42. Wren argues that it is very difficult to make such distinctions and only possible if we remove Scripture from the realm of human experience. Brian Wren, *What Language Shall I Borrow? God-Talk in Worship: A Male Response to Feminist Theology* (New York: Crossroad, 1989), 95–102.
43. Bruce K. Waltke, "The Role of Women in the Bible," *Crux* 31, no. 3 (1995): 30.
44. Bruce K. Waltke, *Creation and Chaos: An Exegetical and Theological Study of Biblical Cosmogony* (Portland: Western Conservative Baptist Seminary, 1974), 5–17.
45. Dorothy Patterson, "Aspects of a Biblical Theology of Womanhood," (DTh diss., University of South Africa, 1997), 149, 159.
46. D. A. Carson, *The Inclusive Language Debate: A Plea for Realism* (Grand Rapids: Baker, 1998), 165–70.
47. Waltke, *Creation and Chaos*.
48. Meredith G. Kline, *Treaty of the Great King: The Covenant Structure of Deuteronomy: Studies and Commentary* (Grand Rapids: Eerdmans, 1963).
49. For example, most would have no problem with Kenneth E. Bailey, *Poet and Peasant: A Literary Cultural Approach to the Parables in Luke* (Grand Rapids: Eerdmans, 1976).
50. Jewett, *God, Creation, and Revelation*, 14.
51. Catharina Halkes, "The Rape of Mother Earth: Ecology and Patriarchy," in *Motherhood: Experience, Institution, Theology*, eds. Anne Carr and Elisabeth Schüssler Fiorenza (Edinburgh: T & T Clark, 1989), 97.
52. Rebecca S. Chopp, *The Power to Speak: Feminism, Language, God* (New York: Crossroad,

1989).
53. Elisabeth Schüssler Fiorenza, *Jesus, Miriam's Child, Sophia's Prophet: Critical Issues in Feminist Christology* (London: SCM, 1995).
54. Mary Daly, *Beyond God the Father* (London: Women's Press, 1986).
55. Paul K. Jewett, *God, Creation, and Revelation: A Neo-Evangelical Theology* (Grand Rapids: Eerdmans, 1991), 336–433.
56. Jean Lyles' impression after hearing Walter Brueggemann preach a sermon where he alternatively referred to God as "he" and "she." Jean C. Lyles, "The God-Language Bind," *The Christian Century*, April 16, 1980, 431.
57. Jürgen Moltmann, "The Motherly Father. Is Trinitarian Patripassianism Replacing Theological Patriarchalism?" in *God as Father?* eds. Johannes-Baptist Metz and Edward Schillebeeckx (New York: Seabury, 1981), 53.
58. Daphne Hampson, *After Christianity* (Valley Forge, PA: Trinity Press International, 1996), 159–63.
59. Carson, *Inclusive Language Debate*, 65–66.
60. On the use of "immanent" and "economic" for the Trinity, Shults writes, "Part of the problem may be the way in which the distinction between an 'immanent' and an 'economic' Trinity functions in the discussion. Even when the distinction is employed for the sake of overcoming the distinction, it brings with it an implicit danger. Insofar as the immanent Trinity and the economic Trinity are dialectically defined concepts, we are too easily forced back into another false dilemma: either they are substantially the same or substantially separate. This way of framing the debate makes it difficult to avoid these pitfalls." F. LeRon Shults, *Reforming the Doctrine of God* (Grand Rapids: Eerdmans, 2005), 164.

Chapter 8: The Eternal Son as God, and Jesus as God Embodied

1. Adrio König, *Menslike Mense* (Halfway House: Orion, 1993), 108.
2. Bruce K. Waltke and M. O'Connor, *An Introduction to Biblical Hebrew Syntax* (Winona Lake, IN: Eisenbrauns, 1990), 108–9.
3. Bruce K. Waltke, "The Role of Women in the Bible," *Crux* 31, no. 3 (1995): 37.
4. Mary A. Kassian, *The Feminist Gospel: The Movement to Unite Feminism with the Church* (Wheaton: Crossway, 1992), 146.
5. James B. Hurley, *Man and Woman in Biblical Perspective* (Leicester: InterVarsity, 1981), 173.
6. Dorothy Patterson, "Aspects of a Biblical Theology of Womanhood," (DTh diss., University of South Africa, 1997), 152.
7. Hurley, *Man and Woman*, 173.
8. John M. Frame, "Men and Women in the Image of God," in *Recovering Biblical Manhood and Womanhood: A Response to Evangelical Feminism*, eds. John Piper and Wayne Grudem (Wheaton: Crossway, 1991), 227–28, 230, 232.
9. Ibid., 231.
10. John M. Frame, *The Doctrine of God* (Phillipsburg, NJ: P&R Publishing Company, 2002), 36–102.
11. Richard A. Norris, "The Ordination of Women and the 'Maleness' of Christ," *Anglican Theological Review Supplement Series*, no. 6 (1976): 72.
12. Kari E. Børresen, "Women's Studies of the Christian Tradition: New Perspectives," in *Religion and Gender*, ed. Ursula King (Oxford: Blackwell, 1995), 248.
13. J. I. Packer, "Let's Stop Making Women Presbyters," *Christianity Today* (February 11, 1991): 20.

Chapter 9: Jesus, Wisdom, and an "Eternal Daughter"?

1. James Barr, *The Semantics of Biblical Language* (London: Oxford University Press, 1961),

39–40.
2. Ibid., 40.
3. Bruce K. Waltke and M. O'Connor, *An Introduction to Biblical Hebrew Syntax* (Winona Lake, IN: Eisenbrauns, 1990), 99.
4. Elizabeth A. Johnson, "Jesus the Wisdom of God: A Biblical Basis for Non-Androcentric Christology," *Ephemerides Theologicae Lovanienses* 61 (1985): 262.
5. Ibid., 271–76.
6. Waltke and O'Connor, *Biblical Hebrew*, 100.
7. Ibid.
8. Lennart Boström, *The God of the Sages: The Portrayal of God in the Book of Proverbs*, Coniectanea Biblica: Old Testament Series, vol. 29, eds. T. N. D. Mettinger and M. Y. Ottosson (Stockholm: Almqvist & Wiksell International, 1990), 58.
9. For parallels between Wisdom and Folly, see Tremper Longman III, *Proverbs* (Grand Rapids: Baker, 2006), 215–23.
10. Bruce K. Waltke, *The Book of Proverbs: Chapters 1–15*, New International Commentary on the Old Testament (Grand Rapids: Eerdmans, 2004), 86–87.
11. Longman, *Proverbs*, 205–6; Waltke, *Book of Proverbs*, 407–8; James L. Crenshaw, *Old Testament Wisdom: An Introduction* (London: SCM, 1982), 97; William McKane, *Proverbs: A New Approach*, Old Testament Library (London: SCM, 1970), 352–54; Boström, *God of the Sages*, 54. Zimmerli argues for Yahweh who "created wisdom at the very beginning, as the first of his works, and how she was present as his darling at creation and played in his presence." Walther Zimmerli, *Old Testament Theology in Outline*, trans. David E. Green (Edinburgh: T & T Clark, 1993), 39.
12. Johnson, "Jesus the Wisdom of God," 289.
13. For example, Rudolf Schnackenburg, *The Gospel According to St John*, vol. 1, *Introduction and Commentary on Chapters 1–4*, trans. Kevin Smyth (New York: Crossroad, 1990), 234–36, 257–59, 481.
14. For example, Jeremias, Bultmann, Schnackenburg, and Käsemann.
15. Rendel Harris, *The Origin of the Prologue to St John's Gospel* (Cambridge: Cambridge University Press, 1917), 3.
16. Ibid., 13.
17. Hartmut Gese, *Der Johannesprolog. In Zur Biblischen Theologie* (Munich: Kaiser, 1977).
18. Hartmut Gese, "Wisdom, Son of Man, and the Origins of Christology: The Consistent Development of Biblical Theology," *Horizons in Biblical Theology* 3 (1981): 51–52.
19. Ibid., 31, 54.
20. Moises Silva, *Biblical Words and Their Meaning: An Introduction to Lexical Semantics* (Grand Rapids: Zondervan, 1983), 139.
21. For instance, Louw and Nida observe that there is no synonymy or hyponymy in the semantic domains of *logos* and *sophia*. It is possible that an illegitimate jump has been made between *sophia* and *logos*, and that the connection has been made by importing the theological concept of "wisdom" into the word *logos*—a process that overloads the word with theological meaning. Johannes P. Louw and Eugene A. Nida, *Greek-English Lexicon of the New Testament Based Upon Semantic Domains*, vol. 2 (New York: United Bible Societies, 1988), 153, 225.
22. Silva, *Biblical Words and Their Meaning*, 106–8; Vern S. Poythress, *Symphonic Theology: The Validity of Multiple Perspectives in Theology* (Grand Rapids: Zondervan, 1987), 74–79.
23. For example, Martin Scott, "Sophia and the Johannine Jesus," *Journal for the Study of the New Testament Supplement Series* 71, ed. S. Porter (Sheffield: JSOT, 1992): 94–115.
24. Robert Kysar, "The Background of the Prologue of the Fourth Gospel: A Critique of Historical Methods," *Canadian Journal of Theology* 16 (1970): 250–55.
25. For example, Edwin D. Freed, *Old Testament Quotations in the Gospel of John* (Leiden: Brill,

        1965).
26. P. Borgen, "Logos Was the True Light: Contributions to the Interpretation of the Prologue of John," *Novum Testamentum* 14 (1972): 119.
27. Louw and Nida, *Greek-English Lexicon*, vol. 2.
28. Oscar Cullmann, *The Christology of the New Testament*, 2nd ed., trans. Shirley C. Guthrie and Charles A. M. Hall (London: SCM, 1963), 262.
29. For example, compare Exodus 33:7–23 and John 1:14, 17, and 18.
30. Ray Anderson writes, "One might also say that God loves as Mother loves Daughter, but then there would be no ontological and semantical link with these terms to the incarnation of God that took place in Jesus the historical person who called God his Father." Ray S. Anderson, "The Incarnation of God in Feminist Christology: A Theological Critique," in *Speaking the Christian God: The Holy Trinity and the Challenge of Feminism*, ed. Alvin F. Kimel (Grand Rapids: Eerdmans, 1992), 310.
31. Jann Aldredge-Clanton, *In Search of the Christ-Sophia: An Inclusive Christology for Liberating Christians* (Mystic, CT: Twenty-Third Publications, 1995), 4. Jewett, who alternates pronouns in reference to God, acknowledges that we can only adopt a masculine pronoun for Jesus. Jewett, *God, Creation, and Revelation*, 46.
32. D. A. Carson, *The Inclusive Language Debate: A Plea for Realism* (Grand Rapids: Baker, 1998), 130–33, 155–56.

Epilogue

1. Thomas C. Oden, *Systematic Theology*, vol. 2, *The Word of Life* (San Francisco: HarperCollins, 1989), 117.

www.ingramcontent.com/pod-product-compliance
Lightning Source LLC
Chambersburg PA
CBHW021652230426
43668CB00008B/601